ERLE STANLEY GARDNER

The Case of the
Real Perry Mason

Erle Stanley Gardner

Erle Stanley Gardner

The Case of the Real Perry Mason

by
DOROTHY B. HUGHES

William Morrow and Company, Inc. • New York
1978

Grateful acknowledgment is made to Jean Gardner and Natalie Grace Naso for permission to quote bibliography of Erle Stanley Gardner, copyright © 1970 by Jean Gardner and Natalie Grace Naso, executrices.

Grateful acknowledgment is also made to Helga Greene for the Estate of Raymond Chandler for permission to quote from the letters of Mr. Chandler to Erle Stanley Gardner.

Library of Congress Cataloging in Publication Data

Hughes, Dorothy Belle Flanagan (date)
    Erle Stanley Gardner: the case of the real Perry Mason.

    "Bibliography of Erle Stanley Gardner, compiled by Ruth Moore": p.
    Includes index.
    1. Gardner, Erle Stanley, 1889–1970—Biography.
2. Authors, American—20th century—Biography.
I. Title.
PS3513.A6322Z68   813'.5'2 [B]   77-16845
ISBN 0-688-03282-6

DESIGN AND BINDING   CARL WEISS

Printed in the United States of America.

2   3   4   5   6   7   8   9   10

FOREWORD

I WAS NOT one of Erle Stanley Gardner's very best friends. There were hundreds who could rightly be so named, for if ever a man had the gift of friendship, it was he. Almost everyone called him Uncle Erle for reasons lost in the annals of long usage, and I came to know him well enough to share that privilege. I met him first in New York, and after that, now and again in Hollywood, which is what outlanders call the Santa Monica, Westwood, and Beverly Hills environs of Los Angeles. And, as writers do, when the spirit moved, we exchanged letters through the years.

That first introduction in New York was at the apartment of Baynard Kendrick, whose books, like Gardner's, were published by William Morrow and Company. I was on my annual working visit to New York, and my editor for many years, Marie Freid Rodell, took me along with her to a pre-Mystery Writers of America meeting there. Gardner had just flown in from the Bahamas, where he had been covering the trial of Alfred de Marigny for the murder of Sir Harry Oakes. I remember him that day as a large, serious man, dressed impeccably in a dark blue suit, and I remember how at once he put his imprint on the gathering. Later, when we met in California, I discovered that he wasn't a big man physically, but that he was, rather, of less than average height; that he was more at home in his usual casual Western attire than a dark blue suit; and that although he was a serious man, he was also a merry one.

My husband, Levi Allen Hughes, and I spent one happy weekend at Gardner's Rancho del Paisano in Temecula. I never thought of posterity at the time or I might have made copious notes of the visit. Instead, I just enjoyed myself. My husband, being a born and bred Westerner, talked hunting and fishing with Erle, and gold and silver mines, and Baja California, which we had just discovered.

Erle and I talked books and authors. In researching for this biography, I was rather surprised to find in one article the statement that Gardner didn't allow people to visit his study. Nothing could be further from the truth. My husband and I spent a good part of our visit in there, with Erle reminiscing about his belongings, gathered from all over the world, and also giving us a firsthand demonstration of how he dictated his books and how his secretaries carried on from there.

From his very first Perry Mason case, to which my young brother introduced me, I was one of Gardner's constant readers. In the early forties in New Mexico, I initiated my mystery review column. The strength of Gardner's appeal was such that, with a stack of new mystery novels just in from the publishers, and with three or four of them from my very favorite writers—and I must interject that I have almost as many very favorite writers as Gardner had very best friends—I invariably chose to read Gardner's new book first.

As the years went on, and I began to hear of his work being taken for granted and even sloughed off by certain critics, I climbed staunchly on my soapbox. I never missed an opportunity in my critiques to point out his importance as a writer. And although I'm a low key, keep-quiet-and-it'll-go-away person, I struck out vocally at some of these critics, including the two who were at that time probably the most important of the lot. Not without temerity did I speak, for they were good friends, but with shame for them, two of the brightest minds in the genre, who didn't bother to evaluate a writer themselves but adopted the opinions of lesser men, and echoed them. Neither Erle nor his publishers ever knew of this encounter or of similar ones. Not for the world would I have hurt Erle's feelings by repeating what I considered thoughtless (meaning "without thought") remarks.

I consider it a special honor that Lawrence Hughes (no relation), the president of William Morrow and Company, asked me to write the biography of Erle Stanley Gardner. I don't know why I was chosen, but I believe that in a circuitous way credit can be traced to Digby Diehl, my book editor at the Los Angeles *Times*, where I have been mystery critic for more than ten years. Digby had the perception to recognize the stature of Gardner, and probably, not surprisingly, the wish to single him out for special tribute. At any rate, I was asked to write "A" reviews on the Gardner books that came out in Gardner's later years. The "A" is the long review at the *Times* and this enabled me to consider the importance of Gardner's work as a whole, not piece by piece. I don't know, but it is entirely possible that it was from reading some of these reviews that Mr. Hughes selected me. I am pleased that one such review, shortly before Gardner's death, elicited a thank-you letter from Erle, a special one in which he wrote at length about his own writing, something he rarely did.

Recently, the forewords of books seem to be patterned on the cliché-ridden acceptance of theatrical awards, those thanking everyone from the honorees' progenitors to the boy who delivers the apples they polish. I shall not follow this custom. Anyone who reads this book well knows that almost every person mentioned within its pages contributed to the making of it. The major contributor is Erle Stanley Gardner, for most of what is written came from his own hand in his own words.

DOROTHY B. HUGHES

Santa Fe, New Mexico
January, 1978

Contents

Part One

INTRODUCING PERRY MASON

Chapter One

THE MOST NOTED lawyer of the twentieth century is a Los Angeles attorney named Perry Mason. This is mentioned without quibble or question or even fear of contradiction. His cases are known throughout the reading world. They have not only been published in all English-speaking countries, but have been translated into Czech, Danish, Dutch, Finnish, French, German, Hebrew, Hungarian, Italian, Japanese, Norwegian, Polish, Portuguese, Russian, Spanish, Slovak, Swedish, and in India into the dialects of Tamil and Urdu, and possibly by now, in answer to frequent requests, Hindi, Gujarati, Malayalam, Telugu, Kannada, and Bengali.

Perry Mason's first recorded appearance as a defense attorney was in *The Case of the Velvet Claws*, published by William Morrow and Company on March 1, 1933. It was written by Erle Stanley Gardner. Gardner was a practicing attorney of Ventura, a small county seat some seventy-five miles north of Los Angeles. Although this was his first book, he was not unknown as a writer. For ten years he had practiced law by day and written stories by night. After a slow start, he had become so much in demand by readers of the pulp magazines, which were flourishing in the twenties and thirties, that the name Erle Stanley Gardner on a magazine cover was guarantee of a sellout.

In his first year of writing, 1921, he earned only $974, less than he made in a month as a lawyer. In his fifth year, his earnings had risen to $6,627. By the early thirties, his sales from writing had mounted to more than $20,000 yearly, a sizable income any day and particularly so in those depression times. At the pulp payment of a few cents a word, this meant a tremendous number of words pounded out on his typewriter night after night. He was prodigiously productive. The quota he set for himself was 1,200,000 words a year, or a 10,000-word novelette every three days, 365 days a year.

Between his commitments to the law and to the magazines, there was never enough time in which to write a novel. Not until it occurred to him that he could dictate one, as he did the real-life cases in his office, did he make the grade. It took three and a half days. He admitted freely and frequently that it would be more accurate to say four days, as he spent an initial half day "thinking up the plot."

With the possible exception of Thayer Hobson, then president of William Morrow and Company, no one was aware that the launching of Perry Mason was to make publishing history. In any event, Hobson rather presciently wrote the following line of copy for the jacket of *Velvet Claws*: "Perry Mason—criminal lawyer. Remember that name. You'll meet him again. He is going to be famous." He was indeed. Gardner wrote eighty-two full-length Mason novels, which in all editions, according to the latest figures, have sold more than 300,000,000 copies. He was the most widely read author of his time. The books continue to sell in astronomical figures. Subsidiary rights, which included magazine serialization, book club, paperback reprints, motion pictures, radio, television, even a comic strip for a number of years, earned a fortune for the author.

And how did Perry Mason come about? It doesn't take much digging and delving to realize that Mason was Gardner and Gardner was Mason, dramatized and glamorized a bit, to be sure. Mason was tall and well built, with "wavy hair" and "long legs." His "rugged features" might have been "carved from granite." In his own words, Gardner had "a fat face," and regarding certain publicity pictures, he stated that he resembled "a middle-aged Kewpie." He was inclined to overweight but he disciplined himself too well to allow himself to become fat. Unlike Mason, his legs were not long, nor were his arms. In his favorite sport of archery, it was necessary for him to compensate by shooting the arrow in a higher arc than most archers do. He must have particularly admired "wavy hair," so many of his characters were given it. His own was just plain straight. Gardner had Mason's "gimlet eyes" and could use the "steely glance" when he chose, although he himself thought of his eyes as round, doubtless because from his youth on he wore round glasses. One physical trait that the two did have in common—and not even Gardner could deny that—was the "boyish grin."

They both had an appreciation of good food. Not fancy food. Perry's dinner of a thick steak broiled rare, a baked potato, and a green salad, mentioned in book after book, was also Erle's favorite.

Erle had others: He could and did grow lyrical over tropical fruits, and was a gourmet of Mexican cooking. Between travels, when he was in residence at his ranch in southern California, he liked to go across the border once a week for such Baja favorites as burritos, enchiladas, chile con carne y frijoles, pollos de Castillo con arroz de Tijuana, bizcochitos, and "Mulege jam."

No matter that they were physically unlike, as a defense lawyer Perry Mason obviously learned his razzle-dazzle from Erle Stanley Gardner. Not one of Mason's methods was ever as outrageous as the time the young Gardner shuffled the Chinese businessmen of Oxnard among shops not their own, in order to foil officials sent to apprehend them.

From cases on record, Gardner could have had no peer in Ventura County. Although he occasionally practiced in Los Angeles and once won a big insurance case there, *Magby* v. *New York Life Insurance Company,* he was foremost, and always proud of being, a small-town lawyer. Nonetheless, he settled his alter ego in the city and made sure that Mason had no peer.

Gardner had admiration for other lawyers but not to the extent of overlooking their weak spots. For instance, he summed up the visiting Clarence Darrow, whose fame was established long before he took on the Leopold and Loeb case, as "dedicated" but "over-rated." Jerry Giesler, the miracle attorney for the motion picture industry, was praised by Gardner for the way in which he "studied details backwards and forwards," but he was "too suave and avuncular" to be a threat to Mason. Earl Rogers, a legend for his brilliant histrionics in the Angeleno courtrooms, may have contributed something to Mason; this Gardner would allow. But he added that all lawyers were actors, and Perry Mason "a helluvan actor." As was, it may be noted, Gardner himself. In and out of the courtroom.

As the Perry Mason books began to proliferate, it was not long before the doubters and detractors became vocal. Each one of them came to the same decision: No one man was capable of turning out such a quantity of work without assistance. Ergo, Erle Stanley Gardner did not write all of his own material; he had a staff of writers assisting him.

This nonsense became so widespread that Thayer Hobson offered an award of $100,000 to anyone who could present proof that any-one other than Erle Stanley Gardner ever wrote one word of Gard-ner's material. On making the offer, Hobson remarked that it would be worth $100,000 to discover another Gardner. Over the many years, there was never a taker.

Unwittingly, Gardner gave substance to the error when early on he referred to himself as a "Fiction Factory." The first time he used the term was in October 1932, prior to the creation of Perry Mason. In discussing the writing of the "smooth type of story stuff" as opposed to his pulp fiction, he wrote his agent, Robert Thomas Hardy, "Let's look at it from this standpoint, Bob. I am a fiction factory, capable of manufacturing quite a quantity of merchandise, and with some knowledge which I have acquired from long years of experience."

An agent was a "fiction salesman" who knew the market and knew what was the best type of story Gardner should "manufacture." On two occasions the young Gardner had entered the business world, and he never recovered from the experience. He always considered himself a businessman and writing one category of business.

By "fiction factory," he did not mean that he hired other persons to turn out a reasonable replica from his story patterns. When he first used the phrase, he was referring to his writing per se, no more than that. Even as late as 1967, when interviewed by Charles Morton, an editor of the *Atlantic Monthly,* Gardner spoke of "my one-man fiction factory."

However, through the years the Fiction Factory assumed a further meaning: He dictated into machines of various kinds, others typed what he had dictated, he edited for continuity of plot, made revisions, and the manuscript was then retyped, proofread by others for final typing, and so on in an assembly line until the book was in hand. This procedure enabled him to turn out the extraordinary amount of material for which he was justly famous.

When he started writing, there was no such organization. In sending his stories to market, he had the help of one young girl, a secretary in his law office. After work she would come to the Gardner home to take care of the correspondence which was a by-product of his writing.

She was Agnes, called Jean, one of the three Walter sisters, who not long before had moved with their mother, Ida Walter, and two brothers from Lancaster in the upper desert country to Ventura. When Erle first met her, Jean was working at the old Pierpont Inn, owned by a friend of her mother, as an assistant desk clerk and also as a hostess in the dining room. Erle and his law partner, Frank Orr,

Honey, Peggy, and Jean

tried to get her to come work for them as a secretary, but she wasn't interested in making the change.

Instead she offered them the second Walter sister, Marguerite, called Peggy. Within a year, Gardner, as usual, had his way, and Jean too became a part of the lawyers' secretarial group. The youngest sister, Ruth, called Honey, was in high school at the time. She often stated quite flatly that after graduation, she had no intention of joining her sisters in working for Mr. Gardner. Nevertheless, in due time she became the third important member of his staff.

When Erle gave up the practice of law after he had firmly established Perry Mason in the profession, the girls also quit the law office. From secretaries transcribing his dictated stories, they became an integral part of the Gardner career.

It was not until almost twenty years later that the fourth member of Gardner's permanent staff materialized. He was Samuel, always Sam, Hicks, a Wyoming cowboy. To call Sam a cowboy is like calling Leonardo da Vinci only a painter. Erle often boasted that Sam could do anything and what he didn't know, he could figure out. After their initial meeting on a hunting expedition, Erle inveigled Sam to California to take over the management of the Temecula ranch. He soon became a fellow explorer, traveling companion, photographer, motor mechanic, amateur archaeologist—name it, it became Sam's accomplishment. He even took over as skipper of Gardner's flotilla

Sam Hicks

on the Sacramento Delta, handling "that fleet of boats as sensitively and knowledgeably as he would a high-strung horse," to quote one of Erle's guests. For a mountain-desert man, this was a prime accomplishment.

At times Peggy and Honey departed to live and work elsewhere, although they always returned when Gardner needed them. Jean, after an early, unsuccessful marriage, made Gardner's work her life. Most of Erle's associates consider her to be the prototype of Della Street, Perry Mason's executive secretary. Erle and Jean were a team, even as Perry and Della. There is no doubt that a goodly part of Della is based on Jean. However, both she and Erle always insisted that Della Street was a composite, that Peggy and Honey were also a part of the character, as were other secretaries. Jean says: "We girls were so much a part of his work, he seldom thought of us as individuals."

Even in the beginning, when story rejections outnumbered acceptances by a hundred to one, Jean was serenely certain that Erle Stanley Gardner would become a major writer. Through the years, it was she who made things mesh, managing the intricacies of the secretarial and household staffs, the business and social engagements, the voluminous correspondence, the details of his constant travel from one site to another, and all the other matters growing out of a multifaceted career. It was she who gave Gardner the freedom to write his way to unprecedented heights in detective fiction.

Chapter Two

PERRY MASON BECAME less of a slightly rough diamond as he progressed through the years; however, there was never a basic change in him as a person. He was a tough antagonist but always a gentleman. His physical looks were never more than suggested. Although Gardner said this was because he preferred to let readers form their own images, there seems little doubt that he did not want to waste time on such relatively unimportant matters as descriptions. They slowed the pace, and the one thing Gardner considered essential was action, the faster the better.

Della Street's appearance was also barely sketched. But book by book a few things were learned about her. She was around twenty-seven years old. At one time she weighed 112 pounds but took steps to get down again to her usual 109 pounds. She must have been extremely attractive, as she received many a wolf whistle.

Perry and Della seem to have arrived full-blown on the Los Angeles scene; no background material was ever given. Gardner was as private about their family lives as he was about his own. When *Velvet Claws* appeared, Della had worked for Perry for five years; he had been a part of the Los Angeles legal profession for at least that long; he was well known there, well thought of, and had good friends among those with whom he was associated professionally.

Paul Drake, who had his own detective agency and did investigative work for Mason, was the third of the trio, and was also introduced in *Velvet Claws*. He was described as tall with a florid complexion, a rather nondescript figure, as befits a detective. However, as he developed in the early books, easygoing yet keen, efficient, unflappable, he could be a prototype of Sam Hicks.

Paul's offices were near Perry's in the same old-fashioned building down by the old courthouse in Los Angeles. He was one of Perry's best friends as well as a colleague. At the end of case after case, the three of them, Perry, Della, and Paul, would go out to dinner together. Or for a late evening supper, if the case ran long, and a bit of dancing. More than once Della and Perry were described as a handsome couple on the dance floor, having "the perfect rhythm of long practice." Gardner himself couldn't dance, and he said so many times; he had never learned how. Yet dancing meant something special to him, and he describes dancing couples often in his books. Jean was dancing with a hotel guest the first time Gardner saw her; he passed her grace on to Della.

Another thing that Gardner must have been obsessed with was straight seams in silk stockings. Not once but over and over again, he wrote of Della "straightening the seams" of her stockings. For the younger generation who would not understand such a reference, let it be said that when stockings were made of silk, before World War II, they had a seam at the back which habitually slid about the leg. The advent of nylon and new methods of knitting made the seam obsolete, giving the fashionable "bare-legged look."

Most detective stories in the thirties, and truly, most since then, were based on the Sherlock Holmes device of a Dr. Watson to ask questions and act as sounding board for the main protagonist's ideas and theories. Gardner eliminated this ploy. Neither Della nor Paul was Watson. Mason didn't need one. He kept things moving too quickly, using dialogue and fast action for explanatory material.

The other Mason regulars came later. Hamilton Burger, district attorney of Los Angeles County, was not introduced until the sixth Mason book, *The Case of the Counterfeit Eye.* As there were D.A.'s who preceded him, so there were any number who appeared after. But for no more than a book or two. He was the one who "took," the one who evidently satisfied the author. With the advent of television, Burger, of course, became as important as the initial trio.

At the start of the Mason cases, members of the Los Angeles police force were strictly stereotyped. Sergeant Holcomb of the Homicide Squad is the officer best remembered, a big, dumb, antagonistic cop who made no bones about his "hate" of Mason. There have been any number of ideas proposed as to why Gardner gradually eliminated Holcomb and his ilk in favor of the personable Lieutenant Arthur Tragg, described as slender, suave, sophisticated, yes, with "wavy hair" and thoughtful eyes. The change came as Gardner moved increasingly toward strengthening the image of the police; it was one of his prime campaigns. Anyone who could weaken that image, such as a Sergeant Holcomb, would no longer be tolerated.

Of all Perry Mason's close associates, the only one who changed drastically was Lieutenant Tragg. This came about in casting the television show, and the small, whimsical, intelligent policeman portrayed by Ray Collins became a perfect foil for Raymond Burr's Perry Mason.

There were innumerable other character actors in the books. Frank E. Robbins, at the time editor of the *Quarterly Review* of the University of Michigan, published in 1950 a delightful article, "The World of Perry Mason," a labor of love and research. He had counted 515 men and 205 women, each named and characterized, in Mason's world up to that year. Numerous junior lawyers came and went in Perry Mason's office in the early days, beginning with Frank Everly, who appeared in the second book and was doubtless a memory of Gardner himself, "a young lawyer who was getting practical experience." Of all the typists, minor secretaries, and switchboard operators, the most memorable was the brash, softhearted, loyal Gertie, who presided over the switchboard in Perry's office for many years.

Frank Robbins also tallied the imaginary cases peripherally referred to in the books, such as the "Dalton, Melrose, Johnson, and Miller cases."

It may be that the best description of Mason as a person came from Della in *The Case of the Howling Dog*. With tender solicitude she told him, "You take too many chances, Chief. Your love of excitement is going to get you into trouble some day. Why don't you simply handle trial work instead of going out and mixing into the cases the way you do?"

He gave her the "boyish grin" as he answered, "In the first place I like the excitement. In the second place because I win my cases by knowing the facts. I beat the prosecution to the punch. It's lots of fun . . ."

It was in this same book that Della told Perry he was "a cross between a saint and a devil," to which he responded unperturbed: "All men are."

It sounded just like Erle Stanley Gardner speaking.

Chapter Three

When *The Case of the Velvet Claws* appeared in 1933, the mystery market was immensely overcrowded, and suffering from the country's economic depression. In the opinion of Robert Thomas Hardy, Gardner's agent, "This type of fiction is not going to lose its popularity for long. The Perry Mason stories ought to be increasingly popular and have a bigger and bigger sale . . ."

Although Perry Mason's bow was to almost unanimous critical applause, Gardner would always give the impression that he didn't get good reviews because Will Cuppy of the New York *Herald Tribune*, who was, in Erle's words, the "High Poo-Bah of mystery critics," did not favor the book.

Good as the reviews were, however, most, like Gerald Johnson's in the Baltimore *Evening Sun*, made a direct or implied comparison of his style with Dashiell Hammett's. This disturbed Gardner and on April 17, 1933, he wrote Thayer Hobson of his concern, ending the letter with a paragraph characteristic of his realistic approach to his work and of his integrity:

"Experience has taught me that a writer knows but damn little about his own work. You probably see things about my work more clearly than I do . . . It may be that the book resembles the Hammett style a whole lot more than is apparent to me . . . I don't want to give up the character of a fighting detective unless I have to, but I don't under any circumstances wish to be a tail to someone else's kite, to imitate or to invade a field which has been legitimately trademarked by some other writer."

By April, *Velvet Claws* had sold thirty-two hundred copies, a very respectable sale in those days. In fact, only one first mystery in the preceding five years had sold more. Nonetheless, Hobson apologized for the small compensation compared to what Gardner received from the magazine market, but added, "Don't get too discouraged. The tide will turn and you are off to a magnificent start."

There was no rest period between the acceptance of the first two Perry Mason books and moving on with the series. Because of Hobson's suggestion for a carry-over from one book to the next, the coming book had to be planned before its predecessor was published. The idea worked beautifully, to have Della come into Perry's office at the end of each story and, in telling him about who was waiting outside, put a title on the next "Case." But it wasn't easy to have the title that far in advance; not only are titles predictably not easy to come by, but magazine serialization can play havoc with book publication of works written in sequence. As indeed happened with *The Case of the Howling Dog*, which, though the third manuscript written, was serialized and became the fourth book published.

Before *The Case of the Sulky Girl* could go to press for a September 13, 1933, publication, there was need for the title of the one to follow. Hobson came up with *The Case of the Howling Dog.*

Gardner was already working on a plot with the basic idea "involving a howling dog who howls mysteriously, and ceases his howling under more mysterious circumstances. There will be plenty of mystery, loads of creeps, and a courtroom scene of dramatic intensity similar to the one in the second book, and if I can work it out there will be a surprise ending by which, when the reader thinks the mystery is entirely solved and is ready to lay down the book, the last two paragraphs will hit him a wallop between the eyes and make him turn a mental flip-flop in which many of the facts will have a different and an added significance."

Meantime, Gardner had been trying to catch up on his novelettes. He could not in those early days devote full time to books; his living was in his pulp sales. He had been trying *not* to think of the *Howling Dog* plot.

There was from the beginning the problem of giving his agent time to check the magazines for serialization before book publication. Hobson was writing Erle at the end of April 1933 that, as Erle worked very fast, if he could have *Howling Dog* finished by June and the fourth book by early autumn, there would be time to work on serialization. From then on they could plan for two Masons a year.

A week later Erle wrote his publisher that he was starting the book on Saturday or Sunday, that dictating would start on Monday, and that he should have it finished in a week and typed to send by the middle of June. Sure enough, on May 19 he could write Hobson that he had just finished dictating the end of *Howling Dog*. He felt it was better than either of the other two, materially better than *Sulky Girl*. He wrote, "I don't think it's anything the smooth paper magazines are going to pick up, and I don't think it's any great masterpiece of literature, but there's quite a plot worked into it, and I've tried to carry it through in such a way that it has quite a wallop at the finish." He had also laid the foundation of the next book with the title *The Case of the Lucky Legs*.

Hobson wrote back, "You know I am not just talking through my hat when I say that if you can turn out really good tales at the speed you are turning them out, the sky's the limit, even in the book field."

Such compliments were good to hear but Gardner was by no means satisfied with what he had written. Of the first two books he commented, "Frankly I think the fighting detective has more appeal, but the strategic detective offers more chance for a genuine mystery in the plot, and if the second book should prove more popular than the first, we could trim our sails accordingly, and with the background of the second book I presume the critics will lay off the Hammett cracks. . . . Naturally I'd like to make a success with these books . . . I always like to give value received and I'm also keenly aware that the generous campaign of advertising and selling which you put back of this first book has been very largely responsible for the sales."

When Erle sent in *Howling Dog* in early June he wrote that he was sorry he hadn't sidetracked the second book because the conflicts weren't really the type to best bring out Perry Mason's character. "However, it has some good features as a mystery yarn . . . Unless I am greatly mistaken, this book I am sending today is by far the best of the outfit from a standpoint of dramatic punch. However, I am a writer not an editor and I may be all wet. You look this over; then if you want me to write *The Case of the Lucky Legs* right away, I'll try to get it dictated during July so you can have it in August. Otherwise we will wait until we see how the second book is received before we play around with the fourth."

Of the two books, *Howling Dog* and *Sulky Girl*, Erle said, "There's one technical defect in both of these . . . and I don't know how to avoid it. The books show the facts leading up to the crime, and then the solution comes in the courtroom. —In the first book (*Velvet Claws*) the characters start from scratch and race breathlessly through to a finish. In the last two books, where the solution comes in the courtroom, it is necessary for a period of time to elapse which gives the reader an unconscious feeling of having lost his stride somewhere along the line. If the period of transition can be handled adroitly enough, and the reader is going fast enough when he hits it, he will simply coast from one period of emotional tension into another, but it's a technical defect, nevertheless. With books that are paced as rapidly as these are, there shouldn't be the interruption of action, but I see no way of avoiding it. I think that Perry Mason's forte lies in his mastery of dramatic courtroom technique, plus his fighting ability, his ingenuity, and his general hardboiled loyalty to his clients."

What is of particular interest in his analysis of his Perry Mason character in these early books is that his own interest was in the "fighting ability" and the "loyalty," whether hardboiled or soft-boiled, whereas it was when Perry met his public and made them his own, with his clever techniques, the matching of wits in and out of the courtroom, that he gained his following. It is also of particular interest that Gardner felt the courtroom scenes slowed the pace, which indeed they may have done in his terms, but his readers couldn't get to the courtroom quickly enough. They raced through the Perry Mason books to arrive at the scene where Mason would pull the razzle-dazzles which made his name world-renowned. According to Gardner, in those early days, the courtroom didn't have enough action "to interest the ordinary reader who likes wood-pulps"; it catered only "to a more highbrow class." Gardner's idea was "to try and catch them all."

Hobson soon dropped the "Mr." Gardner for just plain "Gardner," saying the other seemed much too formal. Erle, of course, was all for it: "Glad you abandoned the 'mister.' In dealing with you New Yorkers I never know whether to bust out and act natural, so I always let you folks make the first advance, but I have a feeling you and I have a good deal in common in our outlook on life, and have been strongly tempted to throw formality overboard for some time . . ."

On July 5, Erle sent two letters to Hobson. In the first, he wrote: "I can recognize something of the opportunity I have in the book field—not so much for money as for a stepping stone to a better type of writing. I want to turn out books that will make people talk and make them buy. I have no natural *gift* as a writer. Everything I've worked out has been through hard work and careful study, which means that I'm chuck full of theories."

The second letter ran to more than seven single-spaced pages. Again, as in all the early letters, he was weighing pros and cons in view of future work. "I don't believe I can create any other character that will be as good as Perry Mason," he wrote. At this time, with only one book published and two more written, he and Hobson were both talking of diversifying. "I have no desire to write an ordinary type of detective story, particularly under my own name. By an ordinary type, I mean the conventional type. I don't like to read them and I don't think I'd care to write them. —There's one other type of dramatic detective story which I believe we could work out . . . in which the appeal would depend on the human interest of the subordinate characters."

This was a little difficult to explain, he said, but he thought it was what made S. S. Van Dine's stories go across. "I think his character, Philo Vance, was a pain in the neck, and that many of the readers also thought so. I think his plotting ability was exaggerated by himself to himself, and for that reason I don't think he knows why it was his stories had a success. —Having now modestly placed myself in the position of knowing more about the stories than the guy who wrote them—and I only read one and skipped through the high spots of one other—I will unblushingly state that I think his success came from his genius in depicting his subordinate characters. He had wonderful ability along those lines."

Unless his memory failed him, he believed it was Dickens's *Christmas Carol* in which the roofs were lifted off the houses and readers permitted to see into the private lives. He would like to write a detective story of this sort in which there would be an underlying mystery, "but an intensely human heart interest on the part of the characters. I may find that I lack the skill to do anything with it when it comes to getting it on paper."

Van Dine had laid down a set of rules, widely circulated in the thirties, that he considered obligatory for detective-story writers to follow. Gardner reacted with immediate pugnacity. It made him so mad "I promptly proceeded to write stories in which I violated as many of the rules as I possibly could. . . . In the average detective story the murder is not a murder—it is simply a corpse, thoroughly sterilized." He then offered his personal credo: "I hate all forms of convention. I believe a man can go further questioning fundamentals than conforming to them." He realized he was making a mess of expressing himself because of dealing in intangibles and largely because "I'm putting myself in a position which makes me sound conceited as hell. Incidentally, I *am* conceited as hell, which is another thing you'll have to put up with." To which Hobson replied, "Of course you are conceited as hell. Why shouldn't you be? So am I."

As this theme, "I *am* conceited," recurs over and again in Gardner's letters and personal writings, it requires more than a passive acceptance of his valuation of himself. Because it simply wasn't true. If anything, as those closest to him recognized, he had a rather sizable inferiority complex particularly where his writing was concerned. He was never sure of its quality. This in part may have been due to some members of his family upping their noses at his writing for the pulps, and undoubtedly resulted in his ready boast about his prowess as a salesman but his disparagement of his abilities as a writer.

Also, in the United States at the time Gardner began writing, mystery and detective fiction were considered lowbrow. It was not so in England, where such intellectuals as Dorothy Sayers and G. K. Chesterton were important in the field. And it is unimaginable why it should have been true here when Mary Roberts Rinehart had for a number of years made of the mystery story a novel of person and place, of character rather than formula. Just prior to Gardner was Van Dine, most definitely a man of intellectual qualities.

Although he may not ever have fully realized it, Gardner was a writer's writer. As early as 1934, G. K. Chesterton wrote admiringly of his work. Sinclair Lewis, in an article on writers in 1937, wrote ". . . the magicians are the authors of literate detective stories: Agatha Christie, Francis Iles, Erle Stanley Gardner, H. C. Bailey." And the mystery buff, Somerset Maugham, in the early forties wrote that he read "Dashiell Hammett and Brett Halliday for rough stuff; Rex Stout, Ellery Queen, Gardner, Christie and H. C. Bailey." Also in the forties, the reviewer of *The Case of the Cautious Coquette* for *Time* quoted Evelyn Waugh, who was a close friend of Graham Greene, as saying he wished he could "write whodunits like Erle Stanley Gardner and Margery Allingham."

Concerning Gardner's inner feelings about his writing, there has never been a real writer who was satisfied with the level he reached, who could say, "I don't have to try to do better, this is the best." And although there are few who would go as far as Gardner did, that is, say out loud "I'm no writer," this simply was in the character of the man. Another would express it differently. Gardner remained the New Englander, too prudent to tempt Fate by praise in any form.

Gardner was competitive; he was always working to prove himself the best. This combative spirit kept him ever on the offensive where his stories and books were concerned. He was prepared to battle it out with no retreat when it came to writing his books his way and no other. He could be a lamb and he could be a devil. He knew it and would don the cap suitable for getting what he wanted. He later wrote that in the early days, when Hobson would try to turn him over to one or another editor, "I would suddenly develop temperament. I could be the most cantankerous so-and-so in the whole literary world. I would get in fights, brawls, and disputes. I would be sarcastic, belligerent and utterly impossible. The harassed editor would go to Thayer and suggest they get rid of that so-and-so Gardner, and Thayer Hobson would look surprised and say, 'Why, I never had any trouble with him. Let me take him back and see if I can't get things straightened out . . .' So Thayer Hobson would take me back and I'd become a lamb."

There would be no second place ever for either Erle Stanley Gardner or Perry Mason. They had to be in top place. Gardner didn't expect to fall into it; he worked like a demon to get there.

Part Two

EARLY YEARS

Chapter Four

WITH HIS HERITAGE, Gardner could only have been a hard worker. New Englanders are not soft. The man who was to make Perry Mason a classic was born on July 17, 1889, in the small town of Malden, Massachusetts. He was the second son of Grace Adelma Waugh and Charles Walter Gardner. His brother, Walter, had arrived some two years previously.

The senior Gardners' hometown was Stoughton, Massachusetts. As a young married couple they had moved to Malden in the interests of Mr. Gardner's profession. Charles Gardner was a high school graduate, an accomplishment not taken for granted in his day, and therefore important. Although he did not go to college, he had the qualifications of a civil engineer.

Both Gardner parents were descendants of Colonial New Englanders and were members of the Sons of the American Revolution and Daughters of the American Revolution respectively. Family is and has always been important in New England, not as a genealogical game but simply as an ordinary piece of knowledge. It didn't take research or researchers for Mrs. Gardner to know she was of Mayflower stock, or for Mr. Gardner to know that the Gardners came from a long line of sea captains, one branch settling in Maine, and his own family line rooted in Nantucket. In a 1930's letter to one of his Maine cousins, Minnie Gardner Spratt, Charles wrote, "You know we are descended from the first white settlers on Nantucket and possibly from some others. Grandfather Richard Gardner's house still stands, made over into a nice summer home, and was illustrated in the *House Beautiful* a couple of years ago. . . ."

The letter continued with the Down East humor which was instilled early into his son Erle: "Grace gets a great kick out of the ghosts of the past and as she is of 'Mayflower' descent, she rather

Charles Walter Gardner

looks down on the Gardners who didn't have the gumption to get over here until 1640. But then I bet they can eat more sour milk biscuit than hers ever did." In the same vein he continued: "I imagine you have the old grandpa clock that belonged to your mother. I came near stealing it the time I was down. We have a Willard Banjo clock about one hundred and fifteen years old that everyone admires."

When the Gardners moved across the continent to California, they didn't ship with them a trainload of antiques. They had few worldly goods. Erle's father was just getting started in his profession. Wherever his work took him, he carried his family along. So it was that his wife packed up the two boys and herself and set out with him sometime in the summer of 1899 for the West Coast. In the hearts of the two deep-dyed New Englanders, it was considered no more than a temporary move for business reasons. They were never again to call Massachusetts home. They became Californians.

In the east, Mr. Gardner had been working as an engineer, building a breakwater in Portland, Maine. The move west came when he was asked to take on a similar project in Portland, Oregon. Oregon evidently made little impression on Erle, although the family lived there for several years, for in his writing about his boyhood, he does not speak of it. It was in Oregon that Kenneth, the

Grace Waugh Gardner

third son, was born in 1901, twelve years after Erle, fourteen years after Walter.

Erle was about ten years old when the family first trekked west, yet he might never have known New England. So complete was his lifelong identification with California, from its Oregon border to Baja, from its northern mountains to its southernmost deserts, that it becomes difficult to remember that he was born back east. He was beyond doubt dichotomous, his instincts as much those of the New Englander as of the Californian. His two sides didn't war with each other; they settled down quite well in tandem, neither the one nor the other ever achieving ascendancy.

In 1902, the family moved to Oroville, California. Oroville was one of the gold-dredging centers of the world. The company for which Erle's father worked had mining interests there, and Mr. Gardner was asked to represent the company. Before long he had made himself an expert in gold-dredging placer mining, and later he devised and proved a more efficient and more successful method of mining by using a drill to determine the pay dirt of a given piece of land.

The little mining town of Oroville must have seemed rough and rude to Mrs. Gardner. But to the older boys, accustomed to New England formality, it was like a storybook. Not that Grace Gardner

His father's mining rig. Gardner on far right

would ever let her sons forget their upbringing. She was a five-foot upright New England lady with red hair and a temperament to match. "Ma," the boys called her, with the same fondness as boys today speak of "Mom."

There was no question about who ran the Gardner household; it was Ma. Even when they were full-grown men, Ma was to be heeded. Her pictures in an album Walter put together one year for her birthday, with rhymes for cutlines, show a slim young woman, pretty, bright, and, the verses say, fond of playacting.

The family structure was built on love. This does not mean there was the permissiveness prevalent today. In nineteenth- and early twentieth-century families, discipline was quite as important as love. Ma was the disciplinarian of the Gardner family; Pa was busy with his work. But Pa's word was never questioned, as hers was sometimes permitted to be.

Erle was devoted to his father and mother. When he was a grown man with a family of his own, he was not embarrassed to write to them, "I love you so much it hurts." And according to his younger brother, Ken, one of San Francisco's most respected physicians, "They adored Erle."

The one flaw in the weave of devotion was the collision of temperament between Erle and his big brother, Walter. It lasted too long for simple sibling jealousy, so it may have been rooted, as Erle believed, in Walter's pushing him around when they were boys, something that Erle, being Erle, never forgave. It very likely was an accumulation of small rankles that grew out of proportion, and also of the vastly different characters of the two brothers.

Walter was a conformist, and there is no criticism attached to the word; conformists are one strength of society. He did well in high school and was a part of the social structure among his peers. He went on to Stanford University where again he did well, was prominent on campus, and graduated with honors. He made his way in the business world and married and raised a family, moving to Illinois in his middle years. In some respects he also was a writer. He wrote poetry at school and later contributed frequent articles to business magazines. "He could have been a damn good writer," Ken believes.

Erle was a maverick and thoroughly enjoyed being one. This may have been a reaction to Walter, the desire to be a person in his own right, but on odds it seems to have been a natural trait. Even as a boy, he must have possessed the high-voltage energy that made him the whirlwind he became in maturity. He could not endure the confinement of four walls, not at school, not even at home. To him the only place to be was out in the open, in the sun by day, under the stars at night. This was how one grew in strength and health. His sleeping under the stars began in his teens at the Oroville home. The rest of the family occupied bedrooms, but he would take his sleeping bag up onto the roof. In spite of his mother's always being afraid he would roll off, he never did. And his mother would shake her head and say of him, as she was to say through all her years, "That Erle! That Erle!"

Erle seems to have done well in school back in Malden. He finished the fourth grade in 1899, the year of the move West. It was also the year of the commemoration of the 150th anniversary of the municipality of Malden, founded in 1649. As a part of the commemoration, the school committee published a City of Malden Public School Souvenir in which appeared the first published work of Gardner. Titled "Atalanta's Race," it is a retelling of the golden apple myth as follows:

> One day there was to be a great race. People came from distant lands to see it. They came because Atalanta was to race. The people said, "No one can beat Atalanta anyway."
> Hippomenes was one of the judges. When he saw Atalanta he wished

he could race. He said, "Atalanta, may I race?" "Yes," said she, "but if you do not beat me you must die."

The story continued through the race until Atalanta, picking up the golden apples given Hippomenes by Venus, discovered Hippomenes had reached the goal and won.

The work is signed: Earle S. Gardner, Grade Four.

When one considers that a fourth-grader couldn't be more than nine or ten years old, it is an accomplished piece. Further, when one also considers that of all the children in the school, not more than a dozen, if that many, had their material printed in the souvenir booklet, one comes to the conclusion that little Erle already had a gift for writing. Also one notes that what impressed him in the story was that you don't stop in a race, because if you do someone else will reach the goal ahead of you. It is evident to him that anybody can be beaten, but if you don't win, you'll die.

At sundry times and places, Gardner explained the varied spellings of his name as it appeared in print. "The name my parents gave me was E-r-l-e. After I started school, however, there was some joshing about the way the name was spelled and I used the spelling E-a-r-l or sometimes E-a-r-l-e until sometime around my high school days, when I changed it back to E-r-l-e."

Gardner mentions no school troubles in any of the grade schools he attended. He may have bottled up inner rebellions in his early school days or it may well be that his behavior problems did not arise until adolescence. It is normal enough that open rebellion against routine begins in high school days; that particular age group begins to feel its oats, to use a good Western expression. It is the age when young people realize that Mom and Dad, or Ma and Pa, can't kill them, that it's against the law.

Erle told the story of his high school days over and again. It rivaled *Peck's Bad Boy*. "At the start, my father thought I would make a good lawyer. It was pretty generally taken for granted that I was going to study law. I would undoubtedly have graduated from high school, gone to college, taken a pre-legal course, then graduated in law and lived a somewhat uneventful life if it hadn't been for certain little things which gradually shaped my existence."

He went on to say the "certain little things" included a certain amount of friction between the principal of the Oroville Union High School and a callow, awkward, self-conscious freshman. The principal, Professor Fogg, as he wished to be called by the students,

"Peck's Bad Boy"

was a thin, nervous but impeccably dressed middle-aged man with a carefully groomed Vandyke beard and a scar on his left cheek. Behind his back, he was known to the students as "Fuzzy" Fogg.

"I had a rudimentary natural talent as a cartoonist," Erle recalled. "Technically, my cartoons were very very bad indeed. I had a certain aptitude for sketching but an astigmatism made it difficult for me to judge my own work. A face which would look all right to me when sketched on paper would look simply terrible if held up in front of a mirror so the sides were reversed. However, my cartoons had one unfailing quality which was never lacking, no matter how bad the cartoon might be from a technical standpoint— it made the man whose picture I had drawn terribly mad."

Erle's partner in crime that year of 1906 was Frank Reardan, for many years now a leading physician of Sacramento. Erle and Frank decided it would be a great idea to have in the school paper Erle's cartoon of Professor Fogg with the caption, "Our Fuzzy," and beneath it the school yell Erle had devised featuring him. A woodcut would cost twenty dollars, as the paper's ads paid only for the cost of printing. In those days, even as today, twenty dollars was a not inconsiderable sum for high school boys to come up with. However, they finally gathered the money, all of their group contributing a little something, and Frank, who was business manager of the paper, had the woodcut made. Now there was an almost greater difficulty. The paper ran to only six pages, plus the front and back covers. As the Professor trusted Frank as little as he did Erle, the page proofs had to be shown to him before the paper went to press. What Frank did was keep the illustrated inner page out of the proofs, which thus went to press with Professor Fogg's okay.

When the paper came out, the two boys were immediately summoned to the Professor's office. According to Dr. Reardan, "Erle, with his ready wit, said that the drawing was not a caricature but a cartoon. The Professor admitted that prominent persons were characterized in cartoons and was apparently satisfied."

But not Erle. He was soon involved as a troublemaker again.

A dictum from the principal changing the name of the school paper put Erle on a soapbox concerning the rights of the student body. "I admit that with my tongue in my cheek, albeit a look of childish innocence on my face, I suggested to the principal that we should have a constitution drawn up which provided that the relations of the principal of the school and that of the student body should be the same as the President of the United States to Congress; that the principal would therefore have the right to veto any action of the student body with which he didn't agree." The principal walked into the trap. The constitution was changed accordingly. Upon which, "I gleefully announced that the next time there was a veto on the part of the principal, we would pass the measure over his head by a two-thirds vote."

The president of the board of trustees heard about the affair. He considered the principal to have been somewhat inept and did not renew his contract. Instead, a disciplinarian was hired to, among other things, "restore discipline and order."

"That meant me," Erle reported. He later learned that the departing principal left a note on his desk for his successor. It said: "Suspended Erle S. Gardner. *Watch him!*"

The suspension had come about as a result of Erle's deciding it would be a great idea to draw his cartoon of Professor Fogg on the front of the school building. Frank vetoed the idea, saying that Erle would be expelled immediately if he did this. However, Frank had a great idea himself. If he could learn to draw the picture, he could do it. Erle would be in the clear and Frank would never be suspected as he had no art talent whatsoever. Under Erle's tutelage, Frank practiced for several weeks until Erle was satisfied that he could do a good job.

Dr. Reardan recalls: "The high school building was the first stucco building in Oroville. So one Sunday night I climbed a ladder, with Erle holding a carbide bicycle lamp, and did the ghost figure, using old-fashioned marking chalk which on the stucco facing was impervious to scrubbing and weather for at least a year or so." The Monday morning following, the Professor went through his regular routine, arriving briskly at 8:30 A.M. and going straight to his office. He emerged quickly to find out why the students were assembled outside looking upward. He joined them and looked upward too.

"Erle and I were immediately summoned from the crowd to his office where he began his interrogation by accusing Erle of drawing the picture. Erle replied that he did not draw it, and was accused of lying. Erle replied that he was not lying and with that the Professor expelled him and turning to me, remarked that he knew I could not draw, but that I certainly had something to do with it, so I was expelled also."

For three weeks the boys pretended to go to school, but actually went to the river. At the end of that time, Frank was allowed to return to school, as he was to graduate in June, but Erle was informed he would have to wait until the next term. Dr. Reardan believes that his folks never knew of the expulsion.

Erle's family must have known, for when his father asked him if he drew the picture, and Erle said no, that was good enough for his father. In one of his letters to Ken later in life, Erle said that his estimate of "the old man" rose high, because his father believed him and asked no further questions.

With the new principal, Erle's trials with authority became greater. He described the incoming disciplinarian as having "a jaw that must have inspired naval architects of the day to design the prows of battleships accordingly."

With predictable results, Erle found the jaw great for an aspiring cartoonist. "Things happened to me which shouldn't have happened to a dog, and during this time I retaliated in ways that I shouldn't," he remembered more than fifty years later, and he hadn't changed his belief that he had been on the receiving end "of petty persecutions which were, at times, not so petty."

For example, malaria was then endemic in the valley of the Sacramento River, and drinking water came from the stream. The high school put down a deep well and the new principal, before going home for lunch or after school, would carry his drinking water home in a two-gallon tin bucket. When the bucket looked a little bedraggled the principal would keep an erring student after school and order him to clean it until he could see his face in it.

There wasn't any doubt in anyone's mind that in due course Erle would get the bucket-polish punishment. Meanwhile, prowling around with a gold pan, he had found an old cleaning house, one he believed went back to the days of forty-nine, when the country was mined by hand, largely by the Chinese. The method then was to wash the gold over plates covered with quicksilver. Under the cleaning house was a layer of clay impregnated with quicksilver which contained a goodly amount of gold. Erle would squeeze the quicksilver through a chamois skin, thus getting quite a bit of the gold and huge quantities of quicksilver.

On the day he was sent to scrub the bucket, he happened to have in his pocket a small phial of quicksilver. In his own words, he did a wonderful job with that tin bucket. He amalgamated it.

"The principal came down in the course of time, quite apparently determined to find fault with the job I had done and to try to break my spirit by making me do it all over. There wasn't anything to do over. The principal took one look at that bucket and tried to conceal his amazement. He did manage to ask me by what secret process I had managed to get it so clean. I looked him in the eye and assured him I had simply worked hard on it and used a lot of elbow grease as he had instructed me to do."

Erle says he never learned what happened after the principal filled the bucket with water and went home. One thing was known: The principal bought a new bucket and Erle was not asked to shine it. But the relationship did not improve.

Erle does not record what finally caused his suspension that year. He does record his farewell to the school. He took his large amount of quicksilver, procured a key which fitted the lock of the school's side door, and one night slipped in to turn loose the mercury on the school's third floor. It went into the cracks, and gradually penetrated from the third floor to the second, from the second to the chemical laboratory, giving some "unconventional results" in connection with certain experiments. Years afterward, when the building burned down, he heard that for some strange reason no one could understand, one of the firemen began to salivate excessively.

Gardner was not one to forgive and forget. Not if he felt he had been wronged. In a letter to Mrs. Alice Biffle, the social editor of the Oroville *Mercury-Register* on November 10, 1954, Gardner wrote in part: "In looking back on it I marvel that the Oroville School had such remarkably capable female teachers and that they were able to work under the domination of the four-flusher who was the principal of the school at the time I severed my academic connections . . ."

At the end of the reprint of his letter in the Oroville paper, there followed an editor's note: "The principal Gardner refers to was . . . last heard from in a southern California high school. Following some sort of a football rally, he was menaced by students throwing oranges. He beat a hasty retreat and did not return to his job. Efforts to trace him since then have failed."

Chapter Five

IN THE SUMMER OF 1906, before Erle's final suspension, Charles Gardner took the family to the Klondike, where he was sent on mining business by his company. In late August Walter and Erle were shipped back to Oroville for the start of school in September. The parents and little Ken would not follow until the freeze-up was due.

Erle was seventeen that summer and Walter nineteen, old enough to take care of themselves for the few weeks. Although he does not write of it, the friction between the brothers must have reached a climax after their return, because Erle moved into a little shack occupied by a friend, and went to school from there.

The friend was called the "Little Swede" as distinguished from his brother, the "Big Swede." In his unpublished memoirs, Erle wrote with remembered glee: "The Big Swede's reputation was rather well known around Oroville. He was a holy terror. If my parents had had any idea that I was to have an association with him, I probably would have missed the opening of high school in September of 1906."

When Erle moved in with the younger brother, the Big Swede was not in Oroville. However, he returned before the elder Gardners came home, and by the time they arrived hero-worship for the Big Swede had been firmly embedded in Erle. It lasted throughout his life.

He wrote, "The Big Swede was somewhat older than I and his life had been one that was well calculated to inspire parents with awe. He had run away from home at an early age, had been a sailor on a windjammer, had taken up prospecting, and had learned fighting and absorbed his morals of life along the waterfronts of various cities of the world. He was a remarkably rough, tough fighter and I doubt if anyone ever bested the Big Swede in any type of two-fisted rough-

The Big Swede

and-tumble combat. While he wasn't very big he was abnormally strong, particularly in his hands and wrists. However, the Swede's mental attitude was the big thing about him. He didn't believe there was anything in life that could conquer him, and as long as he held to that unswerving belief he never met anything that could or did conquer him."

Of himself Gardner wrote, "On the other hand, at that time I was a shy, self-conscious individual who somewhat shunned others because I didn't understand how to comport myself with others."

This picture does not jibe with the one of young Erle up before the student body preaching a new constitution, or of the Erle facing up to the principal and getting across that constitution with its joker clause. It does not jibe with the picture of the prankster who baited the establishment. Nor does it jibe with the one of a boy who was on the staff of the paper, a contributor of humorous material, a boy whose cartooning was so popular with his fellow students that they raised the large sum of twenty dollars to have it printed in the school paper.

Yet one never knows exactly what goes on under the skull of teenagers. Erle probably did think of himself as a "shy, self-conscious individual," doubtless because of the conflict with his older brother. According to Erle, his brother beat him up and bullied him physically as well as emotionally. It would be only natural then that he would dream of the day when he could take on Walter and give it back to him with compound interest. Erle had sent for a book on boxing put out by the Spalding company and had studied this book assiduously. He knew all the technical terms and had carefully memorized the illustrations of punches and counterpunches. With the return of the Big Swede to Oroville, Erle didn't need the book. He had found himself a trainer.

Soon after his arrival in Oroville, the Big Swede formed The Butte Athletic Club. It was his idea of a money-making business, but first he needed money to outfit a gymnasium. He decided to put on an athletic exhibition, charging admission. He arranged the boxing matches, and for some unknown reason, probably because he could only get a star-struck boy to play sucker, he pitted Erle against a trained fighter from Sacramento. He said that Erle could box circles around the other fellow, but once Erle had agreed to take on the fighter, the Big Swede informed Erle that he'd lied, that the opponent was terrific.

"With the attitude of a crook who is proud of his chicanery," Erle later wrote, "the Big Swede offered to teach me something about 'the real art of fighting' so that I wouldn't take too bad a licking." The bout was six weeks off. "I distinctly remember that at the time it seemed far more important to me to get into shape so that I could put up a good fight than to reach any heights of academic scholarship in the Oroville Union High School."

It is clear enough why the boy Gardner would be impressed by the toughness of this man. But it is beyond understanding why, in his mature days, Gardner continued to extol a person whose amorality was such that in order to raise money for his own purposes, he could take a boy for whom he professed friendship and deliberately send him to be beaten up in a prize ring.

The mature Gardner was unswervingly loyal to his friends. Until, or unless, they did him wrong, even a little bit wrong. That ended it. Yet he took the beatings the Big Swede inflicted on him and never once said one word of reproach against this man. The answer may be the one given by a member of Erle's family. The Big Swede amused him.

It happened that prizefighting at that time was "a completely illegal activity which constituted a felony under the laws of California." The Big Swede not only had Erle training constantly but out selling tickets after school. As a result, it wasn't long before Erle was summoned to the office of the deputy district attorney. His efforts to convince the lawman that the fights were what the Big Swede called them, exhibition boxing, and his attempts to find some loophole in California law covering prizefighting so impressed the deputy district attorney that he suggested that Erle might like to study law in his office. Erle said that after he quit training he would certainly like to do that.

The opportunity came sooner than expected, thanks to the Big Swede. He went to the high school principal, put up twenty dollars, and asked the principal to cover it and arrange for a four-round exhibition match with Erle, winner take all.

Erle was dismissed from school and he went to work in the law office of the deputy district attorney of Butte County.

The exceptional caliber of Charles Gardner was never more apparent than in the action he took when he returned from the Klondike. He doubtless knew he had a bright, intelligent boy in Erle, and doubtless he was not willing to have that intelligence and brilliance wasted. On his business trips with businessmen, he had been inquiring as to whether there was an outstanding high school principal in California. More than one person had mentioned Joseph C. Templeton of Palo Alto High School.

Presumably, after weighing many pros and cons, Mr. Gardner confronted Erle, told him he was always in trouble at school, yet put up such a good talk it seemed that the fault lay with the teachers. He ended by saying, "I'm going to send you to Palo Alto. If you have any trouble there, I'll know mighty well where the responsibility lies. Now get your things and get started."

It was arranged he should board and room at the Templeton home. Mr. Templeton had eight children of his own but was willing to add a ninth. He figured that Erle's chief trouble was too much energy, and he arranged a program to keep him busy, too busy to be looking for trouble. As Erle was an early riser, he was encouraged to read Blackstone for two or three hours before breakfast, then after breakfast to make it to school on the run. After school he was to work until 9:30 P.M. in a law office, typing legal papers. He then went back to the Templeton home and did his homework. It was a grueling schedule for a teenage boy but it was what Erle needed.

"The following year was probably the most important of my life," Erle recalled. "J. C. Templeton's understanding of human nature, his patience, his tact, and his ability to command respect changed my entire life.

"As an ex officio member of the Templeton family, I never heard the slightest hint of inharmony in that household. The amount of work done by Mrs. Templeton was prodigious . . . cooking, washing, sewing, shopping, housekeeping, and all before the days of electric appliances. The boys were young huskies with hollow bones, who demanded food and more food. The salary of an educator in those days was hardly adequate to raise such a family . . . Mrs. Templeton managed the household so that there was plenty of good, nourishing food, a homelike atmosphere, and an uncomplaining cooperation.

"Mr. Templeton said grace at every meal. He had a great deal for which to thank the Deity, and he certainly didn't want Heaven to feel that he was ungrateful. With that mastery of the English language which characterized his every schoolroom utterance, he returned *complete* thanks for the food. The boys, brought up in a religious atmosphere, fully appreciated the necessity of saying grace, but being hungry and living in a keenly competitive family, at the final 'Amen,' the simultaneous clatter of forks as they speared through the meat and against the platter sounded like a burst of hail on a tin roof."

After graduating from high school on June 18, 1909, Erle took a full-time summer job as typist, along with reading for the law, at twenty dollars a month in Willows, California. With one son in Stanford, an expensive university, Mr. Gardner did not have the money to send Erle there also. His father planned to borrow for Erle's tuition, now that the younger son had shown what he could do. Erle wouldn't even listen to the idea of his father's going into debt for him. A college degree was not essential to become a lawyer. In fact, there was a continuing debate at that time whether it was better to get a legal education in a lawyer's office or in a university.

"I didn't want to 'waste time' going to college," Erle recalled. "I wanted to study law in offices. I wanted to be free to drift around

California, picking out the attorneys who I felt really had something on the ball, and studying law with them." But his father wished him to attend college.

Valparaiso University in Indiana must have had a high reputation as a law school and was less expensive than Stanford or Mr. Gardner would not have chosen it. That autumn Erle entered its law school. Later Gardner said, "I learned more law there in a period of three or four weeks than I ever learned anywhere in anything like the same amount of time." This was mostly from firsthand experience which sent him escaping from town just one jump ahead of the sheriff.

His short-lived stay stemmed from his determination to keep on with his boxing. As there was no gymnasium at hand, he turned his room in the dormitory into a ring. And as he was on the third floor, the floors below began to complain about the noise. The professor in charge of the dorm gave orders that the boxing was to stop. Gardner rejected the demand. Instead, he and his sparring partners tried boxing without moving their feet. "The experiment was only partially successful," he admitted.

It wasn't too many nights after the dictum that the professor appeared at "the ring." Remarking that he too was a boxer, he ordered everybody out. Standing on Erle's right to invite his friends to his room, one of the students refused to go unless Erle told him to. The professor tried to throw the boy out. "But," Gardner reported, "he failed ignominiously. His knowledge of boxing did not include anything that was practical. It was quite a shambles."

Evidently Erle and his fellow student realized they had gone too far, because they figured they'd better get their action in ahead of the professor. Next day they went to town to swear out a warrant for the professor's arrest. The grounds were, in one version, that he had been the aggressor in the affair and, in another, that he had trespassed on private property by invading Erle's room. Whichever version is fact is of no import. Erle learned that school officials had a warrant out for his arrest, alleging "criminal conspiracy." Oddly enough, this was not for the boxing episode but for a bottle-smashing episode which had happened in the dormitory corridors shortly before in which Erle had not taken part. In fact he had tried to talk the ringleaders out of it. But he was not believed when he denied having anything to do with it.

He realized if he had to testify about the affair, he would either have to commit perjury or admit that he had been asked to take part in the matter. If he admitted the invitation, he would be asked the leaders' names. At which point he'd either have to name them or be guilty of contempt of court.

And so he ducked the cops who were trying to serve the warrant. He caught a train to Chicago and one from there to Eugene, Oregon. How the school officials or the law knew where he was going is not reported. Perhaps he told some friends and the friends talked. At any rate, Erle recalled, "I dodged the sheriff there, who was looking for me on telegraphed instructions from Valparaiso. I went out to the railroad camp and worked on railroad construction, a place so tough that no deputy sheriff would come anywhere near it. I worked there until the thing blew over . . ."

Chapter Six

FROM THEN ON he read for the law in lawyers' offices. It would seem that he went first to Santa Ana to the office of E. E. Keech. Although Gardner kept possibly the most extensive records of anyone of his time, somehow he never did list in order and by date the law offices where he read. Or if he did, such a list hasn't yet come to light. However, as Professor Templeton, his mentor, made the Santa Ana arrangements, this was more than likely the next move.

E. E. Keech, a close friend of Templeton's, was one of the leading water rights attorneys in the state. On arrival in Santa Ana, Erle moved into a rooming house but later he occupied "the attic of the huge Keech residence." Keech not only had a large house but also a large family. Erle must have been made a part of it, as he had been a part of the Templeton family, for he wrote in later years, "There I formed more friendships which were destined to last through the years."

And then, on an afternoon when Erle was closing the law office, he was visited by a man who gave his name as Boxall. He had heard about Erle's boxing experience, and as he himself also boxed, he thought Erle might like to work out with him once in a while. Erle locked up the office and accompanied Boxall to his "residence." This consisted of an unfurnished house in one of the cheaper parts of town. The kitchen, with its stove, table, and cupboard of dishes, served also as the living room. The actual living and dining rooms had been turned into a boxing ring. The house also had two bedrooms, unfurnished except for a few chairs and folding cots.

Boxall worked for California Edison Company, but his main interest was fighting. "He used to bewail the fact that the world had become too civilized to have any more wars . . ." His future was to be World War I, at which time he rushed to Canada to enlist, "had a glorious military career," and was killed in battle. Later Erle learned that he had come from a good English family.

But that was later. When they first met, all Erle knew was that Boxall was a professional fighter, what was called in the trade "a pork-and-beaner." Erle moved into Boxall's "residence." By day he worked in the Keech law office; by night he boxed with Boxall and the "pugs who were on the fringe, rather clever amateurs, and a few pork-and-beaners who came around evenings for a workout." Erle remained there until he took his bar examination. He was admitted to the bar when he was twenty-one years old, probably the only youth on record to have been admitted with two black eyes, faintly disguised with makeup.

He went back to Willows where he had studied the summer after his Palo Alto graduation. Ben F. Geis, who practiced there, had quite a reputation as a trial lawyer. After an interview, Erle became a law clerk in his office. Gardner being Gardner even at twenty-one, he was soon "restive." He wanted to open an office of his own. His father had made real estate investments in Merced, believing it was a community destined to grow. It seemed a good place for a young lawyer to get started. Erle therefore went to Merced, where he rented a one-room office and for the first time "hung out my shingle."

"I had no idea how to build up a legal business," Gardner remembered, "and my pre-legal training had been sufficiently unorthodox so that I had none of the social graces. I had never learned to dance. I didn't know any card games, and I was slow to make friends."

The season of summer in the San Joaquin Valley was notoriously hot. Day after day it was one hundred degrees in the shade. Many days the heat went to more than one hundred and ten degrees. Erle sat in his one-room office, waiting for business which didn't come in. After three or four days, when the situation was becoming intolerable, a well-established Merced attorney asked him to take on a small case which his office was simply too busy to handle.

The "small case" turned out to be a complicated situation. But when the client came in to ask the fee, the inexperienced Erle gulped and to the man's complete surprise said ten dollars.

His break came in a letter from Boxall, who had moved to Oxnard, a town close to the coast in Ventura County. Boxall wrote of walking three miles down to the beach at Port Hueneme to swim, and returning to his bachelors' club where he and a group of congenial young men were living. They even had a Chinese cook to pre-

The young lawyer

pare their meals. Boxall thought there was an opening for a lawyer, as there were only two in town.

In those days before radio, television, and air conditioning, Erle's two Sundays in Merced had been "a nightmare of walking down to the super-heated park, sitting on a bench until I was tired; then going to my room until I got tired; then back to the park bench. So I went to Oxnard."

He intended only to look the situation over but he was fortunate enough to find something worthwhile right away. I. W. Stewart, a prominent corporation lawyer, was bothered by having to handle small justice court claims. He offered Gardner a desk and office room if he would take over this petty work. Gardner could hang out his own shingle.

Gardner grabbed at the opportunity. He mailed the Merced office key to a secondhand furniture dealer there, instructing him to go in and clean out the place. He then unpacked his suitcase and began his practice of law in Ventura County, a practice that was to last some twenty years.

"If anyone with a sixth sense had wanted to pick the one place in California where an attorney could have grown up with the community, and in all probability make a fortune out of the practice of law, Ventura County would have been the place," Gardner wrote in 1969. Oil had recently been discovered nearby. Port Hueneme was to be developed as a harbor. Money came pouring into the communities, "and even today, after many many years, Ventura County is considered a hot spot."

"Stewart was a thoroughly efficient bachelor who was dedicated to his work," Erle remembered. "He spent all of his days and mostly all of his evenings in his office and encouraged me to do likewise. His approach to all problems was highly ethical and conventional . . ." Stewart didn't have to urge Erle to follow his work example. Gardner wanted to learn all the law there was to know. He studied, he boxed, he ate, he slept. Before their relationship terminated, Gardner believed that Mr. Stewart had reason to regret inviting the young man into his office. It is possible, Gardner being unconventional. But it sounds more like a typical Gardner put-down of Gardner.

At the time Erle moved there, Oxnard was the brawling, shocking, young town in the county, a place of brothels, gambling, open saloons, and violence. Ventura, the county seat, some twelve miles away, was "a pinnacle of respectability. Ventura was an old town which dated back to the Spanish forefathers, a town of churches and schools, of dignity and morals. I fitted right into Oxnard," Erle stated.

There were only two or three thousand inhabitants. The economy was supported by the factory of the American Beet Sugar Company. There was also a prosperous teeming Chinatown attached to the town. According to Gardner, the Chinese were too smart to work in the beet fields. Instead they "devised gambling schemes by which they secured a fair percentage of the money earned by those who *did* work in the beet fields." Mr. Stewart had many Chinese clients but he turned more and more of their small cases over to Gardner.

Oxnard was running wide open until the day the grand jury, sitting in Ventura, demanded it should be cleaned up. The sheriff closed the town up tight. The Chinese remained. There was an unwritten understanding that as long as they confined their gambling to Chinese lottery and fan-tan they would be let alone. They lived up to their side of the bargain. But in order for the county to keep check on Oxnard, private detectives were hired, and when they presented a bill for two thousand dollars, it threatened the county budget. Thereupon the detectives were told to arrest twenty-one Chinese lottery sellers, the idea being that if each was fined $100 or $150, the fines would pay off the detectives' bill.

The Chinese were enraged. They wanted to fight. Stewart did not wish to handle the case himself. He did not hand it over to the young and untried Gardner, however, but suggested to his Chinese clients that they get a Los Angeles attorney to act as chief counsel, with Gardner to assist.

Paul W. Schenck was retained. He was, Erle recalled, a remarkable individual, one of the well-known Los Angeles criminal lawyers at a time when the practice of criminal law was unbelievably colorful. In Los Angeles he was considered a specialist in Chinese cases. He carried his own interpreter with him, although he fostered the reputation of being able to read and speak Chinese. Erle learned later that Schenck's knowledge of Chinese was somewhat sketchy. Nevertheless, he used the few words that he did know in a convincing way.

Schenck won the first case, having to do with a lottery ticket. The district attorney then became determined that all the other cases would be won by the county. Under the laws of California, any justice's court in the county had jurisdiction over any offense committed anywhere in the county. A Ventura justice of the peace could issue warrants for arrests in Oxnard. A jury drawn in Oxnard was certain to be sympathetic to the defendants; therefore the D.A. never tried a case in Oxnard. It was his usual custom to hold the trials in Ventura, where the defendants were invariably convicted.

In this present matter, however, because there were twenty-one cases and the D.A. wanted nothing to go wrong, he decided to hold the trials in a town now known as Ojai, but which was called Nordhoff in those days. It was a small, isolated country community about twenty miles from Ventura.

Young Gardner hadn't done much in the first trial but "hold Paul Schenck's coat, so to speak, and act as a legal messenger boy." Being the kind of youth who had no inferiority complex when it came to believing in his ability as a lawyer, he wanted desperately to have a case of his own. A bright idea came to him. He was certain that the D.A. and his detectives couldn't remember the faces of twenty-one Chinese defendants and were simply picking them from the street numbers of their business places. So Erle went to Chinatown and moved the resident of Number 45 Savier's Road to Number 2 China Alley. He moved Number 2 China Alley to another address, "and so on down the line."

Having set the trap, he waited happily for it to be sprung. He had done this thing entirely on his own. He'd been afraid to consult Schenck, as he wasn't sure about the ethics of the plan and felt that the city lawyer might veto it. It began as Gardner hoped. The officials picked up the Chinese man they found at Wong Duck's. The man insisted he was not Wong Duck. This they ignored. But just before they started back to Ventura, a deputy sheriff who was a veteran of Chinese arrests suddenly said, "Wait a minute. That's *not* Wong Duck."

By the time the D.A. and his outfit had assimilated this, the Oxnard paper had already come out with the headline: WONG DUCK MAY BE WRONG DUCK SAYS DEPUTY SHERIFF. The D.A. gave up for the time being and dismissed all the cases against the Chinese.

"Up to that time I had been *chong tze t'oy*," Erle wrote. "This meant the little attorney. From that time on I was *t'ai chong tze*, the big lawyer." He inherited the business of Chinatown.

The chief of police now initiated a big raid, not only on the Chinese but also on the non-Chinese with questionable business activities. Of the latter, when queried as to whether Mr. Gardner was their lawyer, those saying "Yes" were arrested. When the chief asked the same question of the leader of the Chinese community, the reply was that Mr. Gardner was the lawyer for all Chinese.

Shortly before this Erle had written his father, "I am terribly busy. I have clients of all classes except the upper and middle classes." Now he found himself a "legal leper," who would have had no law business left had it not been for the Chinese.

Soon thereafter one of his clients was arrested and charged, under a city ordinance, with conducting a gambling establishment. Another who refused to disown Gardner was charged with running a "blind pig." In his research for the defense of these men, Gardner found a Supreme Court decision holding that a city ordinance which was in the exact language of the state law was actually in conflict with the state law. Not knowing this, the city attorney, when he prepared a series of gambling ordinances which the city of Oxnard passed, had copied them word for word from the state penal code.

When his Chinese client was convicted of gambling, Gardner went to Ventura to a higher court, brought up the illegality of the city ordinance, and knocked out the entire proceedings. The police officials of Oxnard were quite naturally annoyed. "In fact," says Erle proudly, "I realize now that I have annoyed many, many people as I went through life."

Being as smart as, and also as cocky and brash as a future character he would create, one Donald Lam, and being as smart and devious and legally astute as one to be known around the world as Perry Mason, Gardner anticipated that the city of Oxnard wasn't about to let itself be outsmarted for keeps by a young lawyer. Not when the townsfolk were laughing about how he had outmaneuvered the police force and legal eagles of the town. He didn't wait for the next move from the city. He made his own.

When he returned with his client to Oxnard, he let the newspapers know the man was there. Surreptitiously then, he loaded the man into the back of his automobile, covered him with a blanket, and drove him again to Ventura. Once there, he took the man to a justice of the peace, to whom Gardner declared, "Your honor, I have defended a guilty client. I'm satisfied this man was guilty and yet I got him off by a technicality."

The judge was not upset. He assured Gardner that sometimes these things did happen and that a young attorney should not feel upset by it. Gardner continued to press the matter. "I all but cried as I told the judge that my conscience simply wouldn't be satisfied until the man made atonement for his crime."

The judge pointed out that there was no charge against the defendant, so he could do nothing. Gardner then signed a complaint charging his client with violating the state law by running a gambling establishment. The judge called in the district attorney and they all went into the courtroom. Gardner's client pleaded guilty, the judge fined him the nominal ten dollars, and that presumably ended that. Neither the judge nor the D.A. said anything about the matter publicly, it being legal nonsense from the start. Gardner and his client certainly did not mention it. They returned to Oxnard, biding their time.

As Gardner had suspected, the city attorney soon announced that being prosecuted under an illegal ordinance was no prosecution, and that therefore there was no jeopardy attached. The police now re-arrested Gardner's client for the original offense. He was brought to trial at the justice's court. Gardner did not doubt that the justice of the peace would give the man the full amount of the sentence the city authorities wanted, six months in the county jail and a fine of five hundred dollars. This, of course, would fully discredit the upstart young lawyer.

"I pretended to be surprised and indignant," Gardner related in later years. "I went into court and promptly raised a plea of once in jeopardy. That was right down the city attorney's alley. He came into court with a wheelbarrow load of law books and took up some two hours making a very learned argument, citing numerous authorities upon a question which is really elemental . . ."

Repeatedly Gardner tried to interrupt until he was "squelched." The judge told him he could have his say when the city attorney had finished. "Thereafter I didn't say anything. I simply let him argue. I sat and listened and listened and listened."

When the city attorney was finished, the judge was ready to dispose of the case. He started to overrule Gardner's double jeopardy plea. And then Gardner sprang it. The certified copy of the docket of the Ventura court, which stated the defendant had already been prosecuted under *state* law, pleaded guilty, and paid his fine. The judge looked at the copy, unable to believe it. He finally asked, "Who in the world filed the complaint?"

And Erle answered, "I did."

As was expected, this broke up the courtroom. And when the indignant city attorney wanted to know why Gardner hadn't told the court about it at the beginning, instead of wasting all their time, Gardner pointed out that he'd tried more than once to speak but had been instructed not to interrupt but to sit down and wait his turn.

This case ended the attempt of the police to get rid of Gardner. Their strategy of divesting him of clients had boomeranged. Cases began to pour in on him, even some that carried a good fee.

"I started practicing law when I was twenty-one," Gardner was to remember, "with a fund of practical legal knowledge, all the brash impetuosity of youth, and virtually no inferiority complex. I was trained in a hard school. My clients didn't want a lawyer to tell them what they *couldn't* do; most of them had already done it. They wanted a lawyer to tell them to go ahead and do what they wanted to do or to explain to a court that what they had already done was legal. . . .

"In my own case, I was lucky. I didn't have to try too many criminal cases. Those I did handle were exceptional ones. I have lost cases—not too many, but some. All during my career I never suborned perjury, never put a witness on the stand when I knew he was lying, never permitted my clients to 'cut corners,' which isn't saying that I haven't defended and perhaps acquitted several guilty men in my time. But they were for the most part Chinese who were only guilty of a little gambling among themselves and were arrested for it; whereas, if the officers had wanted to 'raid' some of the exclusive homes, or drop in at the club of some of the leading fraternal organizations, they could have found plenty of gambling going on.

"The more successful I became as an attorney, the more I was called on to be in one place, to answer telephones, to draw up contracts and conveyances, which I detested, and to be available at all hours . . . I found out that wasn't what I wanted."

Many years later he was to add, "I dislike the routine practice of 'office law' and I keenly enjoy the trial of cases, particularly in front of a jury. So when I get homesick for a good old rough and tumble courtroom fight, I pull up my dictating machine and turn out another Perry Mason book."

Chapter Seven

IT WAS TO BE many years before Gardner became a vicarious defense attorney. Like it or not, he had to continue practicing law, no matter how much the "office law" might irk him. He had acquired a family.

When he went into I. W. Stewart's law office in Oxnard in 1911, Mr. Stewart had as secretary a talented young Southern woman, Natalie Frances Beatrice Talbert, known to her friends as Nat.

She was from Love Station, a hamlet near Coldwater in Mississippi, and the youngest of ten children. Her father had been a surgeon in the Civil War. Her mother, who died when Natalie was two years old, had had her own gift of writing; she was author of a cookbook. The mother's mother raised the children.

Nat attended Blue Mountain College in Mississippi for some years, not as a college student, but for high school work, quite usual in nineteenth-century education. It was probably while there that she began her stage career. She created a program of "dramatic readings and poetry, with dialect stories in Scotch, Irish, Negro, and others."

But illness beset the Talbert family. There was an infection of tuberculosis which carried off some of the children, after which came the father's death. It was decided to move to a more healthy climate. In 1900 the remaining sisters came to Los Angeles. Nat was fifteen years old.

In those years, it was not so difficult for a young person "to go on the stage." It was, however, considered "unladylike," which is undoubtedly one reason why Natalie treasured a letter from her pastor, who wrote to tell her how proud he was of her. She continued her readings in Los Angeles, evidently with considerable success. She told her granddaughter many years later that she had been offered a screen test by a major studio but turned it down because she didn't care about it.

She had a living to earn and dramatic monologues did not steadily supply it. Nat, therefore, took business training on the side. In 1910 she went to Oxnard to work in Mr. Stewart's office. It was only natural in a rough, wide-open town, such as Gardner described Oxnard to be in those days, that Nat and Erle, both of high moral families, would seek each other's company after the office closed, as well as during working hours. For all of his self-portrayal as a tough guy, Erle was as much the gentleman as Nat was a lady, he from New England stock and she from Southern, perhaps the two most conservative-mannered parts of the United States. She was sweet and pretty—all who knew the young Nat mention these qualities— and also had a bright, inquisitive mind, which Gardner would demand from any woman in whom he was interested. Moreover, with the legal knowledge she gained from her work in Mr. Stewart's office, she could talk over legal matters with Gardner as well as or better than any of his other Oxnard friends.

On April 9, 1912, Nat and Erle went down to San Diego and were married. They called it an "elopement." Not that anyone was going to stop the marriage, but this eliminated a fancy wedding, something Gardner would never have stood still for. Nat was four years and one day older than Erle. It sounds more of a gap than it was. As a successful practicing lawyer, Gardner was older than his twenty-two years. His birthday was July 17, hers July 16, and until her death in 1968 they usually celebrated them together.

Their daughter and only child was born on January 25 of the following year, 1913, in Oxnard. She was named Natalie Grace, for her mother and her paternal grandmother. She was called Grace to avoid confusion in the immediate family. Nat was very ill for some time after Grace's birth, but she tried to keep the seriousness of her illness from Erle. By then he was in such demand as a lawyer that she did not want him worried by domestic matters.

In 1915 Gardner was invited to join Frank Orr, a leading young attorney of Ventura, in a partnership. State Senator Orestes E. Orr had been one of the most prominent attorneys of that county seat. After his son, Harold Francis Orr, had graduated with honors from the University of California and been admitted to the bar, the senator took Frank, as he was called, into his law firm. When the senator died, Frank was left with a leading law practice, a law

Nat and Erle

Kenneth Gardner, the senior Gardners, and grandchild, **Grace**

library, a big office, and a volume of legal work. He didn't like trial work; his interest was in corporation law. The editor of the Ventura *Post*, Fred Davis, had been watching and reporting on Gardner's spectacular career in Oxnard. It was he who promoted the partnership between Frank Orr and Gardner.

There were any number of reasons why Gardner was pleased to make the move. As he put it, the tricks that endeared him to Oxnard's Chinatown had managed to attract quite a bit of not so agreeable attention. "I had secured the enmity of the district attorney of the county, the somewhat respectful antagonism of the city attorney of Oxnard, the ill will of the Oxnard police force and of several members of the City Trustees of Oxnard."

Gardner always said that putting him and Orr together was like mixing oil with water. "Frank Orr was a pillar of respectability in a community which was known for its respectability. He and his wife were among the real four hundred of a very conservative, very socially conscious, very law-abiding community . . . I was a brand from the burning. Not only had I come from the roisterous, brawl-

Frank Orr

ing, wicked city of Oxnard, but my career had been pyrotechnic."

Notwithstanding Erle's oil and water figure of speech, a lasting friendship was formed between the partners. Erle thought Frank Orr had one of the best and most thorough legal minds he ever met. Orr was city attorney of Ventura for many years. He was, in Erle's words, a walking encyclopedia when it came to bond issues, municipal law, and associated matters. He was the Gardner family lawyer for his lifetime.

Orr was entertained by Gardner's dramatics in the courtroom, and joined him in certain cases. It is most likely that he was the former law partner of Gardner's who told an interviewer some years ago, as reported by Albin Krebs in *The New York Times*: "It got so he won all his cases. In the courtroom Erle radiated self-confidence at all times. His voice was resonant and carried well. He was big, stocky, plain-looking. Erle didn't try for the dapper, slick-lawyer look. The jurors probably considered him as ordinary as themselves, which suited him just fine.

"His way with a hostile witness was plain wizardry. He could coax the fellow along, right into telling outright lies, or into confusion so complete the fellow would end up babbling and no jury could possibly take his testimony seriously. In behalf of his clients, he nosed about in forgotten statutes and cases to find just the right precedents to fit his needs. At the proper moment, he would spring the precedent on the judge and jury. No one who had known him as a lawyer ever had to look far or to strain his eyes to find where Perry Mason came from."

After two years of the Orr-Gardner partnership, Joe Templeton came again into Erle's life. This was young Joe, son of Professor Templeton, the unscholarly one of the boys, the one who had left school to make money. By now Joe was a manufacturers' agent with his own business, the Consolidated Sales Company in San Francisco. He came to Gardner with a law problem. "One thing led to another," Erle recalled, "and Joe insisted that I had the makings of a good salesman, that I would find a career in sales would be much more interesting than a career in law. —Naturally, I turned him down cold." But finally, he decided to give it a try. Nat and Grace were installed in an apartment in Oakland and there Grace began school. They didn't see much of Erle; he was kept too busy with the new work.

Neither Templeton nor Gardner was as yet out of his twenties. Where older men might think twice, they didn't. Right off, Joe's presence was required in two places at once, in the Northwest and in Indiana. He took the Northwest and sent Gardner to Indiana.

Gardner had no experience whatsoever. On his arrival he was taken on a tour of the plant, which manufactured automobile accessories, and where he thought he was expected to write a report there and then. Knowing nothing about the business, he took the secretary of the sales manager to dinner and let her tell him the company's needs. He dictated a report "at high speed," and boarded the midnight train out of town. A telegram from San Francisco caught him at Salt Lake City. The manufacturer had been so impressed by the report that he gave Templeton and Gardner a sales contract for the entire country west of the Rockies.

With Joe Templeton, Gardner enjoyed "a hectic career which gave me more education in the course of three years than I ever got out of any book anywhere. We were two young fellows and the world was our oyster." This was, of course, before airplane commuting. The two dashed up and down and around the country by train and motor car. Things were happening so fast they couldn't

Joe Templeton and Gardner

keep up with them. They had suitcases with clean linen in the office. Frequently they would come into town, meet for a conference, pick up the suitcase with fresh clothes, and be off again. They had resident salesmen in Phoenix, Los Angeles, San Francisco, Portland, and Denver. From time to time Gardner would return to Ventura to try a case, but he was "only hitting the high spots of the law."

In the strange way of life, stranger than fiction, the Big Swede turned up again. By now he was a self-taught aviator, one of the barnstormers of early aviation in California. Erle ran into him from time to time as he traveled up and down the coast. "On such occasions we renewed our friendship and went out looking for the unexpected . . . We were only arrested once." Probably Erle's favorite quote from the Big Swede was: "Every damn day of my life something unexpected happens. If it doesn't show up of its own accord by five-thirty, then I go out to look for it."

Gardner had come into the selling game in the big boom which followed World War I. When the economy became depressed, the Templeton-Gardner business went broke. Frank Orr had kept Gardner's office unoccupied while he was away, hoping he would come back and resume his practice of law. Erle thus had a place to which he could return. He and Joe decided that the latter would take what was left of the business to pay off their indebtedness. There was one remaining mainstay, the account for which Erle had written his initial report, but at that point, the plant burned to the ground. It was insured, but until it was rebuilt, there would be no manufacturing, and thus no deliveries, and thus no commissions.

The last meeting of Templeton-Gardner was held in their deserted offices. There Joe found they weren't completely broke. In the stamp drawer was five dollars and forty-two cents. They decided to take these assets to the shooting gallery, hoping to win a prize. "We didn't win any prize," Erle reported. "We were completely and entirely broke."

Gardner didn't know it but actually he wasn't broke. The following day he had a letter from the cashier of the First National Bank at Oxnard. There had been two hundred dollars deposited to his credit by some Chinese man who did not give his name and whom the cashier had never seen before. Gardner and the cashier knew the people in Chinatown, and therefore figured it must be someone from Santa Barbara or Los Angeles who was making the deposits, always in cash. Erle drew on the account. The account remained at two hundred dollars.

In 1969 Erle wrote, "To this day, I have never found out who made the deposit." Or how whoever it was learned he was without funds.

Chapter Eight

AND SO IT WAS that in 1921, nearly broke, but unlike most men whose business had folded, with a profession and an office waiting for him, Gardner returned with his wife and daughter to Ventura. Soon thereafter the partnership of Orr and Gardner was expanded to include the Honorable Louis C. Drapeau, who later became a Justice of the District Court of Appeals, and Robert M. Sheridan, formerly of the district attorney's office.

Gardner had intended to practice on a part-time basis. The firm, however, had so many clients that he had to work full-time. Before long, he found himself working nights and days. He hadn't changed his opinion of office grubbing; he wanted to be out front in the courtroom. It gradually developed that he and Drapeau took over the trial work while Frank Orr and Bob Sheridan handled the probate and corporate practice.

"I had some very wonderful partners," Gardner wrote. "Frank Orr is one of the best counsels I have known. Bob Sheridan had a mind for detail, a careful, conservative counselor. Louis Drapeau had been a court reporter for some years before being admitted to the bar. The training was invaluable. He had been a reporter for the Senate, and had covered many famous murder trials in the East." Drapeau had an "uncanny ability" to judge voices. Once he heard a voice he never forgot it. In the trial, he didn't have to look at who was speaking; he knew.

Gardner used neither pencil nor notes, but relied on his memory. In later years, recalling those days, he wrote, "My memory has always been tricky. I can be introduced to someone in one part of a hall, can study his features carefully, express my pleasure at meeting him, go to some other part of the hall, and if this fellow happens to move over at about the same time I'll expect to be introduced to

Louis Drapeau

him all over again. I simply can't remember people in the aggregate and I have a tendency to forget the faces of people that I should know. I *always* forget their names. This gets worse as I get older and is constantly a source of embarrassment to me. If I meet a person out of context, no matter how well I know him I am completely lost.

"On the other hand, while I was practicing law, I almost never forgot the point made in a legal decision I had read, and I could listen to the testimony of witnesses by the hour and recall almost verbatim what each witness had said. This last was the result of intensive training on my part and I think I owe it largely to Paul Schenck."

In one of the early trials in which Gardner was associated with the Los Angeles attorney, Gardner had an automatic pencil of which he was very proud. In those days, he recalled, he would frantically take notes on the testimony of witnesses. During a recess in a particular case, he went out with Schenck to stand by the winding marble staircase of Ventura County's ornate courthouse.

"That's quite a pencil you have, Erle," Schenck said.

"It's my pride and joy," said Erle.

"Let me see it, please," said Schenck.

Erle passed it over and Schenck calmly broke it in two pieces and tossed them down the deep stairwell. To say that Erle was surprised is to make an understatement. What he wanted to do, he confessed, was smash the guy on the jaw.

Schenck said, "Erle, never use a pencil in the courtroom."

Erle was still furious, of course. "You try this case your way and I'll try it my way," he replied.

Schenck said, "Now listen to an older man. Just answer a few questions before you blow your top."

The questions elucidated the fact that Gardner did not know shorthand, that he couldn't take down every word the witness was saying, and that what Gardner was doing was listening with half his mind to the witness, while the other half was trying to keep up with writing down the material. The result was that he missed significant things. Furthermore, he was a giveaway to the jurors, since every time anything that Erle considered important or anything particularly damaging was said, he started scribbling.

Schenck then gave Erle a bit of advice on a jury trial. As long as the jurors are watching the witness, you don't have too much to fear. But when they have their minds made up about the witness, they start looking at the defense counsel or at the defendant. In all probability, they have decided the defendant is guilty and they want to see what the defense attorneys are going to do about it.

Schenck emphasized the importance of watching the jury. "When they start looking around, don't bolster the testimony of the witness by scribbling frantically on that damn pad of yours. Just wait until you have the attention of the jurors, then turn, look at the courtroom clock, stretch and yawn as much as to say, 'Good heavens! How much longer is this goddamn liar going to sit up there and tell those stories.' "

Throughout his entire career, Gardner was usually astute enough to welcome advice from experts. He never used a pencil in court after that.

Looking back on his practice, a lawyer usually remembers when he has been triumphant or has done something clever or brilliant, and Gardner admitted that he had a great tendency to consign to limbo the cases where the reverse was true. However, he added, "I can not only remember one example where I came a beautiful cropper, I can never forget it."

The case concerned a little girl who had run out into the road and had been struck and killed by a car. Orr and Gardner contended that their client, the driver, was well within the legal speed limit, but that the car did not stop in time. An old farmer who had been driving a wagon and team of horses on the same road at the same time testified that the client had passed him and had not been driving with the care the defense claimed. The farmer further testified that he had stopped his team one hundred and twenty-two feet from where the girl was struck.

Gardner decided to make a point of that one hundred and twenty-two feet. The witness could have measured from the pool of blood, but how did he know where to put the other end of the tape? He ascertained that the witness had not been able to measure the distance on his way into Ventura, but with a tape measure purchased there, he could on his return. By then, some time would have elapsed.

Gardner asked the witness if he measured because he'd read somewhere about a witness so doing because he knew some fool attorney was going to try to mix him up on the distance. The farmer admitted he'd had something like that in mind. Finally, after some preliminary cross-examination on the distance, Erle sprang the clincher. "I leveled my finger at him, raised my voice and shouted, 'Now, just tell the jury how you knew where to put the other end of that tape measure?' "

Erle was good at character imitations. The farmer slowly drawled, "Well, now, I told you *I* didn't mark the place but one of the horses did. At the time of the accident I pulled my team to a stop and wrapped the lines around the brake and one of the horses made water right there in the pavement. So when I came back from town, I measured from the edge of the pool to the edge of the puddle and it was"—and he raised his voice just as loud as Erle had his in questioning—"ONE—HUNDRED—TWENTY—TWO—FEET!"

Part Three

MAKING
OF
A WRITER

Chapter Nine

GARDNER MADE a serious start at writing fiction in 1921. He has two differing versions in his two sets of autobiographical notes as to why he decided to try to write. In the 1959 version he explained that for virtually the first time in his life he had some leisure on his hands. He had long ago decided that unless a person was independently wealthy, only writers, who could take their work with them, or owners of mail order businesses requiring little individual attention could be completely independent. In the later 1969 version, he says that he had heard there was good money in writing, and why couldn't he write?

The answer he gave in his notes is one he gave frequently. "Now, right here and now, I want it understood that I have no natural aptitude as a writer. In fact, I don't consider myself a very good writer. I do consider myself a good plotter. And I consider myself one hell of a good salesman as far as manufacturing merchandise that will sell is concerned." Having developed a certain analytical ability in the sales game, he applied this to the manufacturing of plots. "I eventually became a pretty good plotter although I certainly had to work up the hard way. I had to break down a plot to find out what it consisted of. I had to try to find out what people wanted to read, why they wanted to read, and how they read."

In his 1959 notes, he recalled that having decided in 1921 to explore the possibilities of writing, he took a typewriter and some blank paper and started in. "The stuff I wrote was not only unmarketable, but to my surprise, I found I couldn't construct what I wanted to write and get it on paper. It was like trying to sign my name with my left hand. I knew what I wanted to do but for the life of me I couldn't do it."

He gave up. Not for good; Gardner was not a man easily defeated. But for a short while he decided writing wasn't his métier. The reorganized law firm had so much business, there was actually little time for outside activity.

His daughter remembers how he fussed and fumed about having no time to write, and the point at which his wife told him that if he wanted to he could. All that was necessary was to sit down and do it. To prove her point, she sat down, wrote a story, and sold it to the magazine section of the Los Angeles *Times*.

This may have prodded him to try again. In any event, he went back to pounding away on a typewriter. "I told a few friends I was determined to learn how to write. I well remember the courteously patronizing smiles which greeted the announcement."

He was on his own. As near as Gardner could recall, there were no magazines then devoted to authors and embryo authors. There were few books telling how to write. The pulps hadn't quite come into their own, although Street and Smith was inaugurating a chain of such magazines, so-called because they were printed on rough, tan-colored paper made from wood pulp, as against the refined, white, glossy paper used in high-quality magazines called the "slicks."

He had decided to try to crash the pulp field, as it was comparatively easy for a writer to get started there. "I say it was comparatively easy. To my knowledge it has never been really easy for a writer to get started unless that writer had talent of an extraordinary nature . . . I didn't have any extraordinary talent. I didn't have any talent at all . . . I wrote and typed and I purchased postage, and my stories came back . . . I collected an assorted drawerful of rejection slips . . . Since my sales instinct told me that you could never sell a story while it was parked in a desk drawer, I sent out everything I wrote. As fast as it came back, I sent it bouncing out to collect more rejection slips."

He did have, he believed, remembering his high school paper, a certain talent for writing humorous material. He wrote two jokes which he actually sold to a newspaper for a dollar each. This encouraged him to write a humorous skit. It was entitled " 'The Police of the House' . . . purporting to consist of a story about an experience with a house detective as told by a Frenchman on returning to La Belle France." And, said Erle, "Glory be, I clicked."

In his earlier account, Gardner says it sold for ten dollars, in his later, for fifteen dollars. "I never will forget the thrill when the small envelope came back from the wood pulp magazine containing a check instead of a rejection slip." It is probable that ten dollars was the price, inasmuch as his second skit, "The Game of the Badger," sold for that amount.

As he was paid by the word, clearly there was more money in stories than in skits. "I tried to work out a plot and eventually conceived a story entitled 'Nellie's Naughty Nightie,' which, as I remember it, dealt with a situation which arose when an alluring feminine passenger on a train left her nightie in her berth, and an obliging Pullman porter, thinking that he would put it in her bag, got the wrong bag. So a traveling man came home with Nellie's naughty nightie safely ensconced in his bag. His wife did not have a sense of humor and a situation developed which ripened into what I thought was a story. I think the editors strained a bit over that, but they bought the story. The amount of the check was fifteen dollars."

He gave the check to his mother. He knew what her reaction would be, a daughter of New England and a good Methodist church-woman. She was indeed dismayed by such a shocking story. She refused to cash the check, having no wish to profit by "such naughti-ness." Undoubtedly he was playing his own little joke on her; he was always playing mischief with her. And she'd say the usual, "That Erle! That Erle!" Eventually, as young Ken remembers, her New England thrift got the better of her New England ethics, and she used Naughty Nellie's money.

Gardner had been earning big money both from law and, in its time, with the sales company. These piddling literary sums made him decide, "to hell with it. There wasn't any future in writing and I didn't know how to plot."

Nevertheless, the sobering experience of having seen the pros-perous business which he and Joe Templeton had built up collapse overnight had made him realize the advisability of tying a second economic string to his bow. This was the New England Gardner, a Gardner his friends and associates remember well. There must always be the backup car, the extra ice box—just in case. At any rate, he decided to try his alternate idea, a mail order business.

His plan was to sell "something that could be bought as cheaply as possible, yet something that could be described as an attractive piece of merchandise, and something that would sell in a highly competitive market." He knew that lawyers, especially small-town and rural lawyers, had no set fees and felt it beneath the dignity of their profession to bargain. He decided to sell lawyers a course in salesmanship, not calling it that but something higher-sounding.

Being a practicing lawyer, he knew it would be dubious ethics to sell the course under his name. He therefore asked a business friend in San Francisco to join him in a partnership. They would use the friend's name and address for sending out some trial letters. Gardner took one hundred names from the legal directory, and he and his friend organized the Jim Hibbard Book Company. "Somehow, good old Jim Hibbard seemed to indicate a background of rugged honesty. We sent out a hundred letters. We received no replies."

Gardner then realized that lawyers were accustomed to getting advertisements and dropping them in the wastepaper basket. What was needed was something to command attention. So the two "organized" a statistical company, and, says Gardner, he used some of the sales principles he had learned with Joe Templeton. Instead of cheap stationery with side-opening envelopes inscribed "Office of the President," he got stationery so heavy and so expensive that it indicated "no one could afford to send out form letters on it." At the top, to attract attention, he put "Office of the Vice-President." The opening paragraph went something like this: "Compiling statistics for one of our clients, we were startled to find out that 83.72 percent of lawyers were relatively underpaid . . ."

They sent this version to the one hundred names and not only had a response, but orders, even checks. They hadn't asked for orders, only for inquiries, figuring that if anyone replied, then Erle would compile the course. However, among these orders was one from a district attorney, and Gardner decided he'd better write a course fast.

"So I went without lunch for a couple of days, hammering out lessons on the typewriter. I didn't dictate these because I didn't want anyone to know of my connection with the scheme. The multigraph lessons were all sent out from San Francisco."

The partners realized this was a promising start. His business friend wanted Gardner to quit the law, come up to San Francisco, and manage the office. As Gardner's whole idea of a mail order business was to be free of an office, he refused. Thus ended the business.

The lessons went to those who had ordered them but there was no followup to attract other customers. Some years later came a letter from one of the big universities, which wanted to incorporate some of the lessons in their law course. Would the company grant permission? Gardner says the letter was never answered; he still could not afford to appear in the matter.

Gardner now realized that if he was ever going to be free of the confinement incident to practicing law in a rural community, he would have to stay with his story-writing. "So I went at it seriously . . . I hadn't as yet learned how to 'think on a typewriter.' I had to write my stories laboriously in longhand on legal foolscap with a soft pencil; then copy the stories on a typewriter. . . ."

He didn't want anyone to know what he was doing. He was convinced that being an unsuccessful writer was "not the best way to convince clients that they were dealing with a very successful lawyer . . . The stuff I was going to send out would be pretty lousy. Later on, after I had learned something about writing, I felt that I could use my own name. But in the meantime . . . I chose the pen name of Charles M. Green. I started in collecting rejection slips on a wholesale basis. My stories were terrible.

"Every time I got a rejection slip, in place of getting discouraged I got mad. Some of the rejection slips were lulus. For instance, *Smart Set* had a rejection slip which contained the wisecracking advice: 'Please do not send us stories which were written for and rejected by *The Saturday Evening Post.*' "

In later reminiscing, Gardner was to say, "I wrote the worst stories that ever hit New York City. I have the word of an editor for that, and he hadn't seen the worst stories because the worst ones I wrote under a pen name." He never forgot the occasional friendly editor, who would pencil a note on the margin of the rejection slip saying, "Plot too thin," or some other brief criticism.

"I had always told our salesmen that if a man had drive enough, if he kept on punching doorbells, sooner or later he would make his quota of sales. I guess the same thing applies to story-writing. I know it did in my case. Under the name of Charles M. Green, I wrote a story entitled 'The Shrieking Skeleton.' This was a novelette. It was a major opus as far as I was concerned, and looking back on it, I guess it must have been a dilly."

This was in 1923, and at that time the editor of *Black Mask* was a man named Sutton. According to reports, Sutton had published the first detective story of Dashiell Hammett. He had also published the first detective story of Carroll John Daly. He was to publish the first of Gardner's detective stories. "Yet Sutton never made any claims for having 'discovered' anyone," Gardner recalled. "I gathered that *Black Mask* was something of a sideline with him. But from what I have heard since, I think he was really a great editor."

To *Black Mask* went Charles M. Green's "The Shrieking Skeleton." It was so lousy, Gardner said, "that I understand it caused quite a bit of amusement in the editorial offices. It reached Sutton's desk, not because anyone wanted him to read it as editor, but because someone suggested that, as a gag, they send the story in to Phil Cody and tell him they were planning on using it as the lead story in the magazine and would like a campaign of publicity."

At that time Cody was circulation manager. Later he and Erle became warm personal friends. He was, according to Gardner, inclined to take life seriously, too seriously. He read the first Gardner-Green story and "hit the ceiling." He sent it back to the editorial department saying that the characters talked like dictionaries, that the so-called plot had whiskers on it like unto Spanish moss hanging from a live oak in a Louisiana bayou and adding other "rather uncomplimentary things." He begged them not to use the story. The joke having been successful, the story was returned to "Green" with the usual rejection slip, stating that the fact the story was returned did not necessarily imply that there was any lack of literary merit, it simply did not fit in the schedule.

Inadvertently, Cody's note was trapped between the second and third pages and Gardner found it. "At that time I had never had a criticism of a story. I had one then. People couldn't make me mad by criticizing me. I had been criticized by experts. I had been accustomed to standing up in police courts and dishing it out and taking it on the chin. It never occurred to me to get mad at Cody's caustic criticism. I thought it was all in good faith and that I had simply stumbled onto a routine reader's report. So I sat down and studied the story carefully . . . I realized that I hadn't written what I had thought I had written and I realized that the plot was terrible."

For three nights Gardner was up most of the night revising the story. His typing technique was two-fingered, and he pounded the skin off the ends of his fingers. He covered the fingers with adhesive tape and "kept on hammering away on the blood-spattered keys." When he had revised and revised and finally was satisfied, or as satisfied as it is possible for a writer to be, he wrote "a nice letter" to the editor, signed Charles M. Green, thanking him for including the reader's criticism, and saying that he trusted the revision would make the story acceptable. In retrospect, Gardner believed that

Sutton was so embarrassed by the incident that he bought the story. He paid a hundred and sixty dollars for it.

"That did it," Gardner proclaimed. "I was launched on a literary career."

What followed was an anticlimax. As Erle told it, "I kept hammering away at the *Black Mask* market . . . Every now and then I sold a story. Sutton ceased to be editor. Phil Cody became editor, and Phil Cody heartily disliked my style of writing. But Phil Cody had an assistant editor by the name of Harry North, who was a patient cuss with something of a sense of humor, and Harry wasted his time with me, giving me a little coaching on the margin of rejection slips and in short personal letters. . . . I began to write better stories and now and then *Black Mask* bought one. But I still couldn't plot worth a darn."

After Gardner's first year of writing, *Black Mask,* having noted the endorsement on the checks, knew that Charles M. Green was a pen name. They suggested Gardner now publish under his own name. The stories were getting good enough for him to start building himself.

When his first story appeared in *Black Mask,* Gardner had received a letter from Arthur E. Scott, editor of *Top Notch* magazine, saying he'd be glad to read any material Gardner cared to submit. Although later Gardner figured it was a form letter sent by a competitive magazine to any new writer, at the time it meant a chance at another market. Within a few hours, it so happened, a human fly was going to put on an exhibition in Ventura. He would and he did climb the First National Bank building. "This gave me a great idea," Gardner recalled. "Why not have a detective who would be a human fly? There had been detectives who were dope fiends, detectives who were prissy literary nincompoops, detectives who were too skinny to leave a shadow, detectives who were too fat to walk—why not a human fly detective?"

Thus was born Speed Dash, one of Gardner's most popular characters in his pulp days. Feeling that being a human fly was not quite enough to make the character a major detective, Gardner also gave him a photographic memory. He would climb a building to get into a room containing evidence, and then he would memorize the room as he saw it. Later Gardner invented a "mental gymnasium" where Speed Dash would work on his memory. He started with a record of about five seconds to memorize a room; later he could do it in a blink of a tenth of a second, with a gaze of such steady concentration that "his eyes seemed fairly to glitter."

"In that first story Speed Dash was rather crude, I not only thought that I had to give him this wonderful photographic memory but I had to show just how he had acquired it. This took a bit of explaining. It took too much explaining. . . . It went on and on. Quite naturally an author who never could remember names or faces would tend to overexplain. . . ."

Later Gardner heard the story of how Speed Dash made *Top Notch* the first time out. The editor had read the story, and while thinking it over, went to the office window. There he found for himself that the Street and Smith building had been constructed in such a way that there were handholds with which a human fly could climb it. He sat on the window sill and tried putting his weight on his hand in those grooves. Seeing that it could be done, he went back to his desk, took the story to pieces, cutting back the long, elaborate memory-training course Gardner had included, and returned it with suggestions on how to rewrite. Gardner rewrote it, made a sale, and Speed Dash began his career as part of the pulp world.

According to Gardner, Arthur E. Scott was a patient, understanding editor. He was a huge figure of a man, around six feet five, and he could write the smallest hand Gardner had ever seen. "I believe he could have signed his name with perfect legibility within the diameter of a dime." Gardner and Scott remained friends throughout their working careers.

Street and Smith, publishers of *Top Notch,* were particularly anxious not to have their magazines bear the stigma of the so-called "dime novel," although each magazine sold for a dime. "There was still an aftermath of parental opposition to the reading of trashy fiction! Therefore, when one of the executives of the company read this horrible story of Speed Dash, he noticed that as a part of Speed's training it had been necessary for him to live regularly and that he could neither smoke nor drink."

This was what the executive wanted. He asked Scott to request more stories, providing Gardner would emphasize the fact of Speed's pure life. "Could I emphasize Speed's pure life! The man became so pure that distilled water looked like whiskey in comparison. . . . A six-months old baby could have read my future Speed Dash stories."

Discussing the series character, Gardner said, "It is no secret that many authors who have created series characters have come to hate their guts. This has never been the case with me. I fall in love with the guy and tackle each new story with renewed enthusiasm."

Trying to find things more and more difficult for Speed Dash to do became more and more difficult. Arthur Scott suggested having Speed climb some natural obstacles, so Gardner had him forced down in a parachute at the bottom of the Grand Canyon. "Speed blithely scampered up the perpendicular walls of the Canyon like a squirrel running up a tree. Speed could do this because he neither smoked nor drank. He lived a pure life."

Then there was "The Room of Falling Flies" where Speed had to climb out of a porthole and scale the side of the ship. "The villains stood no chance against him because they didn't lead pure lives." And when Speed climbed the Frye Building in Seattle, about the biggest skyscraper on the Coast, the villains had even sent to the Himalayas for a mountaineer, and in the midst of a raging thunderstorm the two of them were chasing around the side of the building. "But," says Gardner, "that savage had used tobacco or had had an impure thought or something and eventually the strain became too much for his dissipated, tired muscles. He lost a fingerhold, ripped off a fingernail, reached out frantically, slipped, lost his toehold, and hurtled screaming down to the pavement, while Speed leisurely groped with his fingertips along the wet side of the building until he found an open office window."

Alas for True Life versus Fiction. Speed Dash had quite a number of readers who took him seriously. Among these was "one aspiring young pugilist in the Navy who emulated Speed by living a one hundred percent pure life so that he could master all adversaries." Unfortunately, in due time he was flattened in the second round of one of his matches.

He wrote Erle with indignation. "Strangely enough, the man blamed me as an author," Erle recounted. "Unfortunately there was nothing I could do about it except try to avoid the writer of the letter."

About the same time he was establishing Speed Dash, Gardner began writing Western stories. Being experienced in the real West, he felt this was something he could do well. "However," he was to remember, "knowing the West was about the worst qualification a Western writer could have unless he had already acquired a big name for himself." Many of the successful Western writers had never been out of New York. Many of the Western editors were in the same groove. The result was that Erle lost a sale when he told a Western editor that he didn't know what he was talking about, and proved it. After that he deferred to the editor's "knowledge."

The number of markets increased and Gardner kept increasing his sales. He knew he had much more to learn about story-writing. He also knew that his most valuable material was connected with his legal background, but he didn't want "to waste it on cheap stories." In this period, he was still having trouble with plots, yet he didn't have the time "to really think up good ones." The plots were no good, he ruefully recalled, because they were simply event combinations.

Gardner realized that often he would start out selling well and then his relations with magazines would deteriorate. His relations with *Black Mask,* his best market, to his horror began to show signs of the same deterioration. After too many rejections from the magazine, he decided on a gamble. He wrote a story entitled "Three O'Clock in the Morning," and with it he sent a short letter. North bought the story, and when it appeared, he printed the author's letter in an introductory box: " 'Three O'Clock in the Morning' is a damned good story. If you have any comments on it, write them on the back of a check."

Gardner began again to try to find out what a plot was and where it came from. "I reached the conclusion that there were certain situations in which a man can find himself, where his every instinct leads him to a course of conduct the exact opposite of what he should be doing."

In his own case, he would try to think of a plot in terms of story. He would then think of stories he'd written, stories he'd read, and he'd find himself with a tendency to switch characters and situations around in one of these to make a new story. "It is a deadly, dangerous habit of thinking," Gardner averred, and a writer's natural tendency.

"Then I began to realize that a story plot was composed of component parts, just as an automobile is . . ." And he began building stories instead of trying to think them up. He worked out basic ingredients, a method of putting these together, and then worked out a method of coordinating the combination of ingredients.

Perhaps the most successful and certainly the favorite plot machine he devised was a cardboard wheel with spokes radiating from the center. Some of the spokes indicated characters, some situations, some unexpected complications, some the lowest common denominators of public interest. He made the wheels so that, as they revolved, the points of contact where the spokes came together would give the nucleus of a plot. "If I couldn't get a plot within thirty seconds, I thought I was slipping and worked myself into a frenzy of activity."

In those early days, Jean would come to his house after office hours to take dictation on matters connected with his writing. When she left around ten o'clock, Gardner would go for his typewriter and start working, two-fingered, on a story. "I would work until one, one-thirty, or two o'clock in the morning when I would be so dog-tired that whenever I would stop to rest I would fall asleep in the chair and have nightmares, dreaming for the most part about the characters in the story, waking up a few seconds later all confused as to what was in the story and what had been in my dream. At that time I would go to bed. I would sleep about three hours a night, waking up around five or five-thirty in the morning. Then I would take a shower, shave, pull up my typewriter and write until it came time to go to the office.

"It's a wonder that I didn't kill myself with overwork. If I finished one story at twelve-thirty at night, I couldn't go to bed without starting another. For a period of several years I pounded out stories on the typewriter at the rate of a novelette every third day, and at the same time practiced law, much of it trying cases in front of juries, which I can testify is a very exhausting occupation."

He finally had learned to think on the typewriter. This more than doubled his output. He then found out about a new mechanical gadget, the electric typewriter, which further increased his wordage. It was inevitable that he would make the transition to dictating his stories.

When he was with the Consolidated Sales Company, Gardner had used a dictating machine. He introduced it into his law office on his return and became the center of an uproar. "I was one unpopular individual and there was a time when the girls virtually rebelled. But I fought the thing through and eventually they came to like the dictating machines."

Jean remembers that some of the secretarial staff were scared to death of Gardner, the way he ranted and raved as he "fought the thing through." At times he would get so impatient waiting for something to be typed that he would grab the paper out of the typewriter saying, "I'll do it myself," and start punching out his familiar two-fingered but fast typing. Once, hearing him run up the stairs to the office, a secretary burst into tears.

By the time he began dictating his stories, Gardner set himself a quota of one hundred thousand words a month, divided into five thousand words a day. When he couldn't work, such as when he was away on a case, he doubled the wordage on other days. "For some ten years I kept up this man-killing pace of a hundred thousand words a month." Jean had become office manager and executive secretary of the law firm but she continued to come after work to help Gardner.

After his sale of "Three O'Clock in the Morning," Gardner became a fixture of *Black Mask* magazine. "This was long before the days of the decidedly controversial Captain Joseph T. Shaw, the editor who was to publicize himself into being known as 'the creator' of the magazine. Although 'Cap' Shaw permitted the belief that he discovered the three headliners, the truth was that before he came on the scene, Dashiell Hammett, Carroll John Daly, and Erle Stanley Gardner were regular contributors to the magazine."

When Phil C. Cody was editor, he came out to the Pacific Coast on one occasion with disturbing news. Dashiell Hammett was going to quit writing for *Black Mask* unless his rates could be raised. Cody was in a Scylla-and-Charybdis dilemma. The magazine simply couldn't afford to raise Hammett's rates. Yet to prosper, it needed Hammett's stories.

"I found myself in something of an embarrassing situation," Gardner recalled. "I was practicing law and making enough money out of the practice of law so I didn't need to make money out of my writing in order to get by. On the other hand, *Black Mask* was my only really regular market and if *Black Mask* couldn't keep on in business without Dashiell Hammett, which Cody felt was the case, I would suffer along with all the other writers. So I made Cody a business proposition. He could take a cent a word off my rate and add it to Hammett's rate. Cody thought that was most generous on my part, not recognizing the fact that I was making a business proposition from a business viewpoint. Cody went back and told Eltinge Warner, the owner of the magazine, about my generous offer, and Warner never had much use for me afterwards. He said that was a perfectly cockeyed offer and no good businessman would have made it."

To which Erle concluded, "All of which shows you can't win them all."

Before Cody went back East, he asked Gardner to go with him up to San Francisco to talk with Dashiell Hammett about the raise in rates.

They went, but failed to see Hammett. When his wife came to the door and saw two strange businesslike men on the doorstep, she thought they were bill collectors, and told them Hammett was out of town and she didn't know when he'd be back.

"However," Gardner recounts, "it turned out that Hammett was only too glad to continue to write for *Black Mask* magazine at the regular rate which, as I remember it, at that time was three cents a word, or perhaps two cents a word. I continued to write for the magazine. The magazine continued to prosper, and despite the fact that Eltinge F. Warner, the owner of the magazine, had written me off the books as an impractical dreamer, I continued to build up my name in the mystery field."

In 1969 Ellery Queen presented in a paperback reprint quarterly four of Gardner's novelettes and three short stories. For this he compiled an unorthodox introduction out of letters he had had from Gardner over the years. In one, Gardner listed the series characters he had created. He couldn't remember how many there had been, but of those he could remember there were Speed Dash; Señor Arnaz de Lobo, professional soldier of fortune and revolutionist; Jax Bowman, of whom Gardner could remember nothing; Sidney Zoom and his police dog; the Patent Leather Kid, a suave, sinister chap; the firm of Small, Weston and Burke; Ed Jenkins, the Phantom Crook, a lone wolf type who ran in magazines for something over twenty years; Whispering Sand; Major Brane, free-lance secret service man; El Paisano, who could see in the dark; Bob Larkin, a juggler who carried no other weapon than a billiard cue; Black Barr, a typical Western two-gun guy, who felt he was an instrument of divine justice; Bob Crowder; Dane Skarle; Sheriff Bill Eldon; and Lester Leith, who was, with Ed Jenkins, Black Barr, and Speed Dash, among Gardner's particular favorites. These were all characters from the pulp days; the books in due time brought D.A. Douglas Selby, Terry Clane, Gramps Wiggins, Bertha Cool, and Donald Lam, and in Gardner's own words, "of course the one and only Perry Mason."

In this same Queen introduction, Gardner remembered these pen names he had used: A. A. Fair, Charles M. Green, Kyle Corning, Grant Holiday, Robert Parr, Carleton Kendrake, Charles J. Kenny, Arthur Mann Sellers, Les Tillray, Dane Rigley, and Charles M. Stanton. When you were writing a million words a year for twenty or so magazines, you needed a roster of names.

Chapter Ten

In 1925, after four years of handling his material on his own, Gardner took on an agent. It wasn't easy then, any more than it is now, for writers living anywhere other than on Manhattan Island to find a reputable agent. Knowing that Gardner wanted someone to help him expand his markets, Phil Cody of *Black Mask* sent him a brochure from the office of Robert Thomas Hardy.

Hardy, a tall, dignified, quiet man, was highly respected in New York publishing circles. In a line of work which had entertained some fancy chicanery, and had at least two financial scandals taking place at the time, he was scrupulously honest.

Gardner had no idea of the workings of an agency. His own plans included having a special sort of manuscript paper with his name and address on it, and sending a deposit to Hardy to use for Gardner's expenses. Hardy's reply to this was that Gardner should use good plain paper for his manuscripts, that the office would put them in folders with the agent imprint as they did with all manuscripts, and that there was no need to send a deposit. All that Hardy needed at the moment was a list of magazines where Gardner had sold, and the rates he was receiving from each one.

Gardner sent on the list with comments. "Nearly all of my work has been fairly long," he pointed out, "running for the most part to mystery novelettes and detective stories. Have sold something over half a million words and about fifty-three to fifty-five separate stories. As far as I know, I am not in bad with any market."

In another letter he wrote: "My greatest production during any one month was in July of this year, in which I turned out something over sixty thousand words. To date I have received eight hundred and fifty-five dollars from stories written during that month and have two stories unsold. Some months I do not write over fifteen thousand words although my average is twenty-five thousand. I have not as yet acquired the facility of expression necessary to encourage me to even try the *Saturday Evening Post* although I have recently received some very strong encouragement from the lesser markets."

He forwarded a story, "The Mob Buster," saying, "Here's a yarn I like, and damned if I know why the editors don't." Much of the early material he sent to Hardy had been turned down by his own markets. In a discussion of *Black Mask* he wrote, "Here is something about Cody . . . he is doing a lot of hard work, and he has three authors he features pretty steady, Hammett, Daly, and myself. He likes my work because he can always send it to the printer nearly as it is and doesn't have to bother over a lot of interlineations, etc. I like to keep my work so neat and clean for him that he can glance it over and shoot it in."

Throughout November he was sending manuscripts to Hardy with long letters on his ideas and plans. "I've never been mediocre in anything I've done yet, and I want to either go to the top in the fiction game or quit it altogether. I figured on five years when I started before I would have my preparation to a point where I could really do proper work . . . In fact, I figured on writing three years before I would look for an acceptance. I got fooled on that, but it's taking me a while to work up through plot ideas and into the style that reaches the big ones. Still I want to get a foundation. Only remember that I regard it only as a foundation."

At the end of 1925, Gardner was convinced that the agency was disappointed in his sales. Hardy reassured him concerning this: "You have commented several times upon the fact that I am not getting wealthy because of commissions. Just dismiss such thoughts from your mind. I know you have the goods and will deliver them. I have mighty few clients that I'd swap for you. I am sure that 1926 is going to be a good one for both of us!"

The new year started out with Erle concerned about his standing in the magazines for which he was writing: "Incidentally are these magazines paying me scrub rates or are they giving me regular rates?" and "Rates don't bother me unless I think a magazine is giving me a scrub rate, and then I get mad."

A week later, he was writing, "I am endeavoring to arrange my affairs so that next summer I can put in more time upon writing and give you a little better quality and more of it. My writing is done upon a very hurried and peace-meal [sic] basis at the present time. If I could get pretty well established with both *Short Stories* and *West* in addition to *Top Notch* and *Black Mask,* I think I would arrange to put more of my time on the writing game and less in the law business."

By February, he was fighting one of his typical fights. "From now on I am going to write Westerns where the hero is a long, lazy cowpuncher with a 'little hoss,' who unwraps himself, the hero not the hoss, from the upper rail of a corral, gets a job with a tough outfit, finds the owner is an eastern woman who has inherited but never seen the ranch, finds the foreman is crooked, realizes he is working for the owner and not the foreman, battles with temptation in the midst of the purple sage, with only the howls of the coyote to interrupt his meditations, has his conscience triumph, writes to the woman, has her come out, have bandits in the pay of the foreman abduct her so she can't get the evidence, have the cowpuncher chase the bandits, and BANG, BANG, BANG, three of 'em bite the dust, and then have the crooked cowpunchers come to the rescue of the bandits, BANG, BANG, BANG, three crooked cowpunchers bite the dust, then have the crooked foreman decide to reform and walk out of the story with his shoulders hunched forward in thought while the old moon silhouettes his broken form." Erle mentioned more than once that three "bangs," such as "Bang, bang, bang!," meant nine cents to the author, whereas one "bang" was only worth three cents at the rate of payment. "There is a streak of red in the east and the hero turns to find the rosy dawn reflected in the eyes of the heroine, and have one of 'em point to the east and mutter, 'the dawn of a new day for the T bar T.'

"What's more I mean it, while I've been rattling the keys and running off the first damphool ideas that came into my head, I'll bet ten dollars that yarn will sell for more than any yarn with a carefully thought out plot, and just to show you I'm going to pull this letter out of the machine and dash off said yarn and I'd like to have you send it to *Short Stories* . . ." The caps are his: "I AM BLAMED ANXIOUS TO BUILD UP A MARKET FOR ARCHERY ARTICLES. I like to take the trips and would like to make them pay their way, and the writers of that stuff get a chance to pick up good tackle for nothing so keep the archery in mind."

At the end of April, Erle was leaving for several months on a trip to Alaska where he would be out of touch with civilization. To Hardy he wrote, "You'll hear from me from time to time with a batch of manuscript sent on for copying, but you won't be able to reach me . . . Incidentally, just sort of remember I'll be depending on literature (?) for my income on this trip and don't let any editors reach for the rejection slips when they see my stuff." He was still trying to place his archery material. "Give it away if necessary," he instructed Hardy. "I like to see this archery stuff in print."

He was traveling by yacht with Adolph Sutro, grandson of the famous San Franciscan who discovered and developed the Comstock Lode in Virginia City. Adolph and Erle shared many adventures; they enjoyed the same type of humor and their various ramblings brought forth the kind of anecdotes Erle loved to recount.

He was home again on July 21, writing, "Here I am, back on the job, happy, healthy and broke." If one wonders how he could, with his double work schedule, take off for three months of yachting, it wasn't easy. This was made plain in his next letter to Hardy: "Things are a bit unsettled here. Either I will have to give more time to the law business, starting immediately, or else we'll have to take in another partner, and let me go on a half time basis. The boys want me to quit the fiction, but I hate to give it up, and yet I'm not ready to quit the law . . . We have more clients than we know what to do with . . . and yet I like this fiction game."

It is quite evident that Erle was under considerable pressure throughout the rest of 1926. As the letters indicate, he had major decisions to make, with strong doubts as to whether he could make the grade in writing. As he had the responsibility of a family, writing had to furnish him with a living if he was to continue with it.

In November, he was writing Hardy, "Tell me, do ordinary writers get ten thousand dollars a year or is it only the fellows who get in the illustrated magazines who make a good living out of it? I'd like to know what the ordinary author for magazines, such as I write for, can hope to make in a year." For some years he had been clearing twenty thousand dollars a year in law, and in the twenties this was a considerable sum; to come down to ten thousand dollars a year—if he gave up the law—would have meant a distinct change in the Gardners' standard of living. "Just how does my stuff seem to stack up to you?" he asked. "Do you think I am slipping, and can you make any suggestions?"

In reply, Hardy summed up, "You have made good progress in one way during the past few years. You have sold a great deal of stuff and interested a number of markets. But I am inclined to think that after this I would write less stuff. Keep the regular markets well supplied, of course—you don't want to lose these. But try to find room to work on some better stories. Don't write freak stuff. Let's have well rounded plots with plenty of action, suspense and emotional appeal. But put enough time in on them to give them a chance at *Liberty, Collier's,* the *Post,* etc. Most of the material you have been sending me is perfectly all right for the newsprint magazines but it hardly makes the grade for the better paying sheets. I want to get four or five hundred dollars for a short story for you before long, and I can't do it with ordinary Western or Detective stories that you have pounded out at top speed."

Erle had done quite well in 1926. He had ninety-seven sales, including twenty-six to *Black Mask* and fifteen to *Top Notch.* Total words for the year were 906,800. As he was paid by the word, amounts for each story were not large. *Black Mask* was one of the lower-paying markets but Hardy understood Erle's feeling about Phil Cody, and that "even though it may be at some financial loss," Gardner wanted material to go to him.

It was in July of that year that *Black Mask* changed editors. Cody wanted to get away from editorial work and handle only the business end. It was then that Joseph "Cap" Shaw was named editor. Hardy said of him that he "seems a nice person and he isn't the least unfriendly to either of us." Shaw had told Hardy that Carroll John Daly seemed the most popular author with readers, judging from letters received. "You come very close in popularity, and apparently he wants to use your stuff regularly." Hardy concludes, "I believe that it is going to be a better paying market before long."

In November Gardner had a visit from Adela Rogers St. John, daughter of Earl Rogers, the famous Los Angeles lawyer whom Erle admired. She was a prominent newspaper writer who covered the Hollywood scene. She and Erle had discussed the flurry of interest he was having from motion pictures, and he wrote Hardy that he would now be offering carbons of his stories to the studios in advance of publication so "don't let any editor misunderstand us or buy the picture rights."

The new year of 1927 didn't improve Gardner's spirits. In the first week he wrote to Hardy, "On the first-class magazines I'm afraid I haven't got the stuff on the ball. I have a hunch that at the present time I'm a second-class writer and a hell of a lot more typewriter ribbons have got to be worn out before I graduate, but graduate I will."

"We are having rather bad luck at present," Hardy wrote in reply, "but I have been hoping it will change soon. There are so many magazines using Western and Mystery stories one would think it wouldn't be difficult to sell almost any kind of a good yarn. You'd be surprised, however, to see how brash they are in bouncing things back. Be sure I'll do all I can."

On March 12, Gardner dissolved his arrangement with Hardy. There was no rancor on either side. Gardner wanted to return to selling his own material; he was convinced he could do better on his own. He remained on his own until May of 1929, when he went back again with Hardy. Nothing spectacular had happened to him in the interim; he still sold and he still collected rejection slips.

Chapter Eleven

WHEN GARDNER RETURNED to Robert Thomas Hardy the agent began urging him to try a detective novel. Although a first book, with rare exceptions, was not a money-maker, the chances were excellent for larger peripheral returns from serialization in the "big mags," such as the *Saturday Evening Post, Collier's,* or the new one, *Liberty,* and sale to the motion pictures.

Hardy pointed out that three stories of Gardner's in *Black Mask,* featuring the same character, had a total of around sixty thousand words. He suggested that the three might easily make book length with "a little working over to establish the continuity. Please give the matter some thought."

Nothing came of this. At the time Gardner's main interest was to sell *The Log of a Landlubber,* an account of his yachting trip to Alaska. From the start Hardy was dubious about being able to place it. He sent it around but it was turned down by every house. He reminded Gardner, "Of course, it would have a much better chance if you had a widely known name." It never did find a book publisher but in 1927 it did appear as a four-part serial in the magazine *Pacific Motor Boat.* It is perhaps the best humorous piece that Gardner ever wrote.

Hardy's next suggestion was the idea of a book featuring Black Barr, Gardner's Western character and one of his favorites. Hardy thought chances were fair for such a book selling. "If it is published, it will give you a certain amount of prestige," he wrote, "and the publishers will want to bring stuff out regularly, if you can meet their requirements." Nothing came of this, either. Or of putting in book form some of the stories featuring Lester Leith, another of Gardner's favorite pulp characters, an idea broached in 1929.

Gardner wasn't much interested in any of these suggestions. Not only had he the yachting book in his mind, he was still hammering on one about archery. For years he was determined to find a publisher for this latter project, but was never able to arouse interest.

Sometime in early 1930, Gardner told Hardy he was starting a book, but in April he found it necessary to write, "By this time you probably think I am the champion false alarm of the world." An involved law case had come up which kept him busy "for a solid month."

By October he was apologizing again: "God, how I hate to write you and admit that the book is still in the process of construction." Actually, between October 1930 and September 1932 Gardner simply didn't have time to write a book. First of all, there was the law, an essential source of income, since he had a family to support; second, he was, as he admitted, in such demand in the pulps that it took all his extra time to keep his regular markets supplied. The breakthrough came only when he discovered his dictating machine could be used for more than just briefs or correspondence.

When he sent the manuscript of *Reasonable Doubt* * to Hardy in early September, he sent a carbon to *Black Mask* to see if they would be interested in serial rights. For some reason, the carbon arrived in New York before the top copy, and Joe "Cap" Shaw loaned the carbon to Hardy. Both agreed that the agent should try for more money than the pulps were prepared to pay.

After reading it, Hardy wired Gardner: NOVEL WORTHY BIG MAGAZINES MAY I TRY LIBERTY AND OTHERS. He sent a follow-up letter, saying in part, "Your detective novel is distinctly good . . . with chance of selling one of the big magazines."

Gardner rushed back a lengthy letter to Hardy, explaining that he wanted Shaw to have the manuscript for *Black Mask* even if it was good enough to offer the slicks. Shaw apparently didn't want the story for *Black Mask*, so Hardy had a free hand. As it was customary to submit to magazines and book publishers simultaneously, he sent the manuscript to Clifton Fadiman, editor of the young house of Simon and Schuster.

On September 26, Gardner was writing to Hardy, "While I like turning out quantity fiction for the woodpulps, I would like also to turn out something a little better in tone, and I tried to do it with the book length which you have. I hadn't felt that this was particular material for the slicks . . ." and repeated his earlier belief, that it

* Published under the title *The Case of the Velvet Claws*.

had too much guts for a smooth-paper publisher. He continued, "On the other hand I did have every confidence that the book, when put out in book form, would either establish a new school of writing, or at least prove of sufficient novelty to attract some attention. The characters are entirely different from the stereotyped characters usually employed in detective stories. For years I have been studying the technique of the mystery story, and the result of that study is reflected in the yarn—not in the following of the technique but in picking the places where it could be changed for the purpose of introducing a novelty."

Two days later, he wrote Hardy that he was working on another book which should be in New York within the next three weeks. His intention was to try to work out a book every month or six weeks. He knew this was too many, but "Edgar Wallace made quite a financial success putting out books in quantity." If Hardy intended "to experiment with the slicks on first serial rights," Gardner would try to make this next book a little more polished, and a little less blunt in its action.

The *Reasonable Doubt* manuscript was rejected by *Liberty* and went next to *Collier's*. If they bought, *Collier's* would probably pay ten thousand dollars, Hardy believed; big mag writers were getting from ten to fifty thousand dollars for serial rights. He was aware that Gardner's book wasn't typically smooth-paper stuff, but he was hoping its novelty and vigor would enable it to get by. "You may remember that not a great while ago Scribner's published a detective story by Van Dine. . . . What a strange thing this is, when one considers what Scribner's used to be."

In reply to Erle's plan to write a book a month, Hardy wrote, "If all the stories you turn out are as good as *Reasonable Doubt*—and I expect them to be better because of added experience—you ought to be able to place two or three a year anyhow." One of his authors placed six a year, under three different names.

Through October, Hardy and Gardner exchanged frequent letters as *Reasonable Doubt* went the rounds. Finally, *Collier's* rejected, and Hardy suggested, "In line with *Collier's* criticism and my own personal feeling . . . I don't think it will do any harm to give some thought to making one or two of your leading characters more likeable and sympathetic. Your lawyer in *Reasonable Doubt* is pretty hard-boiled and businesslike."

Although the *Saturday Evening Post* was the top of the magazine market, Hardy had not submitted there, doubtless aware that

Gardner's book was not their style. Now, having made the rounds, he gave it a try. Wesley Stout, the editor in chief, rejected, commenting that it had "too unpleasant a setup."

By then the second manuscript, *Silent Verdict*,* had arrived, but Hardy advised Gardner he was not going to try this one on the *Post*. He asked, "Can't you write a story of this type without making your characters all so hard-boiled? Readers like some tenderness, heart interest. Naturally I don't want you to inject this at the expense of the strength of your story. Dashiell Hammett's stuff is rather viciously hard-boiled, and Fred Nebel has been emulating him to some extent. Keep your air of realism but avoid the setup that is too unpleasant so far as you possibly can." It would help sell motion picture rights, he went on. "All producers like sympathetic characters and there are none in *Reasonable Doubt* or *Silent Verdict*, . . . unless it be the secretary in the first-named story, and she doesn't figure to any great extent.

"I don't doubt that writing these two novels has taught you a lot," Hardy continued. "Among other things, they should have taught you that you have a remarkable future as a writer of books. Even though we haven't sold *Reasonable Doubt* as yet, you certainly have had a lot of encouragement. You are going to write much better books than either of these you sent me. Take plenty of time with the plot of your third novel and see if you can't turn out something that will make them sit up and take notice. I want a story that I can send to the *Saturday Evening Post* with some hope of its clicking. I believe we can count on fifteen thousand dollars for the serial rights from this course, and perhaps more."

Eventually, Hardy believed, Gardner would get fifty to seventy-five thousand dollars and would have no trouble with book publication; and the chance of selling the "talkie rights" would be in his favor because of the publicity the stories and their author would have had. "No matter how much money you have made in the past, it will be a small sum compared to what you can make in the future, if you will go ahead as I expect you to go ahead."

Meantime, Fadiman of Simon and Schuster had sent back the manuscript with a covering letter in much the same vein as those of the magazine editors. Hardy knew that Frederick A. Stokes Company wanted a novel and sent the manuscript next to them. He mentioned to Gardner that he was also going down to talk about it with Horace Stokes, president of the firm, who was an old friend.

* Published under the title *The Case of the Sulky Girl*.

Again the manuscript was returned. Stokes liked it but the "consensus" was not in favor. "Which doesn't mean a thing," wrote Hardy, "except they showed damned bad taste." He was not too distressed because he had not liked their terms (only two books a year) and because they would not give permission to do "noms," as he referred to books written under noms de plume, with other houses. Later he learned that the basic reason for their refusing the book was that Stokes had recently taken on a couple of young fellows who were using the pen name Ellery Queen. The editors did not wish to push another author in competition. Gardner commented that he would have thought they'd rather have another author where they were controlling things, than in competition at another house.

In the same letter about the Stokes rejection Hardy reported, "I have just talked to Thayer Hobson, president of William Morrow and Company, and think I have got him very much interested. Anyhow, I am sending the manuscript over to him at once."

Literary agents had just recently had word from Hobson that he wanted no more mysteries; he already had too many. For this reason, Hardy made the point of selling the Gardner manuscript before submitting it. On November 9, when he wrote Gardner that Morrow was deeply interested, he mentioned, "This is a young and growing house, and I believe they will give just as good results as we could get from Stokes." And on November 11, he could wire that Morrow wanted to bring out *Reasonable Doubt* and that he was now taking the second book, *Silent Verdict*, to show them. Both books were accepted.

Whatever jubilation there was at P. O. Drawer Y, Ventura, California, does not appear in Gardner's return letter to Hardy. It was all business, primarily about the contract, and had one unusual stipulation: "There's one thing I will not do, and that is read proof. You will either have to arrange for a professional to do this, if it is an obligation of the author, or else make the publisher stand the gaff. When it comes to reading proof, I am an excellent archer, lawyer, author, or adventurer, but I am not a proofreader." (Many years later he had a change of heart and all galleys were sent to him to be checked.)

Hobson wanted to publish in March, unless there was some "very promising possibility of serialization." The terms were not as good as Hardy would like, but the market was bad at the time. There would be need for "a little minor editing": The first chapter was rather bad, "almost unnecessary"; Hobson did not like the title very well, saying it was "a bit subtle," that a majority of book readers would not understand it, that it ought to be more vigorous. There was also the question of different lead characters in the two books. Hobson suggested that Gardner combine his two lawyers into one, and thus, with the two books, begin a series.

And so it was that Gardner, just like any other first-book author, found the old clichés to be true; books weren't written, they were rewritten. But he'd rewritten before; he knew how to do it and to make a quick deadline.

In the beginning, neither Erle Stanley Gardner nor Thayer Hobson in their wildest imaginings—and both had wild imaginations— could have dreamed of the relationship then coming into being. It was a friendship based on trust, loyalty, and understanding. Their voluminous correspondence, necessary, as they were for most of the time a continent apart, was as lively as any Gardner book. They fought like brothers and cussed each other up one hill and down the other, but the friendship never faltered. Their publisher-author team became one of, if not the most successful in the annals of publishing.

William Morrow and Company had been established in 1926 by William Morrow, who had been at Stokes; Frances Phillips, who came over from Knopf; and Richard Rostron, who, having had the foresight to up his age to the legal limit, landed the job of office boy, and who by the time Gardner's first book was taken on had moved up to production, where copy-editing was part of his job.

In the summer of 1926, Hobson, traveling in Europe, met in Rome a college friend, Ed Knopf, of the publishing family. Hobson decided he too wanted to get into publishing. He was twenty-eight years old and had been teaching at Yale.

Returning to New York, he applied for a job at Morrow, and was turned down not once, but, as he persisted, several times. He was also trying other publishers and after two months landed a job in the production department of Dodd, Mead and Company. He finally made it to Morrow in 1927, and when William Morrow died in 1931, the company was reorganized with Hobson as president. The average age of the staff in the thirties was thirty years; officers other than Hobson in 1933 were Donald M. Stevenson, vice-president, Eva C. Colby, treasurer, and Emily "Polly" Street, secretary. Other members of the board were William Corrigan; Charles Duell,

Thayer Hobson

who joined the company as an officer that year; Frances Phillips, the editor in chief, who would become a legend in her own time in New York publishing; Dorothy Thompson, prominent newspaperwoman and foreign correspondent, wife of Sinclair Lewis; and Henry R. Luce, publisher of *Time* and founder of a publishing empire. Only Thompson and Luce were not working members at Morrow. Marie Freid, later Mrs. John Rodell, was the young and able assistant editor assigned to work on Gardner manuscripts. Because of the unusual prominence of women at Morrow, the term "Hobson's Harem" was gleefully bandied about publishing circles of the time.

It was hard sledding for Hobson in the early years, with the Depression settling in. But, according to *The First Decade*, a house history published by Morrow in 1936, "In 1932 Robert Thomas Hardy, the agent, walked into the office with two Erle Stanley Gardner manuscripts under his arm. That started something."

The opener of the Gardner-Hobson correspondence is dated November 30, 1932, when Hobson wrote directly to Erle about his book. Before replying, Gardner asked Hardy if it would be proper for him to correspond direct with Mr. Hobson. Hardy assured him it was perfectly all right, he was not an agent who tried to keep publisher and author apart.

On December 3 then, Gardner mailed his first letter to Hobson. It was formal and businesslike, and concerned his plans for a complete revision of *Reasonable Doubt* before Christmas. He would hold off the revision of *Silent Verdict* until getting the critics' reaction to the first book. In Gardner's opinion, *Reasonable Doubt* was the far stronger of the two books.

In this same letter, he launched full scale into one of his favorite subjects, salesmanship: "As I see it, I am a manufacturer of fiction. You are a wholesaler of fiction. You don't buy fiction because you want it as such, but because you want the profit to be derived from a resale. Therefore, we are partners in a joint venture, and I am anxious to make my money *through you* rather than *from you.*"

Little wonder that Hobson was to say to Hardy that Gardner was a most unusual man and that it was rare "to find an author who looks at things as he does."

"I know that you are a specialist in the sales end of the book field," Gardner's letter continued, "and I know that I know nothing whatever about this angle, my entire experience having been confined to pulp paper magazines. I also know that if I can make you money, I am bound to make a reasonable share. If I can't, I certainly do not want you to lose money on me. Therefore, I am going to be guided by your wishes on the books.

"However," Gardner continued, and it was a foretaste for Hobson of Gardner the writer, analytical of his material and how he would develop it, "I have these suggestions that I wish you would think over. The orthodox detective story is an arbitrary, intellectual puzzle. I believe there is an opening for a story of conflict in which the protagonist has to fight the forces of crime. Conflict is necessarily grim but it is passionately interesting. There is no love interest in a struggle between two football teams, but, nevertheless, that struggle commands huge financial returns.

"The first book is grim. It presents the character of a lawyer who is true to himself in that he fights for his client regardless of the fact that he is getting the double-cross from that client. The idea of the secretary was to show a contrast of feminine loyalty as opposed to the trickery of the other woman.

"The second book has not the element of conflict to the extent of the first and is, in many respects, a 'trick' book. In other words, authors and publishers continually claim that their detective stories give to the reader the key clue by which the mystery can be solved. Usually this is merely an empty claim, a promise but partially carried out. In the second book the real key clue is actually before the reader all the time.

"The characters necessary to develop these two plots are essentially different. I am afraid we may lose something by trying to combine the characters. On the other hand I can appreciate the advantage to be gained by a uniform series, but in the long run, I feel the reading public will respond more to a book of conflict because the field is less exploited.

"There have been two suggestions that the book imitates Hammett and I am most anxious to avoid any imitation. On the other hand Hammett is not entitled to be given the exclusive use of anything which he did not discover. . . . Jack London wrote stories of grim conflict long before Hammett was ever thought of . . .

"It might be, however, that the character of the secretary be changed somewhat to a less casual and flippant viewpoint and the loyalty emphasized, making apparent that it was loyalty rather than affection which furnished the bond between her and her employer, which is, I think, more true of what happens in real life."

Neither Perry Mason nor Della Street had been formed as yet, but the beginnings were there. Gardner had two lawyers with which to experiment, and a character called Della Street, liked by editorial readers, who could become the lawyer's secretary.

The Hammett comparison was something that was to plague Gardner throughout his early years. In 1930 Hammett had published *The Maltese Falcon*, which made history in the detective field, and which, in Gardner's opinion, turned Cap Shaw, the *Black Mask* editor, into such a worshiper of Hammett that he tried to have all his other authors write like him. Gardner felt that he himself was slighted in the magazine because only those authors who *would* imitate Hammett received first class treatment.

Gardner never imitated anybody. He was his own man. When he was accused of imitation, as he was in those early days by book editors, book critics, and slick magazine editors—in other words by all those who had not followed his development in the pulps—it was, in one of his favorite expressions, a red flag to a bull. His angry refutations were not against Hammett but against those who compared him to Hammett. Although the two were not close personal friends, they were good working friends.

In his return letter Hobson said, "I think if at times you make your lawyer a little more subtle and a little less hard-boiled than he

is in *Reasonable Doubt,* you'll get away from the Hammett atmosphere. As a concrete example, I remember being rather un-
comfortable at some of the short, clipped, staccato dialogue when
there didn't seem to be any reason for it. . . . That's the sort of
thing which suggests Dashiell Hammett."

He enclosed "a hasty and informed report" by one of his editors:
"The dialogue in this story needs pruning. It should be more subtle.
Some of it is just a little too rough. I don't mean by this any question of censorship of language. If the author wants, he can get a lot
nearer four-letter words than he has without running into trouble.
The profanity is perfectly all right but not quite as hard-boiled in
its tempo. . . . The last chapter is very weak." Another excerpt
said, "The first part of this book ought to be speeded up. The first
chapter is weak and the whole opening drags and is awkward. . . .
There are too many ins and outs in quick succession. The characters
follow each other in and out of the lawyer's office as though they
were walking around the wings backstage and popping in at the
other entrance. And most of it is unnecessary." This editor commented: "Della Street is a better character than the secretary.
Couldn't Davis, the detective, become Paul Drake?"

Gardner wrote back to Hobson, thanking him for this letter
which "came in last night and I got up at four o'clock this morning
to start work with a bang. . . . Frankly I think there is more of
an opening for a conflict type of detective story than for an intellectual type of detective story. There hasn't been any real Jack
London style of conflict developed by detective writers. . . .

"I want to make my hero a fighter, not by having him be ruthless
with women and underlings, but by having him wade into the opposition and battle his way through to victory. . . .

"More than that, I want to establish a style of swift motion. I want
to have characters who start from scratch and sprint the whole
darned way to a goal line, instead of having them start out at a fast
pace, and then slow down to pick flowers at the halfway mark.

"I realize that this is a whale of an order. Probably it's far in
advance of such technical skill as I have acquired from my writing,
but it's what I would like to do, and I consider the field is almost
virgin. The Hemingway and Hammett style creates an illusion of
fast motion, but when you analyze the plot and the motion you find
that it's an illusion of motion created through style rather than an
event sequence which swoops breathlessly forward. . . . I'm giving
you my views in detail because I want you to see just what I'm

striving for, and because I am particularly anxious to keep from turning out a book that will be labeled as another imitation of Hammett.

"On the other hand, rereading *Reasonable Doubt* I find that I have made my style far too similar to Hammett's. . . . Anyhow I'll revise it and send it forward and you can go over it." He gets into his Western hat to add, "You folks give me the impression of being up on your toes, know what you are doing, and being square shooters."

By December 6, the contracts were drawn up and signed, and Gardner was sending his copies back to Hardy with the note, "Being nothing but an ordinary lawyer, I haven't the slightest idea of what this is all about or whether the provisions of the contract are at all usual, but in view of your comments and the fact that Mr. Hobson seems to be such a square shooter, I am signing as is without bothering to puzzle out what it's all about."

Nowadays a book can't be put to bed in the rapid time it was in the thirties. Nevertheless, with a November acceptance, a full-scale revision to be accomplished, and the technical work to be processed in New York, things had to move fast if the first Perry Mason was to be published in March 1933.

On December 9, Gardner wrote Hobson about the *Reasonable Doubt* lawyer, "I am making him into a new character, and since your editors apparently disapprove of both Stark and Keene as names, I am calling him Perry Mason, and the character I am trying to create for him is that of a fighter who is possessed of infinite patience. He tries to jockey his enemies into a position where he can deliver one good knockout punch."

The book title was a major concern which kept the mails active between Ventura and New York throughout December. Even the author's name was a matter to be settled. Hobson queried in mid-December, "Also please let us know whether you'd like your full name used on the book. I think from the point of view of publicity, I'd christen you just Stanley Gardner. On the other hand, if I had written two books nearly as good as you have, I wouldn't dream of letting anyone cut part of my name off—I'd want all three names used."

In retrospect, it seems strange that Hobson and his staff wouldn't have realized that Erle Stanley Gardner, just like that, all three names, was one of the best-known names in detective writing. But then, pulps and the book market seldom met face to face.

Early camp wagon

Gardner, meanwhile, had already sent a wire covering most of the suggestions he had subsequently received in Hobson's letter. The wire included the fact that if they wished, they could use the first eight chapters for the dummy they needed for promotion. He followed on December 14 with his letter regarding titles. He was still Mr. Gardner to Mr. Hobson. In this letter, he introduced his camp wagon. "Don't know whether Bob Hardy told you, but I have a camp wagon, a regular house on wheels in which I travel around in the desert getting local color, and in which I retire when interruptions here at the office get too numerous and I have a bunch of work to do.

"I dictated the airmail to you of the ninth, and then climbed into my camp wagon and headed for the desert with the copy of the book length and some other rush stuff, intent upon settling down to some real work, hunting for one of the lost mines, getting some local color, and working out some novelette plots. And I picked the first time it had snowed in the Imperial Valley in thirty years. It froze me out, so I came hightailing back a day ahead of schedule and found your wire which I answered today." There was a postscript of possible interest to today's jet travelers: "I'm sending this airmail, and also a copy regular mail in case the plane should be delayed."

He also sent the entire first chapter instead of a few pages, "as the balance of the chapter illustrates the point I want to make about a title. You understand that I know nothing about book titles, or about the book business. I know something about woodpulp fiction and that's all. . . . I liked your idea about having the last of one book pave the way for the next. If we're going to run a series, that's the way to do it." He takes up briefly the advantages and disadvantages of this idea, then continues: "Now if we're going to make a series of stories we should start out with a title that will fit into the general scheme of the titles to follow. Otherwise we've created a sort of trademark for the books, but the titles are at variance with the scheme."

After discussing various titles, including *The Canary Murder, Murder at Midnight, The Grinning Face Murder*, he wrote, "I'm wondering if we can't break away a bit by having the CASE or AFFAIR featured first. . . . I have two suggestions, *The Case of the Velvet Claws* or *The Case of the Blackmailed Bride* . . . If either title is used, it should be keynoted in the first chapter. . . ."

This wasn't any spur-of-the-moment idea; he had first used the formula *The Case of the* . . . for one of his Speed Dash stories in 1925, "The Case of the Misplaced Thumbs."

He leaves the final selection up to the Morrow staff. "You're the ones who know the market, I don't. And it's your money that you're risking against my time, in this venture, and there's lots of time and not much money these days, so you're the doctor." He asked Hobson to wire him the decision.

After much analyzing and taking apart and putting together again in the Morrow office, the title was decided upon and Thayer wired: CASE OF THE VELVET CLAWS PERFECT FOR TITLE FIRST BOOK STOP PROCEEDING AT ONCE WITH JACKET STOP TITLE FOR SECOND BOOK ALSO NECESSARY BEFORE MANUSCRIPT IS SET SO THAT REFERENCE CAN BE MADE IN LAST CHAPTER.

Hobson's follow-up letter contained the news that publication date was being pushed up to February 15 as they had an April Fool's Day mystery they wanted to publish in March. "It is going to be a close call but we can make it if you get us the mss. as promised." He said also that February is probably a better date than March "for books of this type." Nonetheless, for reasons undisclosed, the final publication date was the first of March.

On December 20, with the heading, "On Board the Camp Wagon, Somewhere around Indio, California," Gardner wrote: "Dear Mr.

Hobson: If you're inclined to be envious, get your envy machine all stoked up for action under forced draft. For I'm sitting out in the middle of the desert, stripped to the waist, sunlight glittering, a blue sky, not a cloud in sight, not a breath of wind, air like wine, yet very warm without being hot."

He describes his camp wagon in full and says, "And if you think that isn't the life, you've just been over-civilized that's all. Do all my hunting with bows and arrows, get up every morning, poke around the desert with bow and arrow, prowl around the mountains looking for rock, do a little panning once in a while, yep, have all that stuff along, also cameras and a portable dark room. Carry enough water so I can get into sections of the desert where most cars never go, and go for days at a time without seeing any humans. Then head in to some out of the way mining camps and turn on the radio, switch on the electric lights, get out the drinking whiskey, and entertain characters who let their reminiscences fall on fertile soil."

This explains why he didn't get the wire asking for the second title until he went into El Centro. He had two to offer, *The Case of the Gilded Lily* and *The Case of the Coffin Girl*. He had mentioned *The Gilded Lily* before; it was his pet at the time but was actually not used as a title until 1956. Of *Velvet Claws* he said, "I completely revised the end chapter of that book as you'll see when you get it. Your editors were right. The ending was very weak—lousy. As it is I have Della Street lose confidence in Perry Mason when he turns in the woman, and she keeps on the outs with him until the very last, when she suddenly realizes he was working for his client all the time instead of against her, and, while they don't exactly go into a clinch, they get back to a basis of Della Street worshipping Mason's fighting loyalty."

On his suggested titles for the second book, the editors were not very keen about either. "We've got to do better than that," Hobson wrote: "You and your camp wagon and the descriptions of the life you lead in it, make me rather sick. I was born and brought up in Colorado, you know, and city life with all its advantages occasionally gets me. I've got a swell idea. Why don't you come east in the camp wagon, we'll set it up in Central Park and all live in it. The hunting will be a little on the short side but you can take some fine pictures of the high buildings."

Erle did "better than that." The title, *The Case of the Sulky Girl*, was offered in time for the first manuscript to go to press, and Hobson to send a Happy New Year wire with congratulations.

Chapter Twelve

WHILE HIS FIRST book was going to press, Gardner was off in his camp wagon turning out his usual gargantuan amount of work. His many pulp markets had to be supplied at the same time he was working on more Perry Mason books. Through most of January 1933, he was out on the desert.

In his own words, "I had started drifting away from the law business." The year before (1932), he had been working only part-time at the law, going from "a half-time basis to a third, then to a quarter, sharing in the firm's earnings on the basis of the time I put in."

By 1933, he had all but given up the law. In recalling this period in later years, Erle wrote, "As I drifted away from the partnership, three sisters who were part of the secretarial staff elected to come with me, and since the girls were highly trained, rapid typists, I was able to turn out a terrific volume of work."

The success of his early books, followed soon thereafter by a slick-magazine sale, turned his "drifting away" into a definite end to his work as a lawyer.

He received his author's copies of the first book, *The Case of the Velvet Claws,* at one of his mail stops that January, and immediately sent an autographed copy to Hardy, whom he always credited with unswerving faith and persistence in urging Erle to write a book. He wasn't giving any other books away until the arrival of the extra copies he had ordered (authors receive only a few complimentaries), as he didn't want anyone to feel bad at not receiving a copy right off.

There was no dedication in the book. It was an oversight; he hadn't thought to write one or the publishers to ask for one until close to publication date. Being on the desert, he hadn't received the reminder in time; although he had then sent one, it arrived too late.

Gardner dictating story to Jean while camping out

However, or so he wrote Bob Hardy, he wasn't in favor of the custom of dedicating a book, "particularly ordinary run of the mill."

He pointed out, "These are detective books, destined to appeal to a passing fancy rather than to make literary milestones, and let's turn them out without dedication." He held to this decision for the first twenty-five Mason books, up until *The Case of the Golddigger's Purse*, which had been written in Yucatán and South America, and was dedicated "To the Friends I have found 'South of the Border.' " He again dropped dedications for six more books and then began his foreword series, honoring those with whom he was associated in legal and crime prevention activities.

Only eight of the mysteries he wrote under the pseudonym A. A. Fair contain dedications; these follow the same pattern as the Masons. Of all his dedications, only three were outside the pattern. Two books, with Chinese backgrounds, were dedicated to his friends, the Lui family and Kit King Lui; and the other one was dedicated to Wood Whitesell, a New Orleans artist-photographer. *The Court of Last Resort* was, of course, dedicated to Henry Steeger, who, with Gardner, founded the organization by that name for the improvement of justice.

Erle was pleased with the appearance of his first book, writing to Hardy, "They did a remarkably fine job . . . I enjoyed the jacket blurbs very much and you have got to admit they went out of their way to give me a good send-off."

In connection with the letters they had exchanged about Erle's wish to write a different kind of book, Hobson had sent a new mystery to Erle. It was Francis Iles's *Before the Fact,* a novel acclaimed critically as a classic. After reading it, Erle wrote, "It's the sort of writing I could never do. I can't polish and trim my stuff . . . That book took a long while to write, has virtually no plot, is a character sketch in which the end was well in view before the book was two-thirds finished." He decided it was written by "rather a plain woman who bared the real facts of her sex life. To me there seems to be a sharp line of demarcation between the fact and fiction of the book. If I'm wrong on this, the sex angle of the book is a masterpiece of imaginative writing." *

Gardner hadn't read five books in the last ten years, he admitted,

* The identity of the nom de plume Francis Iles, a well-kept secret at the time, was eventually admitted to be A. B. Cox, who also wrote mysteries as Anthony Berkeley. He was experienced in journalism and in diplomatic affairs; he was also an authority on intricate historical legal cases and published two books on the subject. For many years he was a literary critic on the London *Times*.

being "too busy writing to read." He went on to say, "Occasionally I overwork and get so tired I can't sleep. Then the fatigue poisons pile up until even my ordinary quota leaves me tired and the stuff I turn out is just lousy. Frankly I'm in one of those spells right now. . . ."

He was still talking about the Iles book a week later, saying he would not be able to write anything that had "its delicacy of handling." His hope was to be able to write between two styles, "dramatic and characters. Naturally I would like, like the devil, to write a detective story that would be destined to live."

His letter brought up another subject, Della Street. She would be a problem to him for years, but here at the beginning he said that "she bothers me a little because some goof pointed out that a whole raft of detective story writers were running to the wisecracking type of secretary, and intimated that Della Street was simply true to type. This made me try to change her into a more conventional mold, and, as I mentioned above, I don't do things well when I try to do them conventionally. In fact, I simply can't do them at all. I'll have another look at Della and see what can be done." Finally, on page seven of his letter, he broke into his own thoughts with, "Honestly, Hobson, I'll get clean off the reservation and talk a leg off of you if I don't quit and you don't put a curb on me, so I'm going to wind this up right now."

It was in the summer of 1933 that Erle decided to put the Fiction Factory "all on wheels." His name for the venture was Podunking, from the old theatrical name of Podunk for the smallest of small towns. The mail, that most important adjunct to the life of a writer, was forwarded to certain pickup points.

In his first eight days of Podunking, he dictated three novelettes and almost all of a book. He started the book on Sunday, dictated eight thousand words that day, fifteen thousand on Monday, and then came a letter from Thayer Hobson commenting on the similarity of the Mason plots.

Gardner wrote in return, "It threw me into a loop and I started to revise the book I was writing, then slept on it and decided to complete it as written. This is once that I have a disagreement with you. It is easy to say the Mason stories are all similar, because they deal with a murder, a woman who is suspected and acquitted, but you can say almost the same thing about every detective story written—a central character apart from the police and subsequently proven innocent. Perry Mason deals with the big, masculine, protective element

Podunk Camp: Charles Gardner, Peggy, Nat, Honey, and Jean

of sex psychology. To bring out his talents it needs a woman who is suspected of crime."

While he was camped out that August, there came the first big magazine break. Fulton Oursler, the editor of *Liberty,* wanted to buy *The Case of the Howling Dog. Liberty* was low man on the totem pole of the slicks, but this was a breakthrough out of by-the-word payment into big-time serialization. Hardy wrote that *Liberty* might offer three thousand dollars. Hardy had not yet okayed the deal with Oursler, as *Scribner's* magazine also wanted to see the manuscript. A sale there would mean more prestige.

Alfred Dashiell wanted *Howling Dog* for *Scribner's* but was out-voted, and the deal was made with *Liberty.* Hardy only managed to get twenty-five hundred dollars, but it was the best single deal Gard-ner had had from his writing. Serialization could not start before February 1934, and in the final negotiation Hardy had to give

Oursler until May 5. This still left time for book publication in July. However, because of the elapsed time, a switch in books was necessary. The one Erle was working on, *The Case of the Lucky Legs*, would have to be published by Morrow ahead of *Howling Dog*.

Lucky Legs was the first Mason book to give Erle trouble. "I've lost my perspective on it," he wrote Hobson, "but think it carries on the driving idea of smash-bang action which is really the basis of Perry Mason's exploits." He had written a double ending, one dealing with a romantic clinch for magazine circulation, the other with the foundation for the following book. He asked Thayer, "Did you ever see a cloud come boiling over a mountain and start to drift across a sun-swept plain on the other side? I've watched 'em come over the big snow-capped ranges and start drifting across the desert lots of times. They get thin and puny while you're watching them, and the first thing you know they've dissolved into deep blue sky."

The book was like that. He thought it was going fine when it came off the "presses," his word for typewriters aboard the portable Fiction Factory, then he saw that it gradually faded from a dramatic conflict into just a detective story, then the detective story became labored as hell, and the first thing he knew there was the end of the book.

So he asked the girls, Jean, Peggy, and Honey, his personal editorial board, and they felt the same way about it. "Therefore, there wasn't anything to do except to dig into it, tear it to pieces and begin all over again. I sat around the campfire nearly all of one night . . . staring into the coals and thinking the thing over. The shadows crept in, the pines turned black against the stars, and then I got the idea, which, after all, was as plain as day. I'd simply let a thread slip through my fingers almost at the first part of the book, and that damned loose thread had unravelled the whole yarn before I got to the end. So I had to redictate almost the whole book. We used about three or four chapters. The rest is revised and redictated." He was satisfied that it was a pretty good job all things considered. He was apologetic for the delay.

To which Hobson replied, "Great God, man, you take yourself seriously. Your absurd letter apologizing for the delay on *The Case of the Lucky Legs* arrived yesterday. Of course you realize the above remarks are really not as insulting as they sound. They merely represent the bewilderment I feel that you should feel apologetic . . ." If Gardner knew how many manuscripts were six months, a year, a year and a half overdue, he'd laugh. "One of the best fiction authors we've got has been trying to finish his novel for two years and can't."

Incidentally, Hobson had been up to visit Red (Sinclair) Lewis and had taken *Velvet Claws* to him. Lewis added Gardner to his list of favorite mystery authors.

Morrow planned to put on "a pretty substantial drive" for the second book, *The Case of the Sulky Girl,* which was nearing publication date. "We are not going to try to make *history* with this book because the time isn't quite ripe and it would be a lot more expensive to do it now than I think it will be in six months."

It was at this time that plans were made firm for Gardner to produce four books a year. "I have only been in publishing seven years and that is nothing," Hobson wrote, "but you are the first mystery story writer that I have felt was good enough to carry a four book a year schedule. I'd like to start the salesmen selling the idea this year that we have *the* American mystery writer . . ." This must have been heady stuff to an author with only one book published, but Gardner took no particular notice of it in any of his letters. He was too involved in turning out the number of words needed to satisfy his quota.

In early September, Hobson had received *Lucky Legs* and thought that it was "swell" and that the new ending which Erle was planning would make it "even sweller." He had from Erle a new beginning and a new end shortly thereafter, and wrote, "It's a lot better. A lot better. All congratulations." By then the second book had been released and Hobson added that Erle needn't worry about the critics' noting a difference in Perry Mason's character in *Sulky Girl.* "They all have and they're all congratulating you on how much he's improved."

It was in September of 1933 that Hobson, with Bob Hardy, began their steady push of Mason toward the *Saturday Evening Post.* Hobson had given *Sulky Girl* to Graeme Lorimer, the editor, but wouldn't give him *Lucky Legs* until Erle had revised it. "You're too old a hand to get excited about anything like this but I thought you'd be interested," he wrote. "The reason I didn't want *Lucky Legs* to go to the *Post* in present form was that I gave Graeme Lorimer a long song and dance about the work that had to be done on it, and how sure I was it could be turned into a better yarn than either of the others etc." Hobson concluded that if the *Post* "by any wild chance should want *Lucky Legs* for immediate publication, you've got to fly on to New York and do the revision here."

The *Post* did not buy it and *Lucky Legs* continued to plague Erle. Hobson wrote him in November, "For Christ's sake stop worrying. . . . Somebody certainly has been riding you and got you nervous as an old woman. Anyway if this book were perfect, there would be an anticlimax on the next one. . . ." In another letter, Hobson was giving *Lucky Legs* to someone "absolutely fresh to the manuscript, to see whether there is any cause for your nervous breakdown about this story. If there is, I'll tell you frankly, but I honestly don't think there is anything to worry about."

In reply Erle wrote, "I know I seem like an old woman on that damned manuscript but the *Post* evidently didn't like it at all . . . Naturally I hated like hell to turn out something like that." By January he expected to get a book to Morrow containing "one of the most interesting plot situations you've dealt with in some time. That's one thing about me, Thayer, I'm so God damned modest!"

He went on, "Ordinarily I never doubt my own ability but sail serenely along with a sublime self-confidence which my friends find particularly irritating." This was his own view of himself. The girls had their own apt name for him: Worrywart.

Gardner had planned to stay camped until winter, but this year winter came early. On October 26, the Fiction Factory had to break camp in a hurry to get out of the High Sierra before they were snowed in. The book he was working on was finished in a Sacramento motel.

Chapter Thirteen

ALTHOUGH THEY HAD become friends through their correspondence, Gardner and Hobson had never met. Jean was first to be introduced when she went East to Washington, D.C., to work with Frank Orr in the autumn following the Podunk summer. Erle's law partner had been called by the government to do special legal work.

Honey and Peggy became friends of Thayer by mail, with postscripts added to the letters by Thayer in New York, and by them in return from California. Erle and Thayer played the game of being Lotharios, which added considerably to the fun and games. One of Erle's remarks to Thayer was, "I read your comments on the postscript to the girls in regard to their boss being a good, pure, and conventional citizen. As a matter of fact, I'm either a damned old rake, or about twenty years in advance of my time."

Through October and November the exchange of postscripts continued. Honey bore the brunt of much of the good-natured banter, doubtless because she could toss back the ball with perhaps more agility than the two men. In that winter, Thayer's curiosity took over and he asked the girls to send him pictures of themselves. In return they asked the same of him. His reaction was, "Send pictures! I'm middle-aged and getting bald, so I won't." But he did, old pictures of peculiar-looking men of the nineties, dug out of some family album. Answering a question from Honey, he wrote, "I have been married as often as you three put together and I know more about marriage than the three of you, plus Erle, will ever know." He had long suspected that "you are just three nice girls who eat bread and milk for supper every night, say your prayers, and sleep in flannel nightgowns with long sleeves and high necks."

Thayer left for England early in January 1934 and by the time he returned in late February Erle had set up his Fiction Factory in San Francisco. He sent Thayer his new book manuscript, *The Hostile Witness*, not a Perry Mason, with instructions that if it wasn't good to let him know, as he'd "been discouraged by experts . . . Honey flashes me a peculiar glance when I say that . . ." Although Erle listened to what all the girls had to say about his work, it was Honey on whom he chiefly depended for the editorial criticism of manuscripts.

When Thayer sent his opinion of the new book, Erle's reply to him began, "We go down to play tennis every day, and the mailman always seems to know just when that is, because he comes while we're away. It's a hell of a game of tennis we play—more like ping-pong, but it gives us a break in the work and a chance to get some fresh air. The girls put on a brand of shorts that dazzles the masculine population, and we smash the ball back and forth with wild abandon. By the time we return, the mail is in. —That was the way we got your letter of March 1, and Honey, Peggy and I, sitting in the automobile, read it over each other's shoulders.

"Honey says, 'You remember I told you that I thought the introduction of the characters was too monotonous and you said that it would be a good thing to trademark an introduction in that particular manner,' and I, not to be outdone, said, 'That's all right, but remember I told you the turban stuff was a little out of place in a novel of that nature . . .' So we talked the thing over, up one side and down the other, getting so damned interested we forgot to go over to the sandwich place across the way and get lunch, which we finally do."

He also wrote to Thayer, "Honey (whose judgement on book matters is pretty damn good) insists that the trouble with *The Forgotten Murder* and some of my other stuff is that I keep approaching it from the angle of a Perry Mason story, that trying to keep from making them like Perry Mason stories, I unconsciously pull my punches . . . She thinks that with *The Hostile Witness* I've worked out a new method of approach which is sufficiently foreign to the dramatic Mason presentation so that I don't unconsciously get to imitating myself and that the style and method of presenting character in that book is the important thing that can be capitalized on in future publications."

At this same time he was telling Thayer, "I have been putting

out these alternate books as straws to see how the wind blows. I am
not satisfied with any of them . . . What I would like to do would
be to get some new departure in detective story writing."

He had the first draft of *The Case of the Curious Bride* dictated
despite many interruptions, mostly writing magazine stories "in order
to get some money into the exchequer because I got flat broke in
New Orleans (in December and January) and while we dragged in
about three thousand bucks, we spent it all coming home and moving
furniture up here etc."

The Case of the Talking Crow, the original title of *Curious Bride*,
was changed when Morrow wrote that it was too close to *The Talking
Sparrow Murders*, a book they were publishing by Darwin Teilhet,
also a San Franciscan. Although *Curious Bride* couldn't be published
before November, Erle wanted to finish it before revising *The Clew
of the Forgotten Murder* * because he thought that *Curious Bride*
was going to be "about forty percent better than any Perry Mason
story to date and when we get it into *Liberty* there's five thousand
bucks, less commission, that will be coming our way and which will
go a long way toward sending the wolf back to where he belongs."

After repeating that he would get to work at whichever Thayer
wanted, Gardner added, "Don't be afraid to tell us what you want,
and for God's sake, don't ever be afraid of hurting my feelings.
Personally I'm so hard-boiled I don't know when my feelings are
hurt—I keep Honey for that. She has a chip on her shoulder for anybody who picks on her Nunky Erle." He concluded, "It's a damn
sight handier all the way around to spit out words straight from the
shoulder and not disguise the pills with too much sugar coating."

In his next letter, Thayer announced that he was coming West.
Big plans were immediately made by Erle for the meeting. He offered his Hupmobile-8 and trailer for Thayer's use. All his possessions, he wrote, were divided into three categories, "sacreds," "semi-
sacreds" and "other stuff." The trailer was a "sacred." It was, of
course, highest honor to be permitted to touch a "sacred." Honey's
comment, sent on by Erle, was that she hoped Thayer could drive a
car.

In reply, Thayer stated that he had driven "eighteen five-ton
Pierce Arrow trucks for six months in the French Army," to which

* A non-Mason originally published under the pseudonym Carleton Kendrake. The
title was later changed to the more conventional *Clue* and the pseudonym abandoned.
The Hostile Witness, on the other hand, was withdrawn and consigned to the morgue.

Honey remarked that if Hobson was "the kind of a driver that wore out eighteen five-ton Pierce Arrow trucks in six months, what would he do to your automobile in six weeks?"

Thayer arrived in Los Angeles on May 1, 1934. Erle had all kinds of advance plans for a welcome, even to the hiring of a brass band to meet the train. In the end, it was Peggy alone, with a flower pinned to her lapel for recognition, who drove down to meet him. Thayer had business to attend to there and Peggy left to return to San Francisco.

Erle wrote to him in Los Angeles, "Peg says you are a regular guy." He had known this from the letters and from Jean, who had okayed him from the East, and Jean was "all wool and a yard wide." When she gave approval, "it was like sterling on silver." He stated, "I'm telling you this is a hard gang to crash, and when a person is elected to membership without a period of probation, you can gamble it's something to be proud of."

Thayer was married at the time to Laura Z. Hobson, later a well-known novelist. He planned to join her in Reno and drive to Tahoe and possibly Yosemite. Erle wrote that he didn't want to interfere with their vacation, that he had a tendency "to get overdone and be a prize nuisance trying to do too much."

By the end of May, the Hobsons were finally on their way to San Francisco. On their arrival, Erle almost at once took them out camping in the desert and initiated them into the art of hunting for lost mines. Erle and Thayer struck it off as well in person as they had by correspondence. By June 12 the Hobsons had returned to New York and the Californians were all recuperating from their visit.

Gardner and his group were off the same month on a South Seas trip. After that Erle repaid the Hobson visit when he and Nat went to New York while the girls moved him to Hollywood. This was the visit from which Erle, Nat, and Jean returned West via the Canal. After they'd departed, Thayer wrote Peg and Honey that the the town seemed empty with Erle gone and that he hadn't seen as much of him as he'd have liked, as Gardner "was tearing around with the movie people and magazine editors and all the friends."

From the Canal, Erle wrote Thayer what might be construed as an apology for the way things evidently got out of hand before sailing. "I like New York and am irritated by it. I'm like a bull in a china shop. Not a bull who doesn't appreciate china, but a bull who thinks he's going to be a nice gentlemanly bull and move very cautiously. Then he whisks his tail, something goes crash, turns and his horn knocks off a shelf of china. He starts to leave, then says, 'Well, to hell with that stuff, if they're making all that commotion over a little busted glassware, I'll go back and really show 'em something.' He goes back, finds your restraining hand upraised, grins, if bulls do grin, and takes a boat home, feeling as though he should have busted a little more china, yet sorta sorry for the stuff he did bust . . . When the daisies bloom I'll come back to the damn town again, and smash some more china."

Erle and Laura had not exactly hit it off on the California mine exploration, and, it would seem, had no more affinity for each other in New York. Erle's letter continued, "And for God's sake don't let me fight with Laura. I get to hanging around a city and knock off some of Laura's china and she takes it so politely I remember I'm a bull after all and want to chase her over a fence. But I'm not going to quit being a bull. I like it. Of course one of these days I may become a steer. That's different." He added that he also had "a perfectly swell fight with *Black Mask.*"

Earlier in 1934, in summing up the one hundred best books of the preceding year, the Los Angeles *Times* included fourteen mysteries. One of these was *The Case of the Velvet Claws,* and Erle was indeed pleased and so wrote to Thayer. Thayer's response was, "Of course you are in the fourteen mystery stories listed by the Los Angeles *Times.* You are also in the first four listed by *Time,* The Weekly News Magazine. What the hell? Don't be so surprised."

By the autumn of 1934, Thayer was working to put together a story on Gardner for *Time,* which would possibly be a "cover story," that is, with Erle's face on the magazine's cover. Erle had little interest in gathering together publicity and hence delayed sending material. This elicited from Thayer the explosive, "Christ Almighty God, I haven't been smoking for three days and I am tearing things to pieces, and where the hell is all that stuff that I ought to have to put over the *Time* story on Erle Stanley Gardner, and when is it coming and how soon?"

When Erle sent information, he included something he rarely spoke of, his contributions to American jurisprudence. Some of his legal theories had been upheld by higher courts. In particular he noted the one on the principle of "limited dedication," which is "probably the only case on record in which a municipality was restrained from declaring trees growing in the middle of a busy street to be a nuisance as an obstruction to traffic."

The profile didn't make *Time,* being edged out by one about that other new writer of mystery, Ellery Queen. Thayer sailed off again for London. It was on this trip that he met Isabelle Garrabrants, whom he later married. It was a long and happy union which brought children and home life to Hobson.

Part Four

GROWTH
OF
A WRITER

Chapter Fourteen

IN DECEMBER 1934 Erle suffered one of his periods of discouragement. He wrote to Thayer, "We might just as well admit that Perry Mason has lost his opportunity of ever startling the world. He could have done it if we had followed out something of the treatment of *The Case of the Velvet Claws*, but when we tried to give the stories a development which will be suitable for serialization in *Liberty*, bearing in mind that *Liberty* is a family magazine, and also the necessity of having certain suitable lengths for the various installments, and also try to get something which will be sufficiently dramatic for motion picture fans, yet also keep somewhere within the line of censorship requirements, we have surrounded ourselves with so many restrictions and inhibitions that the character naturally takes on more of the complexion of all other detectives from the Year One down to date.

"Much against my wishes in this yarn [*The Case of the Counterfeit Eye*], my better judgment prompted me to tone down some of Perry Mason's so-called 'unscrupulous and unethical tactics,' in order to make it appear that he wouldn't defend a man and try to get him off if he thought that person was guilty of cold-blooded murder without any moral justification.

"Nuts!

"The reading public gives me a pain in the vicinity of my hip pocket . . . the public certainly must realize that the burning question which confronts a man accused of crime who enters the office of any reputable criminal attorney is not the question of his guilt or innocence, but the question of whether he has the necessary retainer available in the form of spot cash.

"However, when this same public reads installment stories in a family magazine, it becomes somewhat sanctimonious and insists that the character shall be gold-plated with respectability, and when that character appears in the movies, he has to cleanse out the dark recesses of his mind with formaldehyde and scrub his external anatomy with Ivory soap, Lux, and other toilet preparations ballyhooed as being used by the dear little motion picture beauties who have to go out on wild parties in order to please their public but whose secret ambition is to enter a convent and sew baby clothes for the unemployed."

Erle thought he had managed to retain in *Counterfeit Eye* "the fast-moving story, an unusual plot development, a semblance of reality, and a touch of driving characterization. If I have done this, what more can the bastards ask?"

However, he admitted, he and Thayer were both in the business to make money, and if they could make more money having Mason suit his exploits to magazine and motion picture audiences, "Perry Mason confides to me that he's willing to turn respectable for a little while if I promise him that someday, after the magazines and the motion pictures get done with him, and the publisher finds he's not as much of a drawing card as he was, he can come out for one book with hypocrisy thrown to the winds and be just a damn good criminal attorney."

At the end of December, Erle wrote his New Year letter to Thayer, in which he said in part, "Frankly I am a long ways from being satisfied with any of my work . . . My ambition is to build up and hold a reading public. It's the only way that I can succeed. I will never make a flash of meteoric success." His sign-off was, "Let's plant our feet firmly on the ground, double our right fists, measure the distance with a nice left lead, and sock all competitors right between the eyes. Yours for a belligerently successful 1935."

The new year brought troubles with the motion picture contracts. In 1935 Warner Brothers released three Perry Mason motion pictures, *Howling Dog*, which Gardner considered quite good, and *Curious Bride* and *Lucky Legs*, which pleased him not at all. Also, the company was trying to cut the escalator prices. According to the terms of the contract, if it was terminated he could not sell Mason to another company for three years. He had two other pictures released in 1935, not by Warners and not Perry Masons. *Special Investigator*, based on a short story, "Fugitive Gold," was filmed by RKO, and Eastern Service Studios released *This Is Murder*.

He was also having trouble with his next book, *The Case of the Sleepwalker's Niece*. After getting Thayer's criticism of it, he wrote one of his typical replies: "Anyone who thinks a story is lousy and rotten and can't think of the synonym puerile to add to it just isn't the kind of publisher for me to have. When our twenty-eight book contract runs out, I'm very much afraid I'll have to find a sufficiently masculine publisher who can really talk language that I understand."

He revised and rewrote the book before taking off in summer for the hills with his bow and arrow. He sent word to Thayer that "the editors of *Cosmopolitan* think we're slaving away night and day trying to think up ideas for a lousy serial. As a matter of fact, we're going fifty-fifty, one word for every arrow. We shoot about five thousand arrows and write about five thousand words. This makes a fair day's quota." Quite obviously Gardner needed some relaxation. There was *Cosmopolitan* wanting a first installment, *Popular Publications* wanting a story, *Photoplay* needing an installment on the serial they were running, and *This Week* asking for the summary of another serial.

Troubles continued. In October, *Liberty* returned *The Case of the Sleepwalker's Niece*. Now that it wouldn't be serialized, Erle planned to rewrite it because "stuff that would be highly proper in a book wouldn't work so well in a magazine . . . I don't mean smut or cussing but I do mean guts and a real portrayal of character."

Another point which always plagued him in writing for the magazines was their wanting a love interest. This was, he believed, dangerous for Perry Mason. If he married Della Street, he would lose his sex appeal, yet Gardner, in keeping the two at arms' length, exasperated readers. He told Thayer, "How little you know of human nature. Those who want Della to sleep with her boss are the ones who are afraid she isn't, and those who think she shouldn't are the ones who are certain she is."

By the end of December he had rewritten *Sleepwalker's Niece* and had decided that the whole trouble was that he had been worrying too much about the movie and serial markets when he first wrote it. Although he could prove nothing as yet, Erle was quite sure he was being given the runaround by *Liberty*. They had rejected *The Case of the Counterfeit Eye,* which later made the best-seller list, and now had rejected this one. He was considering "making a quick job" of writing the new Mason, thereby forcing the magazine "to either fish or cut bait."

The editors of *American Magazine* had read *This Is Murder,* published under Gardner's pen name of Charles J. Kenny, and wanted a thirty-thousand-word novelette with the same characters. Concerning this, and the sale he had made to *Cosmopolitan,* he wrote Hobson,

"This will make the highbrow element reluctantly consider that Gardner may be going somewhere . . . There is, at the present time, altogether too much of a patronizing attitude on the part of the intelligentsia toward Perry Mason and, therefore, toward his author."

Erle was still strongly disaffected by Will Cuppy's reviews. Cuppy's column appeared in the prestigious New York *Herald Tribune,* and Cuppy did not like Gardner's books. From Erle's letters about him, it would seem that Erle did not realize that Cuppy was a highly respected critic, who had attained a position where he could say what he liked and what he didn't like. To Erle, it was "a personal feud." In most quarters Erle received rave reviews, but Erle being Erle, he demanded one hundred percent approval.

Among his other troubles was that of titles. Writing as many books as he did, titles were a continuing hassle. Erle sent one memo to Thayer and Marie Freid which began: "Here are our problems in connection with a title:

"1. It *should* scan. This isn't absolutely essential but a title which scans is easier to say than one which doesn't, and, since most of the titles in the series have scanned, it would seem advisable to keep the same basic plan in operation. In view of the fact that our titles invariably start with 'The Case of the,' we have the general meter of the title fixed. It runs something like this—la *la* la la *la* la la *la*. The last word in the title, therefore, should be short and one which is naturally emphasized, unless it is a two syllable word, in which event the first syllable is customarily slurred over. 'Brunette' meets this requirement."

He continued at some length on the need of a title to help market the product.

For the first three months of 1936, the Fiction Factory was on wheels again, camping in the desert. In the spring, Erle, Jean, and a temporary secretary were off to Hawaii where one of his favorite friends, Louise Weissberger, had guest cottages awaiting them. Honey later joined them, and she and Walter Moore were married there.

Erle had met Mrs. Weissberger on his voyage to China in 1931. She had boarded the boat, a Japanese vessel, in Honolulu, and had been assigned a cabin with "a timid little Chinese woman" who spoke scarcely a word of English. An influential Japanese couple had also come on board at Honolulu and they coveted the cabin to which the two women had been assigned. Mrs. Weissberger was told she and her cabin mate would have to move. She refused. Thereupon,

Louise Weissberger and Gardner

the Japanese steward proceeded to move them out of their cabin while they were at lunch. When Mrs. Weissberger discovered what had happened, in Erle's words, "she literally took the ship to pieces." It so happened that she was one of the chief stockholders of an important West Coast shipping company. She used her clout. She cabled San Francisco with orders to ship nothing more on any Japanese line until she gave other instructions. Needless to say, she and the Chinese lady were quickly restored to their original cabin.

Because of her spunk, Erle was entranced, and they became fast friends. It turned out that the timid roommate was the wife of an important Chinese banker. Mrs. Weissberger received the same warm hospitality in China that Erle received from his Chinese hosts. Erle became an always welcome guest at her Hawaiian estate.

While Erle was visiting her in 1936, he received from Thayer a suggested title, *The Case of the Pigheaded Widow*, for the next Mason. Erle hit the ceiling. "My answer: NO!" He was to continue hitting it through the weeks of discussion that ensued. His own choice was *The Case of the Dangerous Dowager*, with which he eventually won the war. He felt the word *Pigheaded* in the title was disgusting; the only two other title phrases that would make more men turn away were *Nagging Wife* and *Visiting Mother-in-law*. After his explosive and definite "NO!" he added, "I'm nervous trying to figure out whether it's time to change the Mason formula. I didn't sleep a wink last night . . . I got up this morning after having fought the bed to a draw, and find a cablegram about pigheaded widows."

He had come to believe, he wrote Thayer, that someone in the Morrow office "has a very definite writing talent, a constructive imagination, definite ideas, a strong individuality, and a sense of the dramatic in a constructive rather than an editorial capacity." If he, Gardner, and "this guy" both write books, they'll be different, and won't mix. "I've felt this for a long time. My gang has felt it for a long time. I know you've done some writing and have a constructive bent, but I don't think it's you. You say this Freid gal likes my stuff so I don't think it's she; but sure as hell there's someone who is right as rain, who just has different tastes from mine; but I'm right as rain, too. You chase down the one who suggested this Pigheaded Widow idea, and you'll have the one who has different tastes from mine. If you originated it, it means you have a side to you that's directly opposite to my reactions. . . . Now you sit down and see if someone who's close to you and handling my work is really more of a writer than an editor, and see if you're trying to take a darned good square peg and make it fit into a damned good round hole—and I'll be either the hole or the peg."

He followed this with a letter full of titles, including that of his upcoming book, *The Case of the Lame Canary*. He wound up, "You're a great trial to me, Thayer Hobson. I'm going to be the greatest mystery writer in the world despite your distracting requests for new titles, however."

Erle was returning soon to the mainland and expected to go right on to New York. There were many things he wanted to discuss in person. And so did Thayer, who wrote him, "It was absolutely nix on giving up Perry Mason or cutting down Perry Mason much. . . . Perry Mason is good for years and it would be a mistake to have less than two a year, or to drop him for a while." All of these points could be solved when Erle reached New York. "However—" And Thayer's was as big a "however" as were Erle's own.

"However, it brings up one thing which I am not going to leave until you get to New York and that is your feeling that there is some mind here in the organization which is temperamentally antagonistic to yours. Pigheaded Widow was my idea, and, whether we use it or whether we don't, I stand up for it and I claim because I think Pigheaded Widow is a good mystery title for a Perry Mason and you don't, doesn't mean our minds see things differently. . . . Marie

Freid and I are the two people who do practically all the editorial work on your books here. Neither one of us could write a mystery story * and we couldn't create a Perry Mason in a thousand years, but when you start talking about being worried that tastes are different from yours, etc., etc., you're spouting just hogwash.

"And all your talk about square pegs and round holes I just don't understand. If you still feel that way after you get to New York and we talk about things, by God from now on we'll shut up. As I said above, we'll publish what you write the way you write it, and let you go your own way."

Erle was in Vancouver, a long way from New York, when this letter reached him. His reply, in part, was: "Apparently all titles fall into two general classifications. The first is that of *Pigheaded Widow*, the second is those you don't like. You damned New York intellectuals are so far ahead of us we're out of touch with you, but don't forget that by the same token you're out of touch with the rest of the country." As Helen King, his editor later on, pointed out, "Erle always spoke of 'you people back there' as if the East were encased in amber *circa* 1492."

"I also note your comments about criticism . . . ," Erle's letter continued. "Now, sweetheart, occasionally a situation arises where an author finds his publisher can't take criticism. Now, if that is the case, I'll quit arguing and put in all of the titles on the book that you want and adopt all of the suggestions you make without changing so much as a comma, because when a writer gets to writing snotty letters back and forth with his publisher instead of writing books, it's an economic waste. —And this, you So and So, is the opening gun of a barrage I'm heading for New York to deliver. There's lots more where this came from. In the meantime, Angel Face, I beg to remain, Respectfully yours, —."

In answer to one such letter, Thayer replied by hand, belaboring Erle's favorite use of " 'em": "Yeah, I begin to understand a lot of things. Among 'em . . . why you had to give up a legitimate occupation (selling spotlights) and turn to writing. Why you didn't really get far as a lawyer either.

"But there are a couple of things I'd like to know, among 'em:

"1. Who really writes the stuff you send out over your name, for it is really inconceivable that the guy who writes such really dumb adolescent letters should be able to create much less handle Perry Mason.

* Marie wrote a number of mysteries under the nom de plume Marion Randolph.

"2. Who you've been running around with who has taught you a lot of new dirty expressions. God you're getting tough!

"Poor Jean, I feel sorry for her. She, I understand, has to spend most of her time with you. The real trouble with you is that you don't read the letters I write you. Why not ask Jean to read 'em and explain to you what I say and mean. She wouldn't mind and then you and I would understand each other a lot better. Just as a starter, get her to read what follows and translate it for you, you sap."

The final paragraph satirized a letter from Erle to his agent at the time, Jane Hardy, wherein he had suggested that her assistant read and explain his letters to her.

After further discussion of books and spotlights, Thayer continued: "As for a revolution in detective stories—change to evolution and trends, yes. But don't try to define 'detective stories' too rigidly. There are different kinds now and there will be different kinds long after you and I are pushing up daisies. Because people have different tastes. . . . Well, well, well—Pull in your horns. Affectionately, Thayer."

The postscript was to Jean: "Understand Erle at his worst? He's always at his worst. For Christ's sake and for his sake, get him to write more books and fewer silly letters."

In November, Thayer was expressing his feelings about the relationship of Perry and Della in the new book, *The Case of the Lame Canary.* He said that the two would never talk as sentimentally as they do. It was right in line with his criticism that Perry Mason "is softening up." Also, "The Della Street that I know, or have interpreted from a good many Gardner books that I have read when I've had nothing better to do, is a gal who would poison her mother, eat unslaked lime, and twist a baby's wrist for the man she cared for. But . . . she wouldn't go sentimental on him. She'd snap, rather than coo."

In December, Erle learned that Warners was not going to renew its motion picture option on Perry Mason. It knocked Erle right back to his intention to phase out the Mason books. For three years he would not be able to sell Mason to the movies. True, he was making good money on serial rights in the slicks, but at present there were few sales in that direction. "Perry Mason has run through ten or twelve books, which is damn near enough." His idea was to create "a brand new character, similar in many respects to Perry Mason, a little more refined, a little less daring, a little more sophisticated."

As Erle had been off-again on-again for some time concerning

Perry Mason, and as apparently there had now developed a sound business reason for dropping the character, Thayer called a conference at the office to discuss the possibility. The consensus was that under the circumstances they couldn't urge Erle to go on with Mason. They didn't know how long the books would hold up, as Erle himself "at heart" hadn't very strong convictions about the lawyer's endurance. The idea of disposing of Mason in a rewrite of *Lame Canary,* as Erle had outlined, and sending him off on a trip to the Orient, seemed sound. Nevertheless, Thayer believed that the new character should be as different as possible from Mason, so that people wouldn't say, "This new lawyer of Gardner's is just like Perry Mason; he's just changed his name."

Later in December, Erle wrote, "Well, I've done it—gone temperamental. I don't like *The Case of the Lame Canary.* I don't like any part of the Goddam thing. Somewhere along the line, these slick paper serializations did things to me, gave me sort of buck fever, I guess, and I got trying too hard. I wanted to get good, novel plots, and more plots, and what the hell do I get? From *The Case of the Sleepwalker's Niece* on, the plots have been weird murder mystery plots like my esteemed contemporaries are trying to do, only with the Gardner touch they became complicated like a Chinese puzzle. *Howling Dog* was about the best of the bunch except for *Velvet Claws,* simply because in those cases the character of Perry Mason was the thing which was in the foreground all the time. I'm going back to the first Mason formulae and write a last story which is going to be simple in plot but strong in characterization and action. I don't know the answer yet, but I do know that when a lawyer gets tangled up in cases with lame canaries and moving vans and silenced rifles and firebugs and trick garages and substituted amnesia victims and what the hell have we, that I'm writing the same old murder yarn under a different tag. No real life lawyer would ever have been mixed in a mess like that."

He took issue with Thayer for saying they couldn't ask him to keep on writing Masons. "As far as the book end is concerned, you say what you want, and you'll get it." Between the lines, obviously he was having second thoughts about phasing out his favorite character.

Chapter Fifteen

IN A LETTER to Gardner after the first *Liberty* sale, Robert Thomas Hardy wrote, "Quality is the thing that counts with you now. You are going to be America's most famous detective story writer in a year or two—and I don't mean maybe, or perhaps. . . ."

It was at this time, without mentioning illness, that Hardy spoke of his young wife giving up her Macmillan job to become his business partner. This was the official entrance of Jane Hardy into agenting. "The way that child has taken hold of things is just nobody's business," Hardy wrote. In September, again saying nothing of his sickness, Hardy informed Erle that he had incorporated the business, making his wife a partner so that she too could sign contracts.

In October 1933, in a long letter to Erle, Jane revealed that Bob was dying of cancer. Most New York editors, including Hobson, knew of the illness, and some clients had guessed. Erle was one who was not at all surprised at her news.

By the next year, she had taken over completely the work of Robert Thomas Hardy, Inc. Bob lingered on, desperately ill, and she cared for him along with handling his business. She made some tremendous deals for Erle, tremendous in that period, both with magazines and motion pictures. What she lacked was the faintest notion of how to be an agent for Erle Stanley Gardner. She tried to "handle" him. Somehow she never realized that you didn't handle Gardner, he handled you.

After she set up an escalating contract with *Liberty* in March 1934, she concluded her letter by telling him about it with her directions to him: "Now, Erle, it's up to you. I have done my damnedest at this thing and you've got to turn out the world's best stories on this *Liberty* contract. Don't give them even a ghost of a chance to dare to turn one down. Make *The Curious Bride* the best yarn you've ever done. I know you can do it. As to the other work—I wish you would try to turn out stronger stories, better fitted for serialization than *The Forgotten Murder* and *The Hostile Witness*. *The Hostile Witness* strikes me as a bit weak; you can do better than this. I wouldn't try to turn out book-lengths between the Perry Mason series that are in any way trivial. I would try to make them just as strong as the Perry Masons. It will pay you to do this in the end. We can't run any serials under your own name in the four competitive magazines while *Liberty* is running the Perry Masons, but if you can get some good strong book-lengths built around another character, we could undoubtedly do something with them under a nom. Think this over seriously—. Congratulations on landing one of the biggest contracts ever put across in New York City."

Perhaps, because of inexperience, she may not have noted what Erle saw immediately: All the options in the magazine contract were in favor of the magazine. Nonetheless, for a beginning writer it was good money, rising from five to ten thousand dollars for the first three serials, with an agreement to renegotiate for the fourth.

Within a few weeks, Jane had made her second big deal, one with Warner Brothers for the motion picture rights to *The Case of the Howling Dog*. Spelled out, the contract was for ten thousand dollars, one third on acceptance, one third in sixty days, and one third after another thirty days. Hobson had asked her to try to get it all on acceptance but the company wouldn't go for that. This too was an escalating contract, ten thousand for the first book, fifteen thousand for the second and third, twenty thousand for the fourth and fifth, and twenty-five for the sixth. After that, renegotiation. If they wished to buy a book not serialized, the prices would hold, less ten percent.

Writing him of this deal, again Jane Hardy gave directions on his work (the italics are hers): "Now, as to the revision of the *Curious Bride*—Erle, it simply won't do for the book to go to them in the shape it's in. I've got to submit the three copies simultaneously, as you see from the contract, and your *whole future* depends on the reception of this book. You'll have enough money soon to tide you over and you *must* take time to follow those suggestions of mine. I want it to be in the best possible shape when it goes to *Liberty* and Warner. Morrow will edit, and help. *Liberty* and Warner may, and may not. Remember always, you are *not* dealing with men like Hobson. You'll see what I mean when you meet Jacob Wilk—a man who can be pleasant over the luncheon table, and who can turn into iron ten minutes later, if he's crossed. You have a perfectly lovely story there—and by the way, I'd keep the title as it is. I don't think the *Guilty Bride* is half so intriguing. . . . Also I like the *Penitent Snob* immensely. Now, give some serious thought to that revision. If need be, cut down expenses for a while —do anything but shirk on that job! If you'll follow what I've written you, you'll clinch that thing. It may mean all the difference between acceptance and rejection. So go after it for all you're worth. You're tired. You were, when you finished the book. All right—rest a day or two. But *hide* that murderer! . . . The pulp stuff is all right, but *this* is your *future*."

It wasn't long before his Warner Brothers contract was becoming increasingly irksome to Gardner. He didn't like what he considered the manhandling of Perry Mason in pictures, and wrote to Jane, "I have been continually available for any type of consultation, which would have been furnished gratuitously, and I have been continually snubbed. . . . I have no temperament to speak of, I don't want the motion pictures to follow a book slavishly, and I recognize that when they have purchased something, they can do what they damn please with it, but good business demands that when they have ruined a character, we should make plans to protect our own interests in the future."

Warner also was considering a reduction in the scale of prices stated in the contract, causing Erle to write Jane, "I made a living before I ever saw Hollywood and I can do it again." He wanted Jane to call their bluff, and hoped they would reject the new books being offered. As for her attempts to get him to talk to one of the Warner officials in Hollywood, Gardner wrote, "Personally, I refuse to meet any representative of any motion picture company to discuss any details of any purchase now or at any time. I am devoting my energy to writing; I don't like commercial transactions; I don't like bargaining. I'm paying you a commission to take these details from my shoulders and I'm not going to pay you a commission and then do the work myself. If you want to sell all the Perry Mason books at ten cents on the dollar, go ahead. If you want to terminate the contract by mutual consent, go ahead."

Robert Thomas Hardy had died and Jane had married the promising young writer, Michael Foster, who was one reason for Erle's increasing disillusionment with the Jane Hardy agency. Rightly or wrongly, he felt that the new husband was interfering in agency matters, and he told Jane so. Whatever he felt, it was no more than a minor cause for dissatisfaction; the major reason was simpler. Jane's ideas of selling Perry Mason were far distant from his.

She made another big deal for him, selling *The Case of the Lame Canary* to the *Saturday Evening Post* for fifteen thousand dollars with an option on the next for seventeen thousand five hundred. But the relationship between the two continued to decline. There was another matter which had come up and which fed the flames: ". . . something funny as hell about that *This Week* situation." He had been in Mexico, where Jane had wired him around the last of February that his check from a recent sale to that market wasn't "due" until the last of the week. Later, on March 10, she had wired that a check for the first half had gone out on March 4 and the balance would be due in about three weeks.

On his return, Gardner looked up the original letter from Mrs. Meloney, editor of *This Week*, promising the first half of the payment three weeks from January 23 and the balance one week later. He had left for Mexico believing a check would be sent to Honey to take care of certain of his obligations. "Now what the hell? A check is due when it's promised," he wrote Jane. He added that if she ever held up a check of his, as he knew some agents did, it would be like a red rag to a bull. "I want my money the day it comes in."

In writing Thayer Hobson of Jane and her motion picture negotiations, he said that, confidentially, her merchandising methods were a pain in the neck to him, and that he had taken steps to see that he would now plan the sales campaigns, "but I think it comes pretty late."

From a third party, Erle learned that Jane was saying he'd acquired such a temperament that her attitude was a well-I-wash-my-hands-of-the-whole-thing. He had it on good authority that she told one editor over the phone that "Gardner has such a swelled head I can't do anything with him. It isn't any use to expect him to make any concessions." To Hobson, Erle wrote that he didn't know how she ranked with other agents as he had no standard of comparison, but "I know damned well that an agent who flies into rages and spreads rumors that the author is suffering from a swelled head is a hell of a detriment."

"I've carried on," his letter continued, "until the dissatisfaction in my own mind, the feeling of futility, and the conviction that she's steadly undermining me has become an ever-present and unwelcome mental background. . . . By this time you know the *Saturday Evening Post* has rejected *Substitute Face*. I know nothing of the details, just a wire from Jane. I don't hold her responsible in any way for that. We'll all know more when we do get details. Personally, I felt absolutely convinced it was not only the best Mason I'd written, but the best I could write."

Meantime he had—without her help—an important new market. Ben Hibbs, the editor of *Country Gentleman*, had written Erle *in care of Morrow*, asking him to create a new character for mystery serialization in his magazine. Although Hibbs called on Jane every few weeks, he did not even know she was Gardner's agent. And when Gardner sent her a copy of Hibbs's letter, she responded, "Yes, I know *Country Gentleman* was in the market for a mystery story, but not from you."

"Analyze that in connection with the fact that I could and did write for them a story they liked," Erle wrote Thayer, "and which opened up a new slick paper market which paid me ten thousand bucks for serial rights, and you have a hell of a lot of answers."

The new character he created was Doug Selby, a small town district attorney, who would become one of his most successful protagonists, and would continue through many serials and books.

"Unfortunately, when I quit," Erle wrote, "Jane . . . will probably feel aggrieved and she has a damned sharp tongue which she cracks around at the trade when her clients leave her. . . . I suppose it won't do me any good and I'll have to battle along for a year or so living the breach down, but it's better to do it that way than have her belittling me in so many ways, failing to cooperate in sales campaigns and gradually antagonizing the trade. —That's the situation in a nutshell. I'm hoping against hope that some solution will appear. I don't think it will. I think the time for that has long past. A desire to let her reap some of the crops she and Bob sowed has held me with her long after I'd have separated from any other agent."

On September 24, 1937, he wrote to Jane that he was terminating their relations for a variety of reasons which he felt there was no use to enumerate, but the cumulative effect of which was sufficiently strong to make him take a step he had hoped would never be necessary. He had no other agent in mind but planned to handle his own work. To Thayer he repeated the hope that Jane would consider the decision as a business one and let it go at that, but was much afraid she would not.

His fears were well grounded. It took many years for him to overcome the harm she was to do him among publishers.

Chapter Sixteen

GARDNER WAS a born bachelor. In the nineteenth century and early twentieth, the bachelor estate was an honorable one. Not until the twentieth moved into its middle years did the Freudian-influenced neo-sophisticates, out of their lack of knowledge and understanding, negate this concept. They didn't change the basic fact that there are born bachelors, they just kept it from being taken for granted.

Gardner was never meant to be a family man. The wonder of it is that he lived a family life for more than twenty years. To be sure, for the most part he lived it in bachelor style. He worked hard and advanced himself in the legal profession. His family had a nice home, set a good table, enjoyed holidays. But he lived life his way. Whenever he had the opportunity, he went off on adventures with his friends, such as the Alaska trip. As for the camp wagon which he devised, it was for him alone, to roam the deserts.

Like many men, Erle was dichotomous. He was a loner, but a most gregarious loner. When he wanted to be alone, he went off alone. When he returned, he wanted to be surrounded by his friends. He was, in a word which was not a part of the vocabulary when he was young, a hyperactive boy. And he grew up to be a hyperactive man.

His daughter, Grace, remembers that when he was not engaged in mental activity, he could not sit still. He was up and agitating about, looking for something physical to engage him. He was very much an outdoor person. He played golf and tennis, as games, not seriously. He rode horseback, was dedicated to archery for many years, which he did take seriously; every chance he got he went to the beach, like most Californians who live on the edge of the Pacific. And he was, of course, a constant traveler to near and far places, his travels being a part of his great curiosity about people and their environments. In the days when he lived a family life, he would keep his travel plans to himself until they were set; then, as if it were on the spur of the moment, he would drop everything and take off. He would go alone or with a male companion to hunt or fish; with Nat on other journeys. When both parents were traveling, Grace would usually stay with her Grandmother and Grandfather Gardner. She remembers her grandmother as a demon on cleanliness. At family dinners, Grace and her cousins, the children of Walter, couldn't eat their cake in the house for fear they might spill it on the carpets. The grandfather, Charles Gardner, a tall, quiet man of wit and wisdom, was a foil for his tiny wife. On his retirement, the elder Gardners moved to Oakland, not far from where Nat and Grace later were to live.

In 1921, when Erle and his family went back from San Francisco to Ventura, they lived at 1703 Buena Vista Avenue, on a hilltop with a fine view of the ocean. There was a board fence around the house, covered with roses. Erle was a photography addict and there are many pictures he took of his daughter, a handsome, tow-headed child with bobbed hair and great hair ribbons, always beautifully dressed for the picture-taking. She is the spitting image of her dad in his young pictures, and according to her mother, was so much like him in temperament and disposition that Nat always had to act as the buffer between them.

More than twenty years later, Gardner wrote to "Dear Dort," as he usually addressed Grace in letters, "Looking back on it I can see where I made a pretty lousy father. Most of your memories of the old man are the ones when he was yelling and cussing around in a hell of a hurry and making decisions which really didn't take into account the way a girl felt. . . . A whole lot of it was a resentment on my part of the way I felt Nat was spoiling you. I tried to be the brake and you always saw me in that capacity . . . and so we bickered and I guess you were pretty much in the middle. I never did have the time or take the time to really get acquainted with you."

Later, writing to her concerning the raising of a child, he said, "I didn't do so hot myself and I sincerely regret I didn't ever get to know you better. Nat was always the ambassador and go-between, and I'd disagree violently with most of her ideas and you always saw me when my foot was being put down on something. . . . I suppose I had too much ambition and having decided I was going to be a writer I subordinated every damn thing to being a writer,

"Dear Dort," Grace Gardner

just as I had previously subordinated every damn thing to being a lawyer."

Erle was an animal lover. He had a peculiar bond with animals and they with him, which came to fulfillment in later years when he lived the ranch life of Temecula. It was only natural that his daughter too would be an animal lover, the point of departure between them being that Grace liked cats and Erle liked birds and the two didn't mix.

There was one bird which Erle rescued that had been coated with tar from an ocean spill. He sat up all night washing down the wings so that the bird could fly again. He used all of Natalie's best embroidered towels for the job, because they were first to come to hand. It never occurred to him that tar was as difficult to get off linen as off wings.

According to all memories of those early days, Nat kept the home in beautiful fashion. Not that she believed in just being a full-time housekeeper. She was an independent woman, and enjoyed outside activities. In a way, her daughter believes, she had a good deal more common sense than her husband had. After she and Erle made a trip to China, she began giving illustrated lectures, adding the South Seas after a subsequent voyage. Still later, when she had spent six months in England, she gave lectures on her experiences there.

Ken, Erle's young brother, worked in Ventura during some of his school vacations. He recalls how Natalie would be busy all day, having the house looking neat and pretty, and a fine dinner on the stove, when in would come Erle announcing, "We're going to the beach, come on!" He would be pulling the sleeping bags and cots and camping equipment out of the closets onto the living room floor, and when Nat would remonstrate, "But Erle, dinner is all ready," he would say, "Bring it along," and it would become a picnic on the sand.

More often than not, they all slept on the beach, or in the hills around Ojai where Erle belonged to the Ojai Valley Country Club. His daughter remembers that he never slept indoors if he could help it. He believed strongly that being out in the fresh air was the way to stay healthy. It is certainly one reason he was determined to get out of that law office.

At other times he would bring home, without advance notice, any number of guests. Nat would always cope with it. She was a Southern lady, very able at preparing the food, and also serving as the perfect hostess. Around 1930, when Grace was a high school senior, Erle decided to buy a house at 2420 Foster Avenue in Ventura. It was in the process of being built and it was finished according to his and Nat's specifications.

After high school, Grace took six months' junior college work in Ventura and then entered the University of California, an English major with a minor in philosophy. As an only child, Grace could have been a spoiled little girl, but there wasn't really a chance for her to be in the unpredictable household.

In June of 1931, when Nat and Erle made the long voyage to China, Grace very much wanted to go along. However, as they planned to be away six months, it would have meant her missing a semester of college, and this her parents did not want. Instead, Erle fixed up his precious camp wagon, which up to that time no one but he had ever been allowed to touch, and turned it over to her for the summer, to tour to Vancouver with some of her girl friends.

The invitation for the Gardners to visit China came through Kit King Lui, the daughter of the eminent "red button" mandarin family of Lui in Canton. Kit King had been coming up to Ventura on weekends to teach Chinese to Erle and Natalie. They had, quite naturally, taken her into the family as an honored guest. This was

Kit King Lui

a rather different reception from that which she had found in Los
Angeles during her studies for her master's degree in sociology at
the University of Southern California. Bigotry against Orientals was
still strong in the thirties and this aristocratic girl had not even been
able to find decent housing.

Because the Gardners had introduced her to American life, she
invited them to accompany her when she returned to her home in
the summer of 1931 so that she could return their hospitality.

It was a dangerous time to visit China. The aggressions of Japan
were at the point where China had appealed to the League of
Nations for assistance. It was also the period when China was moving
into civil war between the northern war lords and the Kuomintang
government.

Although the Gardners were royally entertained as guests of the
family, the Luis were too prominent not to be involved in the political situation. Erle managed to find adventures as dangerous as
those of the new hero he created on this journey, a certain Major
Brane, "who dabbled in international intrigue and dealt with professional spies." Among major dangers for Gardner were being
placed under house arrest; being commanded to appear before the
People's Court with its power of life and death; being accused of
being a spy; being chased by pirates on a boat trip up the Pearl

River. On another occasion, he came close to being kidnapped when he had impatiently ignored a Lui dictum that he never venture out on Canton streets without a member of the family as escort.

In the entire period of the journey, Erle kept up his work. His goal was a novelette every third day; he completed eight of them a month, typing out his own work in the elegance of the Lui home or in native huts, during a Macao typhoon, on a Chinese gunboat—wherever he traveled. And as he wrote in his autobiographical notes, "Travel we did. We went to Shanghai, Peking, Canton, Macao, Tientsin," with a return through the South Seas and with a stopover in the Philippines. His discipline of work was such that here he first "pounded out another novelette" before allowing himself to take off on a journey into the country of the headhunters.

Between the China trip in the summer of 1931 and Erle's decision to put the Fiction Factory on wheels in June 1933, there must have been some sort of growing breach between Erle and Nat. She was not with him when he started Podunking, and when he wrote her of the Podunk plan, he stated, "Personally, I think we're finished here in Ventura."

At the same time he suggested that she keep a city headquarters and he would make his office at the camp. If she didn't wish to be alone, Grace being at the university, Peg would stay with her. At any rate he asked her to let him know what she wanted to do.

On hearing from him, she evidently made a trip to the camp, where she and Erle had words. She left. When the Podunk camp was broken up for the winter, and Gardner and Ray Downs, Peggy's husband, were camping in the lower desert, Erle wrote Nat in November from Calexico concerning the girls, "I don't think they'll ever want to go Podunking again until things are straightened around so you're happy. . . . As far as I am concerned, I have had enough bickering to last a lifetime."

In her return letter on November 23, Nat took all the blame for the trouble at camp, although, "There are some things you said . . . I cannot admit the truth of. One is that I looked down on your work. I have always been immensely proud of your work. I think you are undoubtedly a genius, and your work has always stood head and shoulders over the other fellows'." Another thing she denied was that she went to the camp with the express purpose of breaking it up. It is true that she couldn't quite see making a permanent thing of it, but she figured that since it "appealed to you so strongly and was evidently the thing that you need—the outdoor life—we could work it out some way so that I could leave whenever I got restless."

However it came about, Natalie joined Erle when he and Downs moved to Laguna Beach shortly thereafter. Peggy and Honey also had moved there, and in late December they all went to New Orleans. They took apartments in the French Quarter and remained for two months. Jean was working in Washington, D.C., with Frank Orr. She and her husband, Leslie Bethell, had separated after their return to Ventura from Podunking. When Orr was called East as an expert on city bond issues, he had found no secretary there who was familiar with the subject. Since Jean had worked with Orr on this when he was city attorney in Ventura, he therefore sent out an SOS to her.

Before the move from Laguna to New Orleans, on the first of December, Grace had eloped to Reno where she was married to Alan Robert McKittrick. It was the same sort of "elopement" her parents had had: No one was trying to stop either of the marriages; eloping simply avoided the fuss and feathers of a formal wedding. Alan McKittrick had been born in Wembley, England. His family had moved to Oakland when he was five years old, which made him as Californian as most of the Gardners. He was known and liked by the family. Thirteen years older than Grace, his health was never good; he had a history of heart trouble. He lived until 1962, however, a marriage of almost thirty years. He and Grace had two children, a daughter, Valerie Joan, born in 1941, and a son, Alan Gardner, called "Corky" by all the family, born in 1950. During Alan's lifetime, their home was in the Bay Area.

In February 1934, Erle's friend, Adolph Sutro, made an offer to Ray Downs to come into business with him in San Francisco. Ray had been in charge of an exclusive Santa Barbara restaurant and catering service before the Depression. Acceptance of the offer meant that Peggy and Ray would be moving to San Francisco. Rather than lose Peggy's importance to the Fiction Factory, Erle decided to move his headquarters there, taking a studio apartment. The Downes nad an apartment in the same building, Honey found a place uptown, and Natalie took an apartment farther uptown.

In March of 1934 came word of the big escalating contract with *Liberty* magazine. Erle asked Honey, who had taken over his secretarial work, to go to a travel agency and find out about cruises to the South Seas. He said what he was often to say: "We build castles in the air, and sometimes we put foundations under them." In June they sailed on a six-week cruise, Erle, Nat, Honey, and Peggy. On

Valerie

this trip Honey, whose early first marriage was being dissolved, met Walter Moore, whom she would later marry.

In August they all returned again to San Francisco. This was temporary, for Erle had already decided to move down to Hollywood where friends had been suggesting he come to have a try at writing for the movies. Two of his Mason books were in the process of being filmed, the first, *The Case of the Howling Dog,* to be released in September. Warren William was cast as Perry Mason, with Mary Astor his co-star, and among the supporting players were such well-known ones as Grant Mitchell, Allen Jenkins, and Dorothy Tree.

Erle turned over the actual moving to Peggy and Honey while he flew east on business. Natalie went with him. Jean joined them in New York, her Washington work being completed, and the three traveled back to California by way of the Panama Canal.

On arrival in California, Erle went straight to San Francisco, having had word that his mother was seriously ill. She rallied, and he then proceeded to Hollywood, where he wrote Hobson about the arrangements: "I have an apartment with Nat in San Francisco, a studio hideout in Hollywood, a trailer which is acclimated to the desert, with dictaphones and cylinders in all three places. Whenever anyone is looking for me in one place, I am always somewhere else.

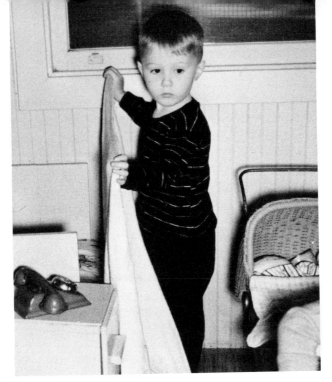

Corky

It makes a swell arrangement. I should be able to work." The mailing address was to be in care of Honey in Hollywood, where she and Peggy, with their children, had already taken a house; Jean had rented an apartment. All three girls were either separated or divorced.

Before he could get into "some real work," his mother died on November 10. It was, of course, not unexpected, but it was a great sadness for Erle. He had loved her dearly and she him. He went to San Francisco for the services, returning the next day and bringing his father with him, to help the elder Gardner adjust to the loss. They took off almost at once for the desert where his father could have "sunshine and clean air," Erle's panacea for all ills. The girls followed him on the first of December. The definite separation of Erle and Nat must have come at this time.

Before this, he had been the only one with a trailer; the others lived in tents. But now he bought two more, one for the girls, with a stove, storage space, and all the works, and one for his Dad, with "a fine double bed, a closet, chemical toilet, abundance of drawer storage space, and a little wood heating stove." Erle put aside his other writing and by the turn of the year had finished *The Case of the Counterfeit Eye.*

Early in 1935, Nat bought a house in Oakland. Erle bought one in Hollywood and set up housekeeping with two Filipino boys to serve him. There was a lot of work done in that house, including the first D.A. story for *Country Gentleman*.

Although they were never divorced, Erle and Nat did not live together again. He gave her an allowance of $225 a month, a generous one in those days. As his earnings increased, he added to it. He also took care of her extras, car insurance, medical expenses, and such. When she wanted to go to Europe that summer, he wrote Hobson, "I think I can send her okay. It will cost about $500 extra for carfare and I will have to increase her allowance to $250 a month." He made the arrangements and she left on May 20 for New York where Thayer saw her off. She planned to stay four or five months, live inexpensively on her allowance, and do it in her own name, not as "the wife of Perry Mason."

On May 31, Erle's father was in the hospital at San Francisco, very weak and not expected to live. He died on June 6, 1935. In less than a year, Erle had lost both of his beloved parents.

He kept on "pounding out" the stories and books. Times were bad. In December, he informed Grace that he was giving no one anything for Christmas. This was a "final, definite and complete announcement." The best thing would be to give a story to an editor "so we can all of us keep fighting Old Man Depression during the coming year." But he sent twenty-five dollars to her, asking her to buy something for Nat, who had by then returned from Europe. He would come to San Francisco for Christmas, arriving the morning of the twenty-fourth and "pulling out the night after Christmas."

He had been helping Grace and her husband, but now he was going to start tapering off, putting them on their own. "I never have, and probably never will, build up any estate," he wrote. "If I should shuffle off, about all you'll have to remember me by will be a few autographed books, a collection of junk scattered around in storage, the old clothes which I wore when I graduated from high school— unless you gave 'em away behind my back—and the memory of a rather queer sort of a dad who never did fit into the position of father, or conform overmuch to the mandate of conventional civilization."

So much for Gardner's prophetic powers.

Chapter Seventeen

THROUGHOUT HIS TROUBLES with Jane Hardy, Erle had given Thayer the complete story, letter by letter, in minute detail. When the break was made, he wrote Thayer: "In view of the highly confidential nature of some correspondence which passed between us, you'd better watch your office files." He hoped Jane wouldn't do anything which would make it necessary for him to come to New York and present his side of the case. She didn't. She undermined.

A year later in a letter to Thayer dated August 6, 1938, Erle enclosed a copy of a letter he had written to Bill Lengel, formerly of *Liberty*, now acting as an agent. It was after Lengel had called on Hobson and quoted Jane on the subject of Gardner. Erle's letter to Thayer was in imitation of Jane's style.

"As my 'closest friend,' Jane is 'worrying about me.' The worrying is being done audibly, apparently in editorial offices and elsewhere. 'Poor Erle,' it seems, 'just can't sell a thing. He really needs an agent. He won't listen to me because of the horrid lies that have been told about me and because he simply *wouldn't* listen to what I had to say. I *told* him that it was going to work out just that way, but he simply *wouldn't* listen. And I'm *so* worried. Don't say a word. This is in the *strictest* confidence but I'm trying to get him and Bill Lengel together. I'm terribly fond of Lengel and if I can help him make more money as an agent, you bet I'll do it—now don't look at my halo. The associate editor of one of the large weekly magazines put it there and I *told* him at the time that it wouldn't fit, but he insisted on putting it on. He's just like a brother to me, and he thinks so much of me. I told him I was worried about Erle and I asked him if he couldn't *please* buy something of Erle's but so far Erle *hasn't* sent in anything that was up to the *Lame Canary*. It really is a *shame* to see a man run down so. I just *can't* understand how he is getting by. I think Thayer must be advancing him money. You just don't see his name *anywhere*. I did see one story in the ——

magazine, and I rushed right over and told the editor how glad I was that he's bought one of Erle's stories. I told him I was so worried about Erle.' etc. etc. etc."

Erle commented, "The funny part of it is that New York editors think she is really worrying about poor Erle. When one of them repeated the blah blah to a friend of mine and that friend suggested that it *might* be a worry caused more by a desire to bring about the condition she was worrying about than actual concern over the condition itself, the editor was simply astounded. Then after thinking over several bits of conversation, he reluctantly agreed that there might be something to it."

Gardner knew he was in a bind. The hell of it was that most of the people Jane talked to were intelligent enough to keep her remarks in confidence and foolish enough to believe that she really was worrying, "which makes it a little difficult to gather evidence." He decided that the only way to stop all this was to get "some big agent to handle my work. And I don't want to be represented by any agent right at present."

Financially he *was* hurting. He had written Thayer in June of 1938, "It sure as hell has been a long time between the financial drinks. . . . I told you a while back and I'm telling you again, that it will take me more than a year to overcome that Hardy situation."

He was that summer thinking of writing a book under a pen name and giving it to Eve Woodburn to handle. Eve had been Jane's assistant before a split-up, for which he felt partially to blame, and was now on her own.

"I'd like very much to write a novel under a pen name which you wouldn't spot," he told Thayer in August. "I'd bet you even money that I could do so." However, he went on to say, although he might be able to write a detective story of that type, it wouldn't be the one he had in mind. He also pointed out the difficulties if Eve were kept in ignorance and it were put in the hands of some reader instead of being given to Hobson when she sent the manuscript to Morrow.

In late September Gardner had the book written. The title was *The Bigger They Come* and the pen name he had devised was A. A. Fair. It was a humorous mystery, featuring not one but two new characters, Bertha Cool and Donald Lam. Bertha was a tough, penny-pinching businesswoman with her own detective agency, whose heart of gold was buried somewhere beneath her avoirdupois. Her assistant, Donald, was a young, smart, "ornery little bastard," who almost, but not quite, got the best of Bertha. They never supplanted

Perry Mason's popularity with either the author or the readers, but they were close runners-up.

Not informing Eve Woodburn that it was a pen name, A. A. Fair sent his first book to her. With it came author instructions to submit it first to Morrow. She didn't; she sent it to *Collier's*, where it was rejected. It was probably the only time in their long relationship that she didn't follow orders.

It was not until after the book was accepted at Morrow that Erle admitted to Thayer that he was A. A. Fair. Even vice-president Charles Duell wasn't to know. Erle made it plain. "I'm particularly anxious to keep your office in the dark on the identity of A. A. Fair. . . . Fair is going to come into competition with Erle Stanley Gardner. Gardner has let his stuff get in conventional ruts and is so tied up with it that he can't quit." Erle bet a new hat Fair would be earning more money than Gardner in a year. This prediction proved false and there was no further mention of the new hat.

"You are going to find Mr. Fair not the easy, amiable bird to deal with that Mr. Gardner is," Erle stated. He and Thayer had considerable discussion as to what the A's stood for, with Erle saying, "I think you have a hell of a crust to criticize Fair's name. A. A. could be Arthur A. but isn't." Gardner liked Artrin but was in a minority. He had decided there was no middle name.

The first Fair book was published in 1939. It didn't take long for the secret to be out, despite all of Hobson's denials. Erle was certain that someone at Morrow had told, but actually, knowledgeable readers didn't have to be told. The touch was there. In Thayer's office, in bookstores, at other publishers, there were "a lot of people" aware that Fair was Gardner. Bill Weber of *Scribner's*, whose pen names as mystery reviewer for the *Saturday Review* and for the *Herald Tribune* were a fairly well-kept secret, laughed in his face when Thayer denied the Fair-Gardner relationship. Thayer denied the nom de plume outright to Jane when she asked him, "Is Erle going to keep on writing those A. A. Fair books?"

In spite of all the palaver about it, Gardner had not closed out Perry Mason. "I'm aware that the change in Mason has been gradual; that he has a certain number of reader friends; that it may be dangerous to rock the boat." There does not seem to be any one firm statement saying he was going to continue with Perry Mason mysteries. It is rather, and fortunately, that he simply couldn't give up Mason. Just the same, he was still determined to write "something which will appeal to the critical school, a story of stark realism without the four-letter words which usually characterize realists."

This in the thirties. "I think that's what the book public wants in detective stories. I think it's a more mature public than those who read detective stories in magazines."

Although Gardner had no New York agent at the time, he did have one in Hollywood. Bill Dozier of Berg Allenberg was representing him for motion picture work. Dozier, who later became a prominent producer in pictures and television, called on Thayer in that winter of 1938 when he was in New York. On his return to Hollywood, he told Gardner he was "greatly concerned"; that far from exaggerating the New York situation which Jane Hardy had created, Gardner had underestimated it. Dozier advised him to get someone immediately to represent him in New York. He suggested one well-known woman but Erle had had it with women agents. This time he intended to find in New York what he appreciated in Berg Allenberg: "They don't peddle bull, and it's a business relationship, pure and simple. The more I see of agencies, the more I have come to distrust an agent who relies on personal charm, appeal, or connections for holding a client on the one hand, or placing his work on the other." He now stated flatly to Thayer: "I think I need an agent."

In December he wrote Thayer, "I am now sold down the river." Dozier had made a deal for him at MGM, six weeks' work on a Nick Carter story for fifteen hundred dollars a week. He would work at home and be free to work on other things if he so wished. After the six weeks, he would receive six thousand dollars more if they wanted a story based on his outline.

In January of 1939 he was still working for MGM. The producer now wanted him to develop a character. For this Dozier intended to ask "plenty." But, wrote Erle, "You can't beat that Hollywood game. I'm probably just a sucker nibbling at the bait."

Thayer was saying that somehow, somewhere, Gardner simply had to cut down on expenses. Erle couldn't see how he could do it, with "my payments to the wife by way of allowance, the property I am buying for the wife, my salaries here, my insurance, income tax, etc. I have to pay out around twenty-five hundred dollars a month."

There was some money coming in, of course, from the movie deal. But this blew up with a bang because of a change of casting. All of Gardner's work was thrown out. The situation caused Gardner to become even more disturbed about finances. He considered closing the Temecula ranch, a recent purchase, and coming east to Connecticut for a year. Through all this period he was borrowing ahead on royalties.

Chapter Eighteen

FROM 1937 to 1941, Gardner did not make a single sale to the *Saturday Evening Post*. He had written his first D.A. story for *Country Gentleman* in 1936, and he sold them another in 1938. From that sale until 1940, he made none to any of the slicks; in 1939, not one line was accepted. In 1940, he again placed a D.A. serial with *Country Gentleman* but the *Post* remained a closed door. His stories were appearing in these magazines during the period, as it was the practice of editors to buy material far in advance of publication, but no new sales were made.

And then, in the spring of 1941, there came the answer to Gardner's troubles. Willis Kingsley Wing. It is small wonder that after his unfortunate experience, Gardner was wary of all agents. Yet he needed someone to handle magazine sales, in particular to try to get him back into the *Saturday Evening Post*. Book after book had been rejected for serialization but he had finally sold them three short stories featuring a new character, Pete Quint. After that, rejection commenced again. He couldn't understand why; he had heard that the Quint stories were immensely popular.

It was Cornwell Jackson, then of Berg Allenberg, who first suggested Willis Wing to Gardner. Gardner queried Thayer and discovered that Thayer knew Wing quite well. They commuted on the same train to Connecticut every workday. In that hour and a half, they frequently talked over literary matters.

Willis Kingsley Wing, who had been at Doubleday and Company, was one of the leading young agents in that year of 1941. He continued as an important and highly respected agent until his retirement in the sixties. Thayer believed Wing could do a good deal for Gardner in the magazine field and approached Wing about handling him.

Willis K. Wing in September 1977

Wing was well aware of how Jane Hardy was maligning Gardner. Hearing the rumor that she was closing her agency, he had lunched with her to inquire about clients, but all he heard about was "poor, dear Erle," and how he could no longer write. As this was considerably before Wing had been approached by Hobson, it was purely gratuitous information.

In December 1941, Erle made an unexpected trip to New York, and Thayer took the opportunity to arrange a meeting between him and Wing. Thayer briefed Wing before the meeting, saying that Erle was "often of quick temper and uninhibited in expressing his views, had a bit of the ham in him for he liked the sound of his own voice, loved to expound a theme at length in person or in correspondence; that often he carried over in his personal relationships some of the techniques of his boxing and added to that the techniques he practiced in the courtroom." Thayer also explained that he and Erle enjoyed verbal sparring, and if this sort of thing occurred in Wing's presence, not to take seriously the language they used with one another.

The first meeting came off well as "the New Haven Railroad bumped and joggled us toward Branchville and West Redding," according to Wing, but there were no decisions made that day. Shortly thereafter Erle was off to business in Boston, and not too long after that he wrote to Wing that he thought they could work together. He was still as suspicious as a forest creature about giving over control of his material. There was considerable correspondence between the two before, in February 1942, Erle made a final decision. He wrote Wing that if the *Post* took *The Case of the Careless Kitten*, which Thayer had sent for serial consideration, he, Gardner, wanted Wing to take over as his agent.

One of Gardner's early disillusionments with the slicks came when an unnamed magazine needed a detective novel in a hurry, and ordered it from him. Before he could finish the story, and no one was a quicker worker, he was told he'd better wait awhile. The while became indefinite. Later he found out that while he was writing the story, an agent had taken the editor to lunch and sold him two novels by another mystery writer.

"He was always," Wing recalls, "very concerned that the contacts, direct and indirect, he had with editors and publishers be maintained. He set great store by the friends he made in all fields. Not, I am sure, because he wanted to 'use' such friends and acquaintances, but because he liked people, respected those he thought deserved respect, and was incurably curious about how and why they did what they were doing." Wing was also certain that the Jane Hardy treatment wasn't something that Gardner would soon forget, a treatment "which implied the agent was more important than the principal."

Because of his being tied up for film and related rights on the Coast, it could have been difficult for Gardner to find a New York agent. Coast film agencies were used to working with New York literary agents on a split commission; where they already had a direct arrangement with a writer "they were no more eager than you would guess to divide a commission with an Eastern agent," as Wing explains.

"I felt I could do Erle good in the magazine field. While Erle wanted to appear in the *Post* and other general magazines, he did not want to neglect his pulp markets and not every literary agency in New York had interest in the pulp field or indeed knew much

about it. I was at home in both areas as well as in the article field,"
a field which was also of prime importance to Erle. "The number
of markets open to Erle and other writers who had interest and
talents as diverse as his were more numerous then than at present."

At the beginning, Wing's main job was to try to promote Perry
Mason with the *Saturday Evening Post*. The editor, George Horace
Lorimer, had found Mary Roberts Rinehart, Leslie Ford, and other
women mystery writers especially popular with *Post* readers. Lorimer
felt the *Post* was making an exception when he bought a Mason
story. Nor did he like the fact that Mason had originally appeared
in *Liberty*.

"It is not easy now to try to describe the Independence Square
attitude," writes Wing, "but through all the *Post* history, from
Lorimer on to the final editor in chief, the *Post* was always right."

Erle felt that its criterion for mystery serials was too narrow. One
day he and Wing sat down and tallied Erle's circulation from both
hardcover and reprint books as against the *Post's* circulation. They
found Gardner surpassed the *Post*. Later, lunching in Philadelphia,
Wing gave Ben Hibbs, who by then had become the *Post* editor in
chief, this information. "After that," Wing states, "it was considerably easier placing a Mason serial with the *Post*."

There was never any continuum of Gardner stories in the *Post*,
a condition Erle would not ever become accustomed to. Everything
would go along fine for a while, then the magazine would reverse
and buy nothing, nor did the condition change when Hibbs became
the *Post* editor. In spite of his difficulties with the magazine, Erle
always held Ben Hibbs as one of his dearest friends.

This friendship was the source of one of Gardner's favorite anecdotes, what he called the "famous Rose luncheon." He was going
east and wrote Hibbs, at that time *Country Gentleman* editor, that
he'd like to stop in Philadelphia and meet the staff of the magazine.
As Hibbs had already visited the Temecula ranch, he knew how Erle
felt about such a thing as formal luncheons. Nevertheless, Hibbs
invited him to lunch in Philadelphia.

Gardner refused the invitation, saying he'd just drop in to say
hello, but Hibbs patiently repeated it, adding that it was a suggestion of the "boss editor," Phil Rose. Hibbs had told Rose about
Erle, and the lunch would be very simple, not a time-waster.

The Curtis Publishing Company had its own dining room and its
own chef, and it was accustomed to serving famous authors. The
Saturday Evening Post was the dominant magazine of the group,

Ladies' Home Journal second, and *Country Gentleman* sort of a country cousin. "The atmosphere," in Erle's opinion, "was that of a very exclusive country club."

Unbeknownst to Phil Rose and Ben Hibbs, Stuart Rose, at that time one of the editors of *Ladies' Home Journal* and later to become "a very important editor" of the *Saturday Evening Post*, was entertaining that day a most prominent woman author of his magazine. With the chef he planned a "special Stuart Rose luncheon."

Stuart Rose was, in Gardner's words, "very much of a gentleman, a man who rides to the hounds, who has all the social graces and all of the urbane polish of a man of the world." And according to Gardner, the special lunch he planned for his author was "squab, hothouse asparagus, artichokes, and all kinds of delicacies."

The inevitable happened. The Phil Rose party arrived first, and were served "the Rose luncheon." When Stuart Rose and his guest arrived, they were served Gardner's mutton chops, canned peas, and baked potatoes. "Years afterward, when I got to know Stuart Rose, and reminded him of the fact that I was the recipient of 'the special Rose luncheon,' I am afraid it all but ruined what was at the time beginning to ripen into a friendship, or at least a friendly tolerance on Rose's part," Erle was to say.

The highlight of it all, Hibbs confided later, was that quite obviously Gardner had no idea that day that he was eating anything special. He was tearing away at the squab, pushing asparagus to one side, trying his best to gulp down the food so they could get back to talking business.

Another *Post* editor Gardner had tremendous liking for, although they frequently crossed swords, was Erd Brandt. In remembering those days, Erle called Erd "one of the best-loved editors in the world . . . sometimes referred to as the wheel-horse of the *Saturday Evening Post* editorial staff." One thing which made him such a good editor in Erle's opinion was his "longing for adventure."

Wing had frequent talks with Erd Brandt, and wrote in part to Gardner, "It is completely clear to everyone in Philadelphia that you are carrying on your book production program with Mason as your first interest. If they like them, they buy; if they don't, they don't. They quite agree that you and Hobson are the best and final judges of what will please Mason fans as books."

Gardner wrote back to Wing, "I realize there is no percentage in an author arguing with the *SEP*. The *SEP* enjoys the position of being infallible because it has the dough, the reputation, and the last word. I am afraid to try and write Mason stories to the *SEP* formula. The past three or four Mason stories, up to and including *Buried Clock*, have been weakened because of a halfhearted attempt to follow that formula. With *Drowsy Mosquito* I decided to forget the *Post* requirements, and I think it's an infinitely better story because of that. I think it is going to be a lot better to simply quit submitting Mason stories to the *Post*."

Wing agreed that it was poor policy to submit a Gardner story if there was risk of rejection on any grounds that would give "Erd a chance to shake his head sadly with the kindly superiority which can be so irritating." As long as Ben Hibbs had Erd heading the fiction department, they'd better skip the *Post*. On rejecting *The Case of the Musical Cow*, Erd had said: "But, of course, it will do very well as a book." Erd was going to the Coast soon and Wing wrote, "You'll have a pleasant lunch, general conversation, but my experience in dealing with Erd since I got on his calling list in the early thirties is that there is rarely an opportunity for any give or take on fiction questions. Erd certainly isn't domineering, he's really gentle, but he's also firm in his own special way and for the most part it comes down to Erd telling you what is 'a good fiction pattern.'" Wing added that other agents had the same feeling.

Erle was keenly interested in having *Collier's* opened up as a market. He had never sold to them, and had an idea that Cap Shaw, during the peak of their dissension, was influencing a top editor against him. The *Post* did not like its authors in *Collier's*, yet Wing managed to place Perry Mason in both magazines. When the *Post* rejected *Musical Cow*, it was bought by *Collier's*, which had a young and able new editor, Knox Burger. Burger had decided *Collier's* would no longer be "a weak sister" to the *Post* and paid the goodly sum of twenty-two thousand dollars. Of the sale, Gardner wrote to Wing, "The thought of having Erd patiently tell me where I missed the market and suggesting I may do better next time makes me feel that the best way to show Erd I can write good mystery stories is to write them for a competitive market. And yet I realize how patiently Erd is trying to educate me for my own good as to what constitutes a mystery story."

As late as the fifties, Erle was still having magazine troubles. By then his A. A. Fair nom de plume had been revealed and he was concerned because every editor everywhere had turned down Bertha Cool and Donald Lam. "I don't want editors to get into the habit of rejecting Gardner stories," he said. "I don't want them to feel that the supply is big enough so they can reject them. I want them to feel that if they want a Gardner story they had better latch onto it as it hits the deck and consider themselves fortunate in getting a good buy." The Cool-Lam books had sold eight million copies. He wanted to work out something where Wing, not Woodburn, could handle them, and perhaps sell *Collier's.*

From the beginning, Wing had his own method of dealing with Gardner, a part of it being his solution to a continuing problem besetting literary agents, the drawing of a line between the professional and the social relationship. By keeping the two separated, Wing knew that the professional relationship was never threatened. Wing did not become a part of the Gardner Temecula ranch gang; he kept his courteous distance.

The business relations between the two men lasted for twenty-seven years. Wing says of it, "I cannot remember a single instance where Erle and I had any friction or mutual difficulties." There was the possible exception when Wing airmailed instead of phoning news of a *Post* acceptance at an advanced price.

When Wing retired in 1968, Gardner wrote, "Your letter of February 13 was not entirely unexpected. I gathered that you were planning to go into retirement, and I'll probably be retiring myself within a short time. I'm trying my best to take life easier, but things keep piling up on me faster than I can unscramble them. . . . I suppose it is the law of life that we are in a stream; that if we have birth, we must have death; that the old must forever give way to the new so that we can have progress. . . . In any event, Willis, we've had a very wonderful association, and I hope we keep the contact alive for many more years—although I think it is time we both started taking life a little easier and took a few more vacations. All the best in the world—."

Chapter Nineteen

DURING HIS MAGAZINE troubles in the thirties, Gardner was of course continuing to write books. Morrow was publishing four a year, two Perry Masons, one D.A., and one A. A. Fair—sometimes others. And he was selling steadily to his old pulp markets.

Quite naturally, he was trying to discover what was wrong with his serial sales, while being well aware of the fact that his former agent was backbiting him to all the big magazines. In analyzing the problem, he wrote to Thayer, "I'm here to tell you, you can't change the so-called Mason formula and have a Mason book. I could write you an encyclopedia now on the plotting of Mason stories. Briefly, it gets down to these simple, fundamental factors: There are two ways of writing a mystery. The first is to build up an attractive character who is affected by the mystery, have him or her in danger, and then bring in the super-sleuth who solves the thing in the nick of time. (These are damned easy to write and is the reason they are a drug on the market—isolated houses in which wayfarers are marooned, islands, country estates, snowbound houses, etc. A dozen people all hating each other, and a series of murders.) —It's the formula for Agatha Christie's latest book, and damned if it doesn't seem to be the formula for the mystery the *Post* is now publishing by Mignon Eberhart. Frankly, I'm Goddamned if I can see them. They're theatrical, unreal, etc. However, readers like them and it seems to be the formula that most slick paper editors fall for, so I may have to take a whirl at it some day—*but* not as a Mason."

The second type of mystery was the protagonist story with a super-sleuth. The reader knows that he (super-sleuth) is going to solve it and there's no suspense. "If you analyze the market, you will find there are Goddamn few protagonist mystery books which have ever been written and have been a success. This is because it takes a lot of damned hard work to plot them."

Then there's a modification of the latter where a Dr. Watson is baffled until about page two hundred when the super-sleuth winds it up in thirty pages of fast action and explains to the reader in thirty more pages. Fairly easy to write, said Erle.

"I have learned a hell of a lot about the Mason stories since I last talked with you. The reason the Mason stories have stood out is because there are just damn few authors who have figured out how to write a protagonist story in which there is any suspense, in which the central character can be dragged into danger, yet preserve for the reader the illusion of masterminded competence which makes the character attractive in the first place."

He went on to say, "Apparently there is a new 'school' of detective writing predicated upon the alarming discovery made in *The Thin Man* that marital relations are not platonic, and murder mysteries are dressed up by taking the reader into the bedchamber, or even between the sheets. I personally am such a simpleminded hick that I was going to write you that the basic plot of a mystery story was the real salad, and the garnishment of novelty was just the dressing.

"But then, I read the Leslie Ford *Saturday Evening Post* serial, in which the whole plot is predicated on the theory that somebody tells a guy the woman he's in love with and who's in love with him doesn't really care for him. . . . There's some very clever writing in that story, some damn nice characterization, and if readers actually fall for plots like that, why in hell should I waste my time analyzing plot fundamentals or your time in making you read through such a hell of a mess of stuff in order to come to the following signature? —Yours, Gardner."

In 1941, Thayer introduced Helen King to Erle. She was to handle his work at Morrow thenceforth, and in time she was to become another member of the Gardner family. But the beginning was stormy with Erle at his temperamental, no pulled-punches best or worst. The beginning was in January 1941. Erle had delivered a story "to fool the reader." He stated that the average reader, "and by that I mean everyone," who reads a mystery story cheats. When he gets to the end, he says, "I knew it all the time." He doesn't realize he is cheating. He simply hypnotizes himself.

In this new story, Erle had Mason give Tragg, and the reader therefore, "a completely cockeyed explanation, pinning the guilt on some innocent person, and then in the last half dozen pages pulling an entirely different rabbit out of the hat. I don't think it's ever been done. I think it's a slick dodge, but I'm God-awful afraid that the reader, hypnotizing himself as he does, will have his mind thrown into a state of confusion which is similar to the reactions of you and Mrs. King."

After some exchange of correspondence about this idea, Erle sent forth one of his blast letters, which was responded to, typically, by Thayer: "Well, I'm glad to see that you're not losing your technique. One of these days you're going to realize that it would be to your advantage to put half the brains into your books that you put in your letters, and then our problem would be halved. By God, you just can't beat Gardner. Of course I'm used to it. This is Mrs. King's first experience with the Gardner blitzkrieg and she's a little breathless." He announced that he was answering the letter, because if she answered it, Erle would learn some new things about women and maybe get a new publisher. Before letting Erle be exposed to her, Thayer intended to wait a bit.

"She is no Lily Maid of Astolat, this King woman. She's hardboiled and she sees red and she can teach you some new words. . . . When I say she's breathless, I don't mean that you made her breathless, I mean she's physically exhausted cursing at you. You're going to like this King woman when you get to know her, even when it hurts."

There was a handwritten postscript the next morning about one of the Quint sales to the *Post*. It ended: "You just button your mouth up, and stay away from writing letters, and devote yourself to writing that makes dollars roll, and everything will be fine."

In February, Thayer wrote that he was making a business trip West. Erle's answer, the third of March, welcomed him: "There's a hell of a lot for us to talk over." Particularly, there was the A. A. Fair problem: The books were not selling as hoped, and Grosset and Dunlap, the reprint house which published Perry Mason, had turned some Fair books down.

Regarding Thayer's usual meanderings before reaching the ranch, Erle wrote: "The normal procedure will be for you to advise me you will be here the first of March or the first of April. About March 17, you will advise me you have been delayed owing to difficulties in lining up other authors, and will arrive about April 10. On April 5, you will wire me you expect to be in Los Angeles on the seventeenth and can I join you for dinner. On the fifteenth, you will wire me you are detained in San Francisco and to make the dinner on the twenty-first. At dinner you will tell me how crazy you are to see the ranch, but you can't get away before the twenty-fifth and can't stay over a couple of days. You will show up on the twenty-sixth with ants in your pants, stating that Trilling (Thayer's secretary) has just sent you a wire, and that you must get into Riverside to take the streamliner east that night.

"I would like to have you stay here long enough to get relaxed, see the Fiction Factory at work, and talk over a few things. Therefore, when the old stalling starts, don't bother to send me all the letters and wires, but just rest assured, sweetheart, that a man who can write murder mysteries will think up some way of having you detained in the immediate vicinity. . . . And if you think I am becoming increasingly snooty, somewhat temperamental, and a little cold-blooded, please be advised that you haven't seen anything yet. Mr. Adolph G. Sutro has just completed a ten-day visit, and I have learned a lot about being snooty."

Thayer's answer on the sixth said, "My God, I don't know whether it will be good to see you or not. It would be my luck to have you have Sutro around for ten days so you could practice doing your stuff before you saw me." As to Erle's agitating about the A. A. Fair books, which had gone on at considerable length, Thayer wrote, ". . . when you can realize that you're no longer a smart lawyer talking to a dumb jury, you'll begin to make sense. The more I study your letter . . . the more I realize that its purpose was to restore my self-respect and give me an opportunity to point out to you just how wrong you are about every subject in the world."

After Thayer had made his visit and returned to New York, Erle wrote to him in re their poker games that it was marvelous to again "work all day for an honest penny, and not have to sit up until two or three o'clock in the morning so your publisher can win it back." But he was agitating again. The Columbia University publication, *The Pleasures of Publishing*, had listed the ten best mystery writers of the past six months in numerical order: 1. Dorothy Sayers by a wide margin; 2. Agatha Christie; 3. Arthur Conan Doyle; 4 Ngaio Marsh; 5. Erle Stanley Gardner; 6. Rex Stout; 7. Ellery Queen; 8. Margery Allingham; 9. Dashiell Hammett; 10. Georges Simenon. Seven of the top ten were women. The favorite fictional detectives were, in order: Lord Peter Wimsey, Sherlock Holmes, Hercule Poirot, Perry Mason, Nero Wolfe; Inspector Alleyn and Ellery Queen, tied; Maigret; Campion and Asey Mayo, tied.

Erle wanted Thayer to find out if the questionnaire on which the listing was based was "genuine or phoney." To what extent was that verdict forced? Was it intended to achieve a certain purpose and the rest of the stuff thrown in gratuitously? If so what was the purpose? This was his usual reaction when he didn't rate first. It was actually nothing but a fun questionnaire, sent to the monthly's readers: librarians, critics, authors, booksellers, publishers, scholars, of whom only 250 out of 2,200 returned it. Those who replied were mystery fans averaging 4.5 mysteries a month (the women read 5.5 a month, the men 3.3). Erle thought it was "strangely significant" that the *Saturday Evening Post*'s favorite women authors of that time, Leslie Ford and Mignon Eberhart, were not mentioned, as, in his opinion, "either of these gals has it all over Agatha Christie four ways for Sunday." He missed the point that the questionnaire was limited to mysteries featuring a series detective.

In mid-June, Erle asked Thayer for advance royalties of four thousand dollars, two thousand then and two thousand the end of July. "I don't know why I ever got in this lousy writing business anyway. I should have been a lawyer. I now either have to cut expenses or increase income. At this writing, both seem to be not only impractical, but impossible."

He had had unusually heavy expenses. Nat had had a detached retina in February; a world-famous surgeon had operated and she had had a long convalescence. In September Jean was to have a serious operation. And sandwiched between them, Erle had, ridiculously, come down with a case of German measles. The stars weren't with him that year. In December his dear New England Aunt Hattie, his father's sister, had a serious operation and he went to Boston to be with her. He took care of her expenses, of course.

Work continued to upset him through July. *The Case of the Turning Tide* had an error which no one had caught, either at Temecula or in New York. Gardner had deleted a wind blowing, and then left in the girl turning to face the wind so her hair would blow back from her face. It "spoiled the book for me, I threw it down in disgust." To make matters worse, when he took up the book again ten days later, he ran smack into a typo where "Boy, oh Boy" was printed "Bob, oh Boy." He says it's "simply a hoodoo."

After a long letter on the next book, explaining one point and another, Erle launched into a serious discussion. "Lately you are getting a little bit on the old womanish side and wanting your *i*'s dotted and your *t*'s crossed. Not that most of the criticisms in your letter aren't sound as a nut, but you want a lot of stuff explained which is already explained. . . . It's only in there once, but it's in-there. . . . Damn near all mystery stories are improbable in motivation. Every mystery story ever written has some loose threads. . . . I am going to try to work out a technique by which loose threads can be tied up as we go along, leaving only one loose thread to be hooked up to bring the whole cloth into a recognizable pattern.

"If you haven't done so, read Agatha Christie's *Body in the Library*. She not only pulls the murderer out of the hat, but the story is just absolutely full of utter improbabilities. The point is she gets by with a good deal of this because there are some very nice spots in the yarn. —I became particularly interested in it because I saw she had got herself into such a position that, to my mind, there was no *logical* way out. —But then she starts her chapter of explanation—Oh, my God! But the point is the *Post* bought this story. More and more readers are reading Agatha Christie. The same is true about half a dozen other writers whose stuff is full of improbabilities. Most of them get by with these things because they utterly ignore them.

"Don't get me wrong. I want to make my stories as airtight as possible. You check me on my mistakes and slipups; but Thayer, for God's sake, don't get to a point where this distorts your perspective. And so help me when anything is in a story once, I'll be damned if I'm going to put it in twice, or three times. —So send me in Mrs. King's reactions, and I'll send you some pages of revision."

Helen King describes the relationship between Gardner and Hobson in those days as "Damon and Pythias fundamentally, but the daily act was nearer Giants *vs.* Dodgers at Ebbets Field." She was, of course, in the middle of it, which she calls "an extraordinary experience—and a helluva privilege."

After they learned each other's ways, this letter to Helen from Erle regarding changes is in the usual vein: "How it can happen that a girl who has such a beautiful body can have a mind that is so contradictory to mine is one of the enigmas of life. You have gone over my foreword and introduction and taken out most of the Gardnerisms and incorporated Kingisms, which is I guess all right except in two instances . . . But I still love you even if you are recalcitrant." (At one time Helen wrote Jean, "I'll make a stern note to myself that I'm to ignore my Purist tendencies in re spelling when Perry Mason is around.")

Their principal running battle was with profanity, at times with Perry Mason but particularly with Bertha Cool. Nancy Harrow, an assistant editor who often handled Gardner material, took plenty of abuse on the matter. Regarding *The Case of the Screaming Woman,*

Helen King

Erle wrote to her, "You don't like profanity. You list 'hell' and 'damn' as profanity. Out here they are adjectives of punctuation." He enlarged, "Perry Mason has used damn and hell for twenty-three years. The readers who don't like hell and damn quit him long ago. I don't want Mason to overdo it, but I want Mason to keep in character.

"I am naturally coarse, rough, crude, and vulgar. I am assuming that Mason got a little out of hand in this story. I am toning him down some, but if the son of a bitch ever gets to be a gentleman, we can sell the serials to the *Atlantic Monthly*, the books to a group of clever professors, and, when you walk past 425 Fourth Avenue, you can nudge your friend and say, 'That place across the street is where I used to work.' Love and kisses."

Helen King has said that Nancy frequently gave Erle a bad time because "she had the eagle-eye of a copy editor, refused to be hurried, and stood her ground as though her feet were part of it." When Thayer and Helen alone worked on a Gardner manuscript, if within forty-eight hours it wasn't "read by both of us, a conference held to compare notes, and our combined efforts typed and sent off (by me, incidentally!), we'd get hell." But when Nancy was handling a Gardner, there would be a ten-day or two-week lapse—"and there is no question that the books she had a hand in were better edited than any before or after."

Concerning the profanity in *Screaming Woman*, Gardner enlarged upon this in a five-page letter to Thayer, opening with, "I have made one hell of a smear of changes in *The Case of the Screaming Woman* to conform to objections. There seems to be an objection to profanity in this book and 'damn' and 'hell' are rated as profanity. . . . If a client asks him if the situation is serious, the Perry Mason the readers have known for twenty-three years would say, 'Damn serious!' rather than 'I am inclined to think that, if the evidence as we now know it is received before the Court with no extenuating facts brought into existence, there is a very strong possibility the verdict of the jury would be adverse. By this I do not mean necessarily that the verdict would be that of first degree murder, but it might be one of the lesser offenses included within the charge, such as second degree murder or manslaughter.' "

"The question is," wrote Erle, "Shall we do anything that materially changes Perry Mason's character after all this time? The next question is: What the hell are we going to do with Gardner? Gardner says he can't interrupt one book to edit another. Yet he is always writing a book. On the other hand if we make the changes ourselves, Gardner screams his head off, writes abusive letters, sarcastic letters, undermines the morale of the personnel and raises hell in his own inimitable, vulgar manner."

After considerable wordage about the Perry Mason stories, Gardner continued: "I do know certain things about writing. One of these is that all three of you must subordinate your individual tastes to those of the mass reader market. . . . I am writing for a mass market."

The reader he is "aiming at" is the guy traveling on a nonstop plane, the doctor tired after a day at the office, the lawyer tired of the red tape of his profession who "wants to read about a man who cuts corners and gets away with it. . . ." A part of Gardner's wrath was that he had just emerged from a session in Hollywood where he dealt with Hollywood writers, "each and every one of whom wants to change Perry Mason. None of these writers thinks he is changing the character. At least he won't admit it. He is 'adapting the character to television.' Each one of them is writing Mason as he sees Mason. It is the God-damndest assortment of crap you have ever witnessed. Mason becomes a smart aleck, a wisecracker, a man who looks upon murder only as an opportunity for a new quip. —Think this thing over carefully because it may be damned important. Show the letter to Helen King and Nancy Harrow if you feel you should."

In spite of all his arguments, nothing changed. Hobson and King and Harrow did their job of reading manuscripts and making suggestions. Gardner blasted his barrages right back at them when they tried to alter his characters and his pace, although he was good as gold about necessary revisions.

Of four pages of corrections Helen sent on the Fair book, *Some Slips Don't Show,* herewith a few of his remarks:

"Page 33: I liked it as is—a lot.

"Page 58: No dates in any Gardner story. Twenty years later in reprint it makes 'em old-fashioned.

"Page 66: Don't see anything wrong with this myself. He'd told her what he was going to do to get the bacon hot, so when I say it was hot it's to be assumed he'd done it. Trouble with you and Thayer is you have no imagination on things which happen when boy and girl are cooking.

"Page 80: Hell no!

"Page 111: The bitch doesn't dare tell when and how she really received the letter. Strike out lines seven and eight if it will make you feel any better.

"Page 125: I don't know and the reader won't care. As the zoo keeper said to the old maid who was so interested in the sex of the rhinoceros, 'Who the hell cares except another rhino?' "

A more than eight-page memo to Helen King on *Pass the Gravy* begins with: "Now let's you and your Uncle Erle quit kidding each other and get down to brass tacks. Dammit to hell I cuss. My friends cuss. Some of them, like Bill Pemberton, have dropped into a habit of profanity where goddamn is an almost indispensable adjective used to qualify nearly every goddamn noun they use in speech. Others are like Louie Roripaugh who use profanity in a semi-picturesque sort of way. . . . I have always cussed."

After some anecdotal paragraphs about his camping days, he continued: "The old bookkeeper out of our law office, Maude McGonigle, who is now seventy-eight, a devout Catholic and who rebels against the infirmities of age, has just been visiting me." According to Erle, she pleaded tearfully with him not to be so profane, as she'd have to go to church "and get down on her old rheumatic knees and pray and pray and pray so that my soul would be purged of all my sins. I told her to hell with it. Let her keep on praying. No rheumatic knees on God's earth can last long enough to even inventory my sins, let alone get a purge."

From this discussion, he launched into "the things which are referred to in the vernacular as falsies." He says that girls should have realized they couldn't keep this a secret. "Personally I don't know how the boys discovered about them but the big boys did discover it by one means or another and they passed the information on to the rest of us." Another "personally" says he can't understand women decking themselves out in sponge rubber and a sweater, and getting upset if you look at it. "Personally" again, he thinks this is to attract a future husband but "imagine the look on the guy's face when he sees for the first time that he has been romantic over a product of the Goodrich Rubber Company."

One thing his editors were particularly firm about was a correct "time chart." Every writer makes one when writing to insure that a character does not, for example, take ten minutes to reach a place which under no circumstances could be reached by him in less than two hours. Erle violated time laws over and again—whenever he felt that hewing to the fact would slow down his story. Neither Nancy Harrow nor Helen King ever let him get by with it, even if, as a usual thing, he ignored their findings.

Gardner did not change his tactics with the years and increasing fame. In 1959, he was writing to Helen about *The Case of the Singing Skirt,* "I am afraid, my dear girl, you are overlooking the facts of life. Of course the bet was fifty dollars earlier in the story. But you must remember that we have taxes and inflation and by page 234 the Goddamn fifty dollars has become more than fifty. I am surprised that you don't realize this. Go down and try to buy a pair of stockings that you got for a dollar sixty-five when we started to write a timetable on this book and see what they cost now. . . . You be a good little girl and unscramble this mess for Uncle Erle and I'll get the hell out of here and write you another book as soon as I get back. The book will only have one gun, the corpse will only have one bullet hole, and I hope to God the story has only one rewrite. . . ."

Concerning this same manuscript, to answer Helen's doubt that a gunshot could not be heard when fired in the adjoining office,

Gardner took a revolver of the same model, extracted bullet and powder from the shell, went into the bathroom adjoining the office at the ranch, and discharged the percussion cap. To Helen he wrote, "The girls thought it was something I had eaten. If it had been in a law library, with books to isolate the sound, I doubt if they'd heard anything." To this length Erle would always go, to verify his facts.

His final words regarding this book were, "I think I am overworking but I can't take time to look back over my shoulder to make sure. As Satchel Paige so aptly remarked, 'Never look back, something might be gaining on you.'"

Part Five

TEMECULA

Chapter Twenty

It WAS NOT Erle who discovered Temecula. It was his dog, Rip, a German shepherd who always traveled with him. Erle and his caravan had been living a nomad life for more than a year. He had sold his Hollywood house in late 1936. Louise Weissberger, who had been his hostess in Hawaii earlier in the year, had come to California to return the visit, and he indoctrinated her into camp life with two house trailers, one for Louise and Jean, and one for himself. "We went north in summer and south in winter," he recalled. Before long he enlarged the caravan with two more trailers, one for a handyman and a cook, the other for an extra secretary. During this wandering, Honey was living in Redwood City, where she kept an office for Erle. Peggy was working elsewhere.

Louise eventually went back home but the caravan continued its wanderings through most of 1937. In early autumn, on their way to Encinitas, they came to Temecula. Because of Rip's pointing, Erle decided to stop for the night with Albert "Gramp" Nienke, an elderly German who had a trailer park there. He had no intention of staying longer than the night.

Rip knew better. He'd chosen the spot. They stayed on. On the first of October Erle sent Thayer a post office box address in Temecula which was "probably for thirty days," and only for their private correspondence; other mail was to go to Redwood City. They were still there after the thirty days, Erle heading his letters: Temecula Camp.

Temecula was peaceful. Erle liked the country thereabouts. Before he broke camp to go to New York on the annual winter business trip, Erle had made his decision to buy a piece of land in the vicinity. He left the trailers at the campsite and asked Mr. Nienke to look around for a small ranch for him.

Rip

Gramp Nienke and Gardner

From New York, as was winter custom, Erle and his secretaries were off to New Orleans. Sometime in that winter, the Rancho del Paisano became available. When he decided to buy it, Erle was still determined not to be tied to a home. The ranch was simply to serve as a place to park the trailers on an occasional stopover; he wanted nothing that "didn't have wheels under it." His feelings about a house to live in were most clearly expressed in one letter to his daughter, Grace: "I'm a cabin fever guy. When I have to live with anyone in close daily contact, I get cabin fever and can't take it."

However, for convenience, he decided to build a shower-laundry at the Rancho. Moreover, he needed a storage place to house all the material accumulating from his work. The Rancho began to grow, as did all Erle's projects. He built a study for his books and papers. Then a place for secretaries to work was needed, so the original main building was put up, with kitchen, dining room, living room, and two bedrooms. This wasn't exactly right for working, so an office building was next.

In time there were houses for permanent residents, houses for guests, any number of buildings for trucks and cars and ranch equipment and for storage. In later years there were fireproof vaults for Erle's papers. "Altogether I think we wound up with twenty-seven buildings," Jean says.

But that first year, Erle wrote Thayer with disgust at "this business of building cabins, roads, putting in my own electric light plant, gas, etc., etc." It had pretty much disrupted his schedule for the past few months. "But I'm gradually getting squared away so

Ranch in the early days

I can get down to work once more." Ranch life was rather quiet but interesting at that, he decided. This was after moving in. Of that effort, he addressed Thayer, "Don't ever move. . . . I've been moving and darn near haven't been doing anything else. One of these days I'm going to get sufficient elbow room and opportunity to write stories without dictating one cylinder, pausing to receive a truck load of furniture, dictating another, stopping to lay out the ground floor plan of the new cabin, and then dash to town for more nails. . . ." Without planning it, Erle had found a home.

When he first came there, Temecula was a crossroads, boasting a general store, which served as the post office and had the only telephone in the area, Gramp Nienke's gas station and trailer camp, and a population between two hundred and two hundred fifty residents.

The big town was nearby Elsinore, whose population today is only in the six thousands, and it wasn't that big back in the thirties. Riverside was the "big city," some forty miles northeast, the place where you went for shopping or for doctors' care or like necessities. Today Riverside has a population of one hundred and forty thousand; it most likely had no more than half that in 1938. San Diego, sixty miles southwest, is the really big city of the area; Los Angeles, about one hundred miles northwest, is too far for influence.

Temecula is in some of the most beautiful country of southern California. The San Bernardino mountains rise above the horizon. The hamlet is due east as the swallow flies from San Juan Capistrano, but the main road doesn't follow the swallow's flight. From Oceanside, over for the most part a two-lane highway, the road to Temecula wanders east and north some thirty-five miles through

Gardner at work in his new quarters

Meg Downs

green rolling hills. Down from Corona or from Riverside the highway is still in part two lanes, green hills alternating with brown hills studded with great and wondrous boulders. It is ranch country. Fallbrook, a nearby town where Jean now lives, is the avocado capital of the world as well as being a large citrus area. Sixty-five miles east and slightly north is Palm Springs and the great lower desert country. In Temecula, Gardner was close to both ocean and desert, each one important to his way of life.

When Erle acquired Rancho del Paisano, his adjoining neighbors were the Pala Indians. Across the road were the Vail brothers with their old-style cattle ranch, one of the last of the great ranches of southern California. The Vails had ninety-six thousand acres. Erle started with only one hundred and fifty but this was added to on several occasions, becoming nine hundred, a thousand, and eventually three thousand acres.

Temecula has grown considerably since Gardner's early days. The greatest change is a development called Rancho California, which is being built on the old Vail ranch plus its perimeter, totaling one hundred thousand acres of land. It covers most of southwestern Riverside County. Until very recently Nancy Hicks Carmichael, a daughter of Sam Hicks, Gardner's ranch manager, was Temecula postmistress and serviced more than nine hundred boxes, both post office and rural. Estimating three persons per box, the Temecula area then had some 2,700 persons.

The best word-picture of Rancho del Paisano as Erle developed it, was in Charles W. Morton's "The World of Erle Stanley Gardner" in the *Atlantic Monthly* of January 1967. In part he wrote: "About halfway up the side of a small mountain are the buildings of the thousand-acre Rancho del Paisano, in a grove of live oaks, affording solid shade from the hot desert sun. The trees, whose vast and twisting limbs indicate their great age, are forever shedding from their dark green abundance quantities of small leaves that have turned dry. It is characteristic of Gardner's standard of maintenance that the first visible activity around the place of a morning is a complete sweepup . . . so that one sees, on strolling from a guest house over to breakfast in the main house, nary a dead leaf but only the tidying marks of the broom . . . one hesitates to leave a footprint on it. . . . Everything about the ranch represents the carefully contrived fulfillment of some pertinent want on the part of the owner. It all works perfectly and apparently without human effort. Meals seem magically to serve themselves on the long refectory table at one side of the living room, a stout and immaculately polished piece of furniture, which, like everything else in the room, is made to withstand hard use for another century or two. The guest houses, partly hidden from one another in the grove of live oaks, are each equipped with reading matter, bar supplies and a thermos bucket of ice, and electric heaters against the morning chill. . . ."

The magical quality, as anyone who ever visited the Rancho well knew, was Jean. She was Erle's right hand; she managed the entire establishment for him. After camping out with the Gardner outfit on one occasion, Helen King wrote of Jean, "She is the only woman in the world who can drop a frying pan, pick up the telephone, take down the conversation between Erle and the caller, and five minutes later have a perfect breakfast on the table; no overcooked eggs or burnt toast or boiled-over coffee."

And Charles Morton said what everyone who had ever been a guest of Jean's at dinner would say: "Her cooking goes far beyond breakfast, and she can put a superb dinner on the table, if some kitchen crisis arises, without the rest of the company even being aware that it was she who did all the work from start to finish."

Jean enjoyed camp life as much as Erle did and was quite as inveterate a traveler as he. The only area where they didn't seem to see eye to eye was grand opera. As Jean once wrote to Helen, ". . . I've been losing some sleep due to the opera season. I get stubborn once a year and go back and forth to L.A. whether it kills me or ruins Uncle Erle's life. He sighs and bears it . . ."

Another view of the ranch was given by Lee Mortimer, a feature writer on the Sunday New York *Mirror* who came on an assignment to Hollywood and was invited to lunch with Gardner. Mortimer figured lunch would be the block or so to Romanoff's or the Brown Derby. "Gardner, it developed, lives on an estate of several thousand acres called Rancho del Paisano. It is near—and the word 'near' is used loosely—a town known, but not known to many, as Temecula, California. 'Somewhere between L.A. and San Diego,' an explorer friend told us." To be on the safe side, said Mortimer, he took along "as companion, bodyguard and guide, the brilliant college-bred nemesis of the Los Angeles underworld, Detective-Captain James Hamilton. After traveling for hours down back roads, through desert wastes, and ever-forbidding mountains, we reached clue number one, a filling station run by a little old Mexican woman who couldn't speak English. Through our interpreter, she gave us a series of directions which delayed us at least two hours longer than was necessary. Finally, by means of blind reckoning, we hit the Gardner estate just as luncheon was being cleared away."

It was 1951 before Erle permitted a phone at the ranch. "After fighting it for years, and then fighting for a few more years," he informed Thayer, "we now have a phone at Rancho del Paisano. The number is Temecula 201."

Prior to that, the usual procedure for Thayer to get word in a hurry to Erle was described by Erle to "Dear Three" (Thayer, Isabelle, and their first child) in December 1938. "Up in Elsinore they have a railroad station and a railroad. The railroad used to carry passengers. It doesn't carry passengers anymore because passengers won't ride on it. It takes too long to go from where you are to where you want to be. However, the railroad has to hold its franchise and so once or twice a week they run a locomotive over the rails with a combination freight and express car on behind. The choochoo has a whistle and a bell and everything. And, of course, there's a railroad station at Elsinore, and a heck of a nice young chap in the station. And because there's a railroad telegraph line running into the place, he's a telegraph operator. And the place is a Western Union station, and he takes down things in dots and dashes.

"When long telegrams come in . . . Scotty, 'that guy in Elsinore,' unscrambles the dots and dashes and writes them down on a sheet of paper, and then reaches for the telephone and telephones nineteen miles to Temecula where a woman in a restaurant slips off her

Hedy Roripaugh

apron and runs into the post office to try and take down what it's about.

"Now on short, simple wires like the one Thayer sent when he said, 'Cosmopolitan has rejected your story. I am so sorry for you,' there's not the least difficulty. Everyone in the valley knew that *Cosmopolitan* didn't like my story and were all sorry for me. And when Thayer sends wires about why he doesn't like mystery authors, the whole machinery bogs down."

The ranch was Jean's home all the time, Peggy's most of the time. Peggy's only child, Meg, was a great favorite of her Uncle Erle's and visited often. Honey and her husband lived nearby. Honey, like Peggy, had the sort of integral independence which enabled her to make part of her life outside the orbit. Yet she was always available to take over Erle's business matters whenever needed. By her first marriage, she had a daughter, Judith Ellen, called Judy. Today Honey has three grandchildren, Denise, Colleen, and Marc, and two great-grandchildren, Nicolle, daughter of Denise, and Shawna, daughter of Marc. She is surely one of the youngest great-grandmothers on record. As is Peggy with her eleven great-grandchildren! Of Peggy's three grandchildren, Duane has six children, Charles two, and Diane three.

At the end of the Ventura days, the girls' mother, Mrs. Walter, moved to Hollywood, where she lived in an apartment on Bronson for many years. Later she lived in Van Nuys near her son, Paul, and his wife. When illness came upon her late in life, she too had her own cabin at the ranch near her daughters. She was Erle's guest until her death.

Louis Roripaugh

There were innumerable secretaries. Some stayed a long time and others didn't stay long as they didn't measure up to Erle's devotion to work standard. Some lived at the ranch, others in nearby communities. And more than one married one of Erle's Temecula friends, in spite of the shotgun he kept handy after Hedy Burger married Louis Roripaugh. Hedy had become part of the family. Louis was manager of the Vail ranch. He had grown up with the job, his father having previously handled it. He was a good cowpuncher, always on the move from Montana to Mexico, buying cattle, then home to fatten the cattle and prepare them for the Vail spring and summer sales.

Erle and the Vail brothers became good neighbors; their poker games were legendary, principally because Erle never gambled more than a dollar's worth. But Louie and Erle were even better friends. Louie initiated Erle into cattle drives and on occasion took him on cattle-buying expeditions. Louie's salty cowboy sayings were a particular delight to Erle, such as this one concerning a spoiled boy who visited the Vails: "And his parents didn't do a thing to him, just let him grow bigger." Another acquaintance he described as "kind of a preacher-acting son-of-a-bitch." And the tag line of his account of a cattle deal: "Hell, if you won't buy 'em, I'll sell 'em to you."

Louie joined Erle's first Baja California expedition with his own truck, as he had to return earlier than the others. Before they left, Erle, "not being entirely blind," had noticed that Louie was coming more and more frequently to the Gardner ranch in the evenings, and if Erle was working, he would drift over to talk with Hedy.

Gardner, Evangeline Rausch, and Mahlon Vail
listening to the horse races on which they all bet

It wasn't until after the return from Baja, however, that Erle was rudely awakened to the realities of life. On an evening after he heard Louie and Hedy say good-night, the clump, clump of Louie's high-heeled boots came down to Erle's cabin. Louie settled himself on the edge of a chair, began to squirm uncomfortably, and finally, after several false starts, told Uncle Erle he and Hedy were going to be married. "Hedy, who had become invaluable to me," Erle mourned. And it was then that he decided "to keep a shotgun handy." The Roripaughs now live not far from Jean in Fallbrook; Louie is still a rancher.

Before Hedy, the first assistant secretary was Nonie Bibler, who shared the New Orleans days. One winter when she and Jean had an apartment in the Vieux Carré across from the Cabildo, tourists would point to them as glamorous artists, little knowing that they were two hardworking secretaries. Erle would drop Dictaphone records at their door after his night's stint. Then he would go out on the town with his friend, Jack Simpson, while the girls went to bed in order to be up early to transcribe his work.

Lilie MacLean joined the Gardner entourage in England in 1949. Erle and Dr. LeMoyne Snyder had gone to London to study Scot-

Secretarial staff circa 1958: Helene Seay, Ruth (Honey) Moore, Peggy Downs, Gardner, Jean Bethell, Millie Conarroe (seated)

land Yard methods. Erle met Jean later in France and they visited publishers there and in Switzerland and Italy. Foreign rights to the Perry Mason books had been sold to England, Spain, France, Hungary, Holland, Germany, Denmark, and Russia before this time.

Not one to let go of a good secretary, and Lilie was an excellent one with the shorthand competence of a court reporter, he took her with them to the Continent, and convinced her also that she should return to the States with them. On their return, Erle brought her mother over to join her in California. Lilie is another who married from the ranch. Her first husband was Erle's Elsinore physician, Dr. Westfall.

And there was Millie Conarroe, a Santa Monica girl, who lived in Temecula with her husband, who was with the State Forestry Department. She later remarried and moved north to Sacramento, working in law offices for many years. She gave up her vacation time one Delta summer to help Erle out on some work. In his opinion, published in one of his Delta books, Millie is "an employer's dream of a secretary."

There was Thelma Pons, who commuted from Fallbrook, and Betty Burke, whose husband was Erle's pharmacist in Elsinore. Both

Betty Burke and Thelma Pons

are still close friends of Jean Gardner and her sisters. Betty says it well, how it was to work for Uncle Erle. From the first day she was entirely devoted to turning out as fine a job as she could because "Uncle Erle made you want to be the best." She was, she says, "overwhelmed with the amount of work he produced between the time we left in the afternoon and arrived the next morning. He would have something for everyone to keep busy steadily all through the next day. I found myself living, eating, and sleeping whatever book, article, or travel book he was creating . . . it was hard not to become involved. Uncle Erle always made his secretaries feel he was interested in their enthusiasm about whatever story they were typing. And he always told them to make a note of anything they wondered about in the manuscripts. He hardly ever took time for conversation but of his great intuitive power we were all keenly conscious. I felt in tune with him always and never once felt I had displeased him or that he was critical of me." And Betty adds the tribute which so many have tried to express, "I loved everything about him. He was very dear."

Part of the family for more than twenty years was Margaret Powvall, a Pala Indian woman, who was the Rancho del Paisano housekeeper. Upon her retirement, Julie Rodriguez, also from Pala, and whom Margaret had trained, took over the household. Julie and her happy smile are still with Jean. Mary Gomez, of Mexican-German ancestry, was cook for Gardner for more than twenty years. She had grown up on the Vail ranch and her husband was a Vail cowman. She continues to live in Temecula. Yet another who was a housekeeper-cook at the ranch was Sadie Covington. She was an

Mary Gomez and Margaret Powvall

accomplished artist and many of her pictures hung in Gardner's living quarters.

David (pronounced Spanish-style) Hurtado, of Mexican-Indian descent, came up from Yecora, Mexico, and worked first at the Vail ranch. He moved to the Gardner outfit at Erle's invitation, and Erle helped him bring in from Mexico his wife, Goya, a highly educated young woman from a fine Mexican family. Sam Hicks was supposed to teach them English; instead he learned Spanish from them and speaks it almost as a second language. There were four Hurtado children, Rosa, José David, Lionel, and Jaime, called Jimmy. The two older boys, José and Lionel, attended Santa Caterina's Indian School in Sante Fe, New Mexico, one of the best known Indian preparatory schools in the West. José was married in Santa Fe after finishing prep school and is now attending medical school. Lionel is also in college, studying computer electronics. And David takes care of Jean's orchard in Fallbrook.

And there was, of course, Sam Hicks. Sam, the soft-spoken, lean and rangy Westerner, the type Gary Cooper so often portrayed on the screen. Sam was born and brought up on his family's ranch near Bondurant, Wyoming. As a very young man, he and his brother had the last official snowshoe-and-sled mail delivery in the continental United States. Among his other youthful accomplishments were horse wrangling and bronc riding, in which, as Erle so often bragged of him, he took awards. Sam was everything Erle would have liked to have been in his youth and what he would have liked in a son. And, says Sam, Erle was everything he would like to be.

David Hurtado

After Sam took over as manager of the ranch, Erle built a home on a hill at the Rancho for him and his family. Here his four children, Nancy, Sam Junior, Susan, and Linda were raised. Today Sam is an associate editor and frequent contributor to *The High Country*, a quarterly published in Temecula, which devotes most of its attention to the history of the California West. He is also an elected official of the Temecula district with the title of constable.

Sam became one of Erle's closest friends. He rode with him, drove him on his camping and business trips, traveled with him wherever he wandered. In more than one book, Erle has written that Sam could do anything.

Both Jean and Sam are strong of spirit, gentle, serenely unflappable, and highly efficient. These qualities Erle must have particularly cherished, although he personally took pride in being a peppery, impatient, hell-raising individual. At least he put on a good act in being just that.

With Rancho del Paisano, Erle was able to live with animals, something that meant much to him but which he could not do when perambulating from pillar to post on wheels. On those travels, to be sure, he always had his good dog, Rip. But he couldn't run a zoo on wheels.

Once he had moved in at Temecula, he used to say that like the old-time story of tramps making an X on the gate of a friendly hand-out house, the dogs marked his gate. Enough of them came to make the story believable. They had found out that he was running some kind of dog heaven, and when abandoned or lost they found

Gardner and a few canine denizens of the ranch

their way to Rancho del Paisano. For twenty years all of his dogs were strays. After Rip's death from old age, Yankee and Rebel were the two top dogs. One belonged to Erle, and one to Jean, who was as devoted to animals as Erle.

Editor Ben Hibbs, a favorite visitor at the ranch, told of the Paisano dogs in an article in the August 1963 issue of *Reader's Digest*: "In this main ranch house, dogs occupy all the choicest chairs and sofas. Since it is an unwritten law that nobody shall eject a dog from his resting place, the trick is to beat the dog to the chair." There was one girl, trying out as secretary, who ordered a dog out of a chair in which she wished to sit. "The dog looked at her over his shoulder with stunned amazement," Erle related, "and the other secretaries gasped with horror. We don't treat dogs that way." She didn't get the job.

The first time Hibbs came to the ranch, he was charged by one of the dogs, who drew blood. Erle declared that when authors "temporarily down on their luck" came in steady streams to borrow money, the dog would wag his tail in ecstatic greeting. But the minute an honest-to-God editor came, the dog bit him.

Hibbs's version of the incident went as follows: "You grabbed the little dog and gave him a couple of mild whacks on the funda-ment—supposedly punishment but actually love-pats—and then you sat down, took him between your knees and delivered a very fine soliloquy. It went something like this—" As Erle reported this hap-pening in his memoirs, it begins to sound more like Gardner's rendition of Hibbs than like Hibbs speaking. "Now look here, you goddam little S.O.B., you can't go around biting editors. I know,

I know. All these years you have heard me cursing editors, and I don't wonder you got the wrong idea. But, dammit all, pooch, I didn't mean it—that is to say I didn't mean all of it. What you don't understand is that there are editors and there are editors. Some of them deserve to be bitten. As a matter of fact, some of them deserve to be . . . Oh well, we won't go into that."

"The above was only the introduction," according to Hibbs as reported by Gardner, and this we can take as Hibbs speaking. "You went on and on for about five minutes while I stood there with a bleeding ankle, and every line of your discourse was as perfect as if it had been rehearsed. In fact, I think maybe it was. I have always suspected that you planned the whole thing, dictated and memorized your speech, and then when the proper moment came you sicked the dog on me."

Some years later, another stray came to the ranch who, to Erle, looked exactly like Ben Hibbs, and this he named him. When Ben and his wife came again to the Coast, Erle met them in Los Angeles to break the news of Ben's namesake. In view of past experiences, it wasn't surprising that the editor expected the worst. But, according to Erle, Benhibbs, the dog, took one look at Ben Hibbs, the editor, and there was a meeting of the minds. The dog wasn't a particularly friendly one but as soon as Ben Hibbs sat down, he jumped into the editor's lap.

Erle wanted a picture of the two but Hibbs explained that the Eastern Seaboard wasn't Temecula and the joke might not be appreciated in Philadelphia. The next year when the Hibbses came to the ranch, Erle told Ben, "I've decided that I'm not going to sell the *Saturday Evening Post* another story as long as I live. I'm going to take a picture of Ben Hibbs and Benhibbs." He did.

"Some day I'm going to ask him if it will be all right to publish the picture," Erle said when he first related the story. "In the meantime, since the *Saturday Evening Post* has become the official outlet for first serial rights on the Perry Mason stories, I think I had better wait a little while." Many years later, the picture did appear with the story in one of Gardner's travel books.

As for selling stories through friendship, Erle once wrote: "Quite naturally, as a beginning writer I got the idea that if I could only meet the editors of the *Saturday Evening Post*, I, too, would become friendly with them and my work would appear in the *Saturday Evening Post*. —This is an intellectual fallacy which seems to be held by virtually all beginning writers. —Actually you become friendly

Ben Hibbs with Benhibbs

with an editor because he buys your material, learns to like it, and finally meets you and then learns to like you."

Horses were as important as dogs to Erle. He and Jean each had their own, Peggy and Honey had theirs, and there were mounts for the other secretaries in residence. The one domestic animal lacking at the ranch was a cat. Cats hunted birds and Erle was a bird lover. The birds reciprocated this affection. One was the blue jay which kept jabbering at him along a road at the Rancho, and not until Erle came upon a rattlesnake did he realize that the jay had been determined to warn him. Some of his photographs of birds are quite astonishing. There is one of a quail who proudly posed for its photograph. Another is of a wild bird eating out of Erle's hand. Meg, Peggy's daughter, says that because Erle never doubted they would, of course the birds ate from his hand. She believes he had such an identification with animals that he never thought of them as being of another species. Everything living, and that included the land and the rocks and the trees, was to him an interchangeable part of a mysterious plan.

Among his pets for a time was a mouse who lived in his study. Gardner fed it with special tidbits, until the day the mouse went off on a holiday, only to return with a girl friend whom he introduced in mouse talk. That was enough. Erle didn't want to raise a mouse family. His little friend was banished to another home.

There was the chipmunk, much photographed, who, although he had the run of the ranch, also had his own special enclosure for a private preserve. He was part of the family until his death from old age.

Gardner riding Nuisance

Bravo and Gardner

Then there was the little coyote, the dear and favorite pet above all others. When Erle and Jean found the tiny cub in the hills, not even the Palas knew what species it was. They took it home to care for, and as the little fellow grew, his snout lengthened, his ears became pointed, and it became evident that he was a coyote. They named him Bravo, which in the language of Mexico has nothing to do with enthusiasm but means a big important fellow. He teased the dogs, stole the girls' sun hats, slept in Erle's room. Raymond Chandler, a frequent ranch visitor at the time, was much taken with Bravo and asked about him in every letter.

The time came when Bravo made it plain he was ready to return to the wilds. He was encouraged to take off and did, but he came around frequently to visit. To this day, everyone who knew Bravo can't speak of his death without becoming tearful. Bravo had never known fear of man. He was shot and killed by illegal hunters, trespassers on the ranch, as he ran to greet them.

Gardner's travel books are filled with stories of animals he had known. The most unusual tale is of the horse he met in Argentina on his South American tour in 1945. Horacio Beccar Varela, "an important lawyer and polished gentleman," one of their hosts, invited Erle, Jean, and Peggy to the races. "We went in with the elite," Erle wrote, and, before the race, were escorted down to the ring to look over the entries. As Erle was considered knowledgeable about horses, he was asked to pick the winner. He chose Number Seven. The horses were exercising in the circle at the time, and the second time around, Number Seven came over to the crowded rail and put his head against Erle's. That was enough for the hosts. If the

The serious archer

horse came over to tell Erle he was going to win, they would plunge on it. Number Seven came romping in three lengths ahead of all comers. Erle, being the New Englander who had never before in his life bet on a horse race, had one two-dollar ticket for himself and one each for the girls.

Rancho del Paisano also gave Erle the room and space and atmosphere for one of his avocations, which went back to his boyhood: stargazing. Astronomy had always fascinated him and always he carried his telescope along when he was out on the desert. By chance, or perhaps more than that, one of the neighboring mountains to his ranch was Palomar. Gardner best explained this interest of his in a January 1959 article for *TV Guide*. "As a writer of mystery stories, I have long been fascinated by the mind of the astronomer. He is essentially a detective. Walking along the crust of the earth, seldom rising more than six feet in height, he is able to look out at the distant stars and tell whether those stars are approaching or receding; what the stars are made of, their mass, their temperature, the elements which compose them. And he does this because of detective ability, a shrewd reasoning from clues. —We learn as we are interested."

Archery was another of Erle's special avocations, going back to early days. He has written: "Bow and arrow hunters, whether for game or trophies, are a breed unto themselves. It is not a sport for them; it is an addiction."

Both he and Jean were proficient enough to be featured on the front cover of the magazine *Archery* in March 1949. Jean holds trophies for her shooting.

Walt and Ken Wilhelm

Among his favorite bow and arrow companions from his earliest days were the famous Wilhelm brothers, Walt and Ken. These two were pros, doubling for actors in motion pictures, and also being featured in a series of sports films for Grantland Rice at Paramount. Walt contributed a regular column to *Archery,* and through the urging of Gardner, wrote the story of his family's trek west in a covered wagon in the late nineteenth century, living for sixteen years off the land. The book, *Last Rig to Battle Mountain,* published by Morrow, had a foreword by Erle. As the two explored the deserts for some forty years, Walt also became an expert photographer.

Two more of Erle's best friends who came out of archery were Dr. Paul Klopsteg and Walter Buchen. George Brommers, a good friend of all three and the editor of *Archery* magazine, introduced Gardner to Klopsteg and Buchen in 1935 at a tournament held at the UCLA campus in Westwood. Buchen had been an English professor before entering advertising in Chicago. As well as having bow and arrow adventures, he and Gardner were also given to long debates about semantics. Dr. Klopsteg, an internationally renowned physicist, first became interested in archery through his Girl Scout daughter. It was the ballistics of the shooting which initially intrigued him. He began to build his own equipment as his interest grew, equipment now in the Smithsonian Institution in Washington, D.C. Dr. Klopsteg holds about all the degrees and honors a scientist can be awarded, topped by the rosette he wears in his buttonhole of the highest civilian honor given by the United States, the Medal of Merit with Presidential Citation.

The three men went on many archery expeditions together, but

Dr. Paul Klopsteg

the best fun, in Dr. Klopsteg's opinion, was playing archery golf at the ranch. This was a game which Gardner invented and which all guests were commandeered to play. Few could beat him on this course.

Above all, Temecula was for friends. Over the more than thirty years that Gardner made it his home, the number of friends who came to visit was indeed legion. Some were regulars, almost part of the family. And some were his family, such as his daughter and his grandchildren. And of course, his dear brother, Dr. Kenneth, and his wife, Dorothy, who were frequent guests not only at Temecula but also at all the other "hideouts" Gardner acquired. He had to add hideouts as the quiet Rancho, planned as a place to retreat and work, became not so quiet because of his propensity for filling it with favorite people.

His second retreat was in northern California, a place called Paradise. Gramp Nienke, who with his wife was the first new member of Erle's Temecula family, had eventually moved up north, timber country being Gramp's first love. Gardner went to visit them and decided this was for him also. He bought property and set up the kind of housekeeping he had originally planned for Temecula, a main house as a gathering place and dining hall, a small office for the secretaries (Helen McGehee, who lived there, was a resident secretary), and another for Erle, with everyone living out of trailers. For years, Paradise was his summer home. A cook-housekeeper maintained the place when he and his staff returned to Temecula.

There were to follow many other hideouts, among them a house

Kenneth Gardner and family

at Oceanside, about forty miles from the ranch, for time on the beach; land at Yucca in the upper desert for desert living; a place at Shasta Lake where he kept trailers and boats; briefly, another ocean property in Oregon at Port Orford; a camp on the Hood Canal in Washington; a small date ranch on the lower desert; a Palm Springs house for sun in winter; a house near the mountain village of Idyllwild. There may have been others; these are the ones he mentioned. He was a restless man, as hyperactives are, always wanting to be moving on to another setting. And enjoying each in its turn.

When he bought a piece of property in the vicinity of Joshua Tree Monument, he explained to Thayer why he kept acquiring more and more land. "I have reluctantly come to the conclusion that the days when a person can go park a trailer almost anywhere have just about passed, and so I'm buying chunks of completely unimproved property in various places where I can roll in my trailers and make a camp. When I get out in the complete silence of the desert and settle down in my trailer, I have a feeling of tranquillity that I don't get any place else."

Each hideout began with the idea of getting away from people and having a quiet place to work. But actually, they were only to get away from *some* people. As Ben Hibbs wrote, "He lives and works intermittently, in all his hideouts. But in each one he soon grows lonely and starts writing letters to friends urging them to come for a visit."

And they came.

Among his closest friends were the people who published his stories and books. They became members of the "Gardner Family"

Gardner emerging from cabin hideout with finished dictation

Maude McGonigle

and included Thayer Hobson, Freeman "Doc" Lewis, publisher of the paperback reprint editions at Pocket Books, Inc., Larry Hughes, who succeeded Hobson as president of Morrow, Corney Jackson and his wife, Gail Patrick, who were the producers of the Perry Mason television series, Ben Hibbs, Harry Steeger, publisher of *Argosy* magazine, and their wives and families.

But paramount in the family were the Ventura friends: Frank Orr, Gardner's law partner in those early years, whom Erle characterized as "one of the most loyal, one of the most devoted friends I ever had. Frank Orr and I had a companionship which is one of the treasured, one of the sacred things in life;" Maude McGonigle, the bookkeeper of the firm, whom Erle pretended to shock; and Gordon J. "Gordie" Miller.

Everyone loved Gordie. He went bow and arrow hunting with Erle, jeep-touring the back roads with Sam, and was relied on in general for whatever came up.

In 1928, when Gordon first came to read law at the firm of Sheridan, Orr, Drapeau and Gardner, Gardner was out of town. Gordon was "confused, depressed and *dumb*," ready to give up, when on the second Monday, the law library door opened with a crash and in came a young man talking to himself, "The code—the code—what does the code say?" He grabbed an armful of books, dropped several, and disappeared, only to reappear and get more books, a process repeated again and again. Each time, thought young Gordon, the man frowned at him. Then without warning, he came back in and sat down beside Gordon. "Miller, old kid," he said, "you have been

Anita Haskell Jones

here for a week and no one has had the courtesy to introduce us. My name is Gardner."

"That was it," Gordon recalls. "Never before had I met such a person—never since." After Gardner left the firm, he asked Gordon to take care of his tax affairs, which he did throughout Erle's lifetime. Not once were the returns in error. "For forty years (yes, *forty* years), Erle and I never lost a case." Sam Hicks states forthrightly: "Without reservation Gordon is the most ethical, professional, thoroughly dedicated businessman I have ever known."

Erle's teaching himself survey engineering was a feat that every one of the family mentions with something close to awe. As everyone knows, surveying takes a knowledge of geometry and mathematics, which are not usually a writer's strong points. Erle buckled down to learn to survey when a new neighbor made the claim that Gardner's water spring was on the neighbor's property. Gardner borrowed all needed equipment from his friend, Adolph Sutro. Gordon Miller just happened to be at the ranch on vacation, and he was chosen to "hold the stick at a distance," and to have all the technical terms explained to him each day, his favorite being "triangular strangulation," coined after a round of mint juleps. When Gardner finished the survey and submitted it to the county engineer it tallied exactly with the one in that office, establishing that the spring was legally on his property. Later, with added acreage, Erle and Sam surveyed the ranch. Erle's readings didn't deviate the smallest percentage from the established boundaries.

A very special ranch regular, first met in Ventura days, was Anita

Pinky Brier with Gardner and desert explorer Bill Bryan

Haskell Jones, a neighbor from nearby Palm Springs. She was home folks rather than guest, a girl of spirit who could and did yell at Erle on one camping expedition when he was storming about, "Don't you say one word to me! I don't work for you!" She was the only one of Uncle Erle's girls who could make that claim. Efficient, lively, and smart, she was ready to travel with the outfit at the drop of a hat, whether off to the South Seas by ship or down to Baja in a camper.

It is Anita who tells the story, which just might be apocryphal but which Erle cherished, of her riding ahead one day into an arroyo on the Rancho. While she waited for the others, who were atop the hill, two locals rode by. "Who's that?" asked one, indicating Erle. The other replied, "That's that fellow who lives up there with those four women."

Another regular was Evelyn Brier from San Bernardino, called Pinky by one and all, who flies now and has flown for years the VIPs of southern California. She also flew charter for Erle. Her list of the equipment he usually took with him includes dictating machines, typewriters, cameras, and briefcases, as well as regular luggage for the party. On one particular flight, when they neared Los Angeles International, she asked Uncle Erle if he'd like her to radio ahead for a skycap. Sam said, "Never mind, Pinky, I can take care of Uncle Erle and the luggage." Pinky had a mental picture of big Sam "fidgeting around" while some skycap picked up his luggage. However, in his thoughtful way, Uncle Erle said, "Now Sam, let Pinky call a skycap. You know that is the way they make a living." Pinky

Sam Hicks, Francisco Muñoz, Jean, and Gardner

Sam Hicks, Gardner, J. W. Black, and Bob Boughton

herself, though tiny and feminine, could have handled the load one-handed. Jean has said, "I've seen Pinky toss heavy baggage into her plane and then pull Uncle Erle up by sheer strength."

Other frequent guests at the ranch were Capitán Francisco Muñoz, Erle's Baja pilot and an intrepid explorer like Erle, Robert M. "Bob" Boughton, chief pilot of the helicopters with which Erle explored the Baja wilderness, and his wife, Jill, and J. W. Black, inventor of the Butterfly and other vehicles for desert exploration, and his wife, Lois. Erle had many friends from below the border, whose guest he was there and to whom he returned the hospitality at the ranch. Among them were Colonel José M. Gutiérrez of Mexicali, Mexican consul, and his wife, Emily; Gilberto Gonzáles Muz-

José M. Gutiérrez and Jean

Blanca and Gilberto Muzquiz, Gardner, and Jean

Bob Masson of Goodyear Blimp, Gardner, Wulfrano Ruiz, Jean, Ricardo Castillo, and Terry Elms

Alicia Ruiz, Gardner, and a decoration she made

quiz of Chihuahua, first met on the Barranca visits, and his wife, Blanca; the diplomat, Wulfrano Ruiz and his exquisite wife, Alicia, from Tijuana, and also from Tijuana, Ricardo Castillo, amateur archaeologist and restaurateur, and his brother, Oswaldo, who explored inner Baja with Gardner on many occasions, and who fed him royally whenever he crossed the border. And also Alfonso Martínez, "Pluma Blanca," so-called by Erle because of his prematurely white plume of hair, owner of a *botica* in Tijuana and founder of a small hospital there. In Spanish, translated by Sam for the Temeculans, who have as little Spanish as Señor Martínez has English, it is he who has told so well why Gardner means what he does to the people of Baja: "It is because he cared about all of them; there was no difference to him between the rich or the poor, the famous or the nobody. To all he gave his love."

Art Bernard and Gardner

There were a host of new friends after Gardner formed the Court of Last Resort, an organization to improve the administration of justice. A few became friends beyond the Court, and were welcomed at his hideouts: Dr. LeMoyne Snyder, prominent criminologist, doctor *and* lawyer, and his wife, Louise, who built a home at Paradise after visiting Gardner there; Marshall Houts, a fine medicolegal expert and teacher, author of many books, brought by Gardner to California with his wife Mary and children, where they too became Californians; and of course, Naomi and Arthur Bernard, the prison warden who tricked Gardner into taking a case, and since his retirement from criminology, a newspaperman in Nevada who speaks his mind with refreshing gumption.

Erle had so many friends. Too many to call each by name and to tell of them. They appear by name and face and through anecdotes in his travel books, which have proved an invaluable source of information, as he had no time to write his autobiography.

Rancho del Paisano was first and foremost a center for Erle's work. But when the morning's quota was done, it became a home where he could relax and enjoy the pleasure of friends, with good food, good talk, and good fun out on the Rancho's hillsides. The thoughtful care and the work involved in making it a special place were so well hidden behind the scenes that not many guests gave a thought to that aspect. It is well known that Erle himself knew he had created something special, for when a Chinese friend once asked him what he would like to be in his next life, he promptly replied, "I'd like to be a guest on the ranch of Erle Stanley Gardner."

Chapter Twenty-one

THERE WERE FEW writers among Gardner's friends. He seemed to think that most of them besides himself were *artistes,* or at any rate considered themselves such whereas he was a hardheaded, business-man-lawyer who, due to circumstances he couldn't control, happened to write. He also had the fixed idea that writers, being *artistes,* were not explorers, adventurers, men to yarn with around the campfire. Of course, neither were the half dozen of his most intimate friends in the profession, including Thayer Hobson and Corney Jackson.

However, there was one writer who won Gardner's admiration and respect with his first published story and an enduring friendship developed. His name was Raymond Chandler.

Chandler was exceptional because he too had been a hardheaded businessman before starting to write. Gardner discovered him in the December 1933 issue of *Black Mask.* Gardner had a story in the same issue. He at once began writing editors about his discovery. Gardner was always ready and waiting to give beginners a boost, but in the case of Chandler, it was more than just wanting to help. He saw Chandler as a special talent. He was going to do what he could to see that this new writer had proper recognition.

In the autumn of 1934 he learned that Chandler was a neighbor of his in Hollywood. At the time both of them were involved in writing for motion pictures. Gardner asked Jean to get in touch and invite the Chandlers to come by for an evening.

Chandler replied by letter, "I should consider it a great privilege to meet Erle Stanley Gardner, even though a man who uses three secretaries and has to be flagged as he whizzes through, would un-doubtedly be far too fast company for anyone of my rather pensive habits. Also I am the merest beginner in writing and spend most of my time looking out of the window and trying to think of something to write about. . . . But I appreciate your kindness in asking me to drop in just the same and shall hope to call you up very soon and pay my respects. I live not far from your address."

The meeting came off most successfully at Gardner's house. It is not surprising that they became friends. Both had had sound and successful careers in business. Gardner had had twenty years' law practice and was almost forty-five years old when his first book was published in the preceding year of 1933. Chandler had been the president of various companies in a California oil syndicate before, at the age of forty-five, his first story was published. It would be another six years, when he was fifty-one, before he published his first book.

Neither man had any patience with artistic temperament although each had his own goodly share of it. They could speak the same language, being businessmen, and could find few others in the trade who took a business approach to writing. From then, until the death of Mrs. Chandler in 1954, after which Chandler returned to England, their friendship remained active.

Both were restless men. The Chandlers moved from house to house and from town to town. While they were in Riverside, Gardner discovered Temecula and in the California sense, they became neighbors. Later the Chandlers moved to La Jolla, also near Temecula. They visited each other frequently through these years.

The Big Sleep, Chandler's first book, was published in February of 1939. In their advertising the publishers quoted Gardner: "In my opinion Raymond Chandler is a star of the first magnitude in the constellation of modern mystery writers. I think you will find discriminating detective fans are already familiar with Chandler's work, even though this is his first book."

Less formally, he wrote: "I know this chap. It's my prediction he's going places. You can put any endorsement of mine you want on any book Chandler writes. . . . The kid is *good.*"

By spring the Chandlers were moving on to Big Bear in the nearby mountains. They had been at Rancho del Paisano and had hoped to return when the "moon was at the half." Cissy, Ray's wife, was, like Erle, a lunar telescope enthusiast. In thanking Gardner for their visit, Ray gave the new address, "Box something or other, but that's not important. You promised to come up sometime—remember. When you get ready, I'll send you directions. . . . I forgot to tell you that I learned to write a novelette on one of yours about a man named Rex Kane, who was an alter ego of Ed Jenkins and got mixed up with some flowery dame in a hilltop house in Hollywood who was running an anti-blackmail organization. You wouldn't remember. It's probably in your file No. 54276-84. . . . I simply made an extremely detailed synopsis of your story and from that rewrote it and then compared what I had with yours, and then went back and rewrote it some more, and so on. In the end I was a bit sore because I couldn't try to sell it. It looked pretty good. Incidentally, I found out that the trickiest part of your technique was the ability to put over situations which verged on the implausible but which in the reading seemed quite real. I hope you understand that I mean this as a compliment. I have never come even near to doing it myself. Dumas had this quality in a very strong degree. Also Dickens. It's probably the fundamental of all rapid work, because naturally rapid work has a large element of improvisation, and to make an improvised scene inevitable is quite a trick. At least I think so. And here I am at 2:30 A.M. writing about technique, in spite of a strong conviction that the moment a man begins to talk about technique, that's proof he is fresh out of ideas. . . ."

By autumn of the next year, the Chandlers were living in an apartment on San Vincente Boulevard in Santa Monica. His second book, *Farewell, My Lovely,* had just been published, and he wrote to Erle, "Am sending you a copy of my latest atrocity, not with the idea that I am passing along anything of value, but just because I wanted to. Much of it is old stuff. All that could be said for it and against it has already been said. The net result to me is a conviction that this sort of writing is in need of modification."

In reply Gardner wrote, "You've done a damn sweet job with your book. You even stirred Will Cuppy's pulse, and anyone who can do this with a book that isn't a dry-as-dust English type of deductive reasoning is a marvel." He went on to give Chandler "some dope from Brentano's" which a New York friend had sent him. It was a system where their readers voted on books they had read, a simple *yes* or *no.* "Your book certainly has a splendid rating on this, and as it is an actual reader barometer, these votes really mean a good deal. I think this book will sell better than your first book and if you can get out a third book without waiting too long, I think you will find a splendid reader reception."

Not long after, Ray wrote from Pacific Palisades, "Good God, we have moved again. Thanks very much indeed for sending me that Brentano list, but who is this guy A. A. Fair who heads the list? I got the book and read it and it held one of the three or four unmistakable techniques of detective story writing. And done to the nice crisp light brown that melts in your mouth. What goes on here? I suppose you know what I mean?

"Living, if you call it that, in a big apartment house in Santa Monica, brand new and all that, I longed for your ranch. I longed for some place where I could go out at night and listen and hear the grass growing. . . . Regards to your gang, Ray."

Within the next few years, between work and travel on both sides, letter-writing waned. But in November of 1945, Ray wrote to Erle: "It seems ages since I saw you and I hope this still finds you at Temecula or somewhere. The occasion of this is that a few weeks ago I went up to Big Bear Lake to get over a case of complete exhaustion such as you will never know, you dynamo. I'd done a script for MGM in thirteen weeks and hated every bit of it, especially as it was one of my own stories. I was completely sunk. The only thing I could read was the Perry Mason stories. There were a whole flock of them I hadn't read—I don't know why. Perhaps my tastes have changed, perhaps my constant legal battles over contracts have made me enamored of the law. Anyhow I read one a night and loved them. It was interesting also to see how as time went on they became so much smoother and more adept. But the way you keep that girl Della Street hanging around is a crime. You told me once you considered Edgar Wallace the greatest man that ever lived; I hope you have changed your mind. You can write the pants off him. But the things that make you come back and back, the irresistible things are the movement, the guys you love to hate, and the legal twists. Every damn one of them ought to end in the courtroom. I feel defrauded when they don't. All the best, Ray."

Erle wrote back his thanks for "the good things you say about Perry Mason. . . . I've been following your career of late with a great deal of interest. Getting quite a kick out of the fact that Hollywood has at last progressed to the point where it recognizes real merit and noting what you have done in connection with the development of mystery story adaptation. . . . Hollywood learned early in the game how to adapt the romantic story to the screen but it never made even a start at adapting mystery stories. Then you came along and gave them one terrific boost. It is going to be interesting to see what happens in the next year or so. . . . If you are ever down in this neck of the woods, be sure to drop in. I have some riding horses now, a mountain ranch that has a cute little house on it (added to the original acres), a phonograph and some old time records and am

TEMECULA

growing my own beef. . . . Here's congratulations on your success, the splendid work you've been doing and the best of luck for the future."

Neither Gardner nor Chandler took their writing troubles with only a whimper; they were fighters. In 1946, both were involved in a sizable ruckus with their former *Black Mask* editor, Joe "Cap" Shaw. The difficulties arose with *Hard-boiled Omnibus*, an anthology which Shaw was projecting. Gardner had refused to be associated with it; Chandler had given permission for the use of a story. Gardner wrote Chandler fully about his Shaw difficulties and his opinion of the man as an editor. In reply, Chandler opened with, "Most of what you write is a complete surprise to me—including the idea that you are a lousy writer. I may later ask the privilege of addressing the Court on that point." After discussion of Shaw, Hammett, Norbert Davis, the fact that neither Cornell Woolrich nor Cleve Adams to his knowledge had made *Black Mask* under Shaw, and his own difficulties in that direction, Chandler turned to another subject.

"I now address the Court, by permission, on the subject of one Gardner, an alleged writer of mysteries. As I speak I have two solid rows of Gardners in front of me, and am still trying to shop around to complete the collection. I probably know as much about the essential qualities of good writing as anybody now discussing it. I do not discuss these things professionally for the simple reason that I do not consider it worthwhile. I am not interested in pleasing the intellectuals by writing literary criticism, because literary criticism as an art has in these days too narrow a scope and too limited a public, just as has poetry. . . . The critics of today are tired Bostonians like Van Wyck Brooks or smart-alecks like Fadiman or honest men confused by the futility of their job like Edmund Wilson. The reading public is intellectually adolescent at best, and it is obvious that what is called 'significant literature' will be sold to this public by exactly the same methods as are used to sell it toothpaste, cathartics and automobiles. It is equally obvious that since this public has been taught to read by brute force, it will, in between its bouts with the latest 'significant' bestseller, want to read books that are fun and excitement. So like all half-educated publics in all ages it turns with relief to the man who tells a story and nothing else. To say that what this man writes is not literature is just like saying that a book can't be any good if it makes you want to read it. When a book, any sort of book, reaches a certain intensity of artistic performance it becomes literature. That intensity may be a matter of style, situation, character, emotional tone, or idea, or half a dozen other things. It may also be a perfection of control over the movement of a story similar to the control a great pitcher has over the ball. That is to me what you have more than anything else and more than anyone else. Dumas Père had it. Dickens, allowing for his Victorian muddle, had it; begging your pardon I don't think Edgar Wallace approached it. His stories died all along the line and had to be revived. Yours don't. Every page throws the hook for the next. I call this a kind of genius. I regard myself as a pretty exacting reader; detective stories as such don't mean a thing to me. But it must be obvious that if I have a dozen unread books beside my chair and one of them is a Perry Mason, and I reach for the Perry Mason and let the others wait, that book must have quality.

"Strangely enough I didn't always feel this way, and I think for the same reason Cap Shaw didn't. I was so steeped in the rugged stuff that I didn't realize how stupid it can be unless it is superbly well done. Today I could no more read a book by Coxe or Adams than I could eat a kangaroo. I think also that I do agree you didn't do your best work for *BM*. In fact you've only been doing it at the peak the last four or five years. It's pretty obvious to me why that is, too. You never were a *Black Mask* writer in Shaw's meaning of the term. You never really were tough. You owed nothing to Hammett or Hemingway. Your books have no brutality or sadism, very little sex, and the blood doesn't count. What counts, at least for me, is a supremely skilful combination of the mental quality of the detective story and the movement of the mystery-adventure story. I read the Doug Selby stories and like them and try to guess where the hell Madison City is (the nearest I can come is Riverside, and that isn't quite right) but there is something missing. I like the A. A. Fair stories, especially the first ones, but they have in the end the same defect the Nero Wolfe stories have: an eccentric character wears out its welcome. The character that lasts is an ordinary guy with some extraordinary qualities. Perry Mason is the perfect detective because he has the intellectual approach of the juridical mind and at the same time the restless quality of the adventurer who won't stay put. I think he is just about perfect. So let's not have any more of that phooey about 'as literature my stuff still stinks.' Who says so—William Dean Howells?"

In late April of 1947, Chandler was considering seriously using a Dictaphone, something Gardner had been urging for some time. He wrote Erle, "I think I should like to come over and talk to you one day towards the end of next week or the beginning of the following week, if you have the time. I would get there in time for lunch and come back in the same evening." He not only was sold on the Dictaphone on this visit, but writing again in mid-May he already had the equipment Gardner had recommended.

Gardner was off to Wyoming in late summer of 1947. He had two more books out, *The Case of the Lazy Lover* and *Fools Die on Friday*. He sent copies to Chandler, who wrote him, "The last two were corkers, damn it, the last two I got anyhow. *Fools Die on Friday* is about the best of the series since the first two. Perhaps since the very first."

For these two men, both of strong opinions and voluble with them, it must have been a true satisfaction to be able to speak their minds with no fear of their opinions being passed to others in or out of the business. They pulled no punches. There was, for example, an aspiring writer who had deliberately copied Chandler and had been praised for it in a newspaper interview. Ray read the piece and sent it to Erle, saying he'd never met the man and wasn't the least interested in him, but "a supposedly reputable agent, a reputable publisher, more or less conspire with a writer to steal another man's bag of tricks, acknowledge it openly, and the newspaper lady sees nothing in the situation requiring comment. And my agent sends it to me as though it might please me."

Shortly thereafter, writing to Jean in place of Erle, who was off on one of his journeys, Ray continued, "Tell Erle, I never had any idea of suing the guy. For what? I could name at least three others in Hollywood who have done exactly the same thing. The only really interesting question involved is where you draw the line between a legitimate imitation (since all writers imitate at first) and an unfair practice. . . ."

On his return, Erle wrote, "You missed the point I was trying to make on this chap. The guy is so completely a type that I was interested in seeing his picture, and have become very much interested in his work. The big question is whether a man, who is so frankly an imitator, can ever develop enough originality to command a following, and whether editors are so completely obsessed on the point of style that they will go for a story that has nothing to commend it except a style which has been established by dint of some other writer's hard work.

"You can just see from his picture the type he is. Mentally alert, abnormally conceited, quick on the trigger, demanding worshipful adoration from his adoring wife, yet withal having that quickness of mind which is a very definite factor to be reckoned with. Or perhaps I am guessing the guy all wrong from his picture."

To which Ray replied, "I did not miss the point you were trying to make about him because you did not make a point. However, if you had, it is quite possible that I should have missed it. . . . I agree with the impression that you get from the photograph except for the abnormally conceited. Considering the success the man has had in so very short a time, a little conceit seems to me to be normal rather than abnormal. . . ."

Of another book- and screen-writer, a woman whom both knew, Erle responded to a note from Ray, "I didn't get nauseated over her business in *Time*. I don't blame the gal for getting publicity where it's legitimate, and, of course, having featured her on the cover as the most important mystery writer of the times the magazine would naturally want to follow up to prove its point. The thing that made me furious, however, was the fact that when a story blew up on her back in Chicago and she had to think of something else quick, she decided to interview her various 'competitors' about the case. I received through the mail a copy of the paper containing my picture and the things I had said to her about the case, the interview making me seem to be very much of a stuffed shirt. She explained to me that she didn't have any opportunity to get in touch with me, so she had an imaginary interview and tried to think of the things I would have said if I had been talking at the other end of the line.

"I blew up and gave it to her with both barrels. I am still so damn mad about it I can't see straight. . . . To my mind the irritating part of all this publicity stuff is not the legitimate publicity but the attempt to push herself into the limelight and milk the situation dry. I knew as soon as I saw the article that we could count on one or more letters to the magazine trying to enhance the publicity value. Sure enough, you will notice the letter in the current issue. . . ."

The end of World War II brought a period of agitation among writers. They had determination to improve their lot, both financially and in stature. James Cain was proposing an American Authors' Authority to which members of both the Authors' Guild and Screen Writers Guild would turn over their copyrights. Gardner and Chandler agreed that there were good points to the idea but both were opposed because of less good, even dangerous, points at issue. They discussed it back and forth in their correspondence. The Screen

Writers, "of which I am a reluctant member," put Chandler on the committee but he refused to serve.

At about the same time, the Mystery Writers of America was working on improving the author's position on reprint royalties. Ray wrote: "I understand that you did not agree with the position of Rex Stout's committee on reprint royalties, but I don't think I have heard why."

Erle replied, "I'm afraid someone has misinterpreted my position on this reprint business. . . . As a matter of fact, I get quite a kick out of Rex Stout and am inclined to be somewhat influenced by his thinking. However, on this reprint business my contention is that the boys are just about two years too late.

"What irritates me is the fact that writers can't appreciate that their money doesn't come from the publishers but does come from the reading public. The reprint books have opened up a marvelous new field. Gradually they're changing the reading habits of the nation. Properly encouraged, there is no reason why writers of books can't be sitting on top of the world in another three or four years."

In August 1946 Erle was writing to "Raymond," as he sometimes addressed him, of having had a very interesting chat with "the chap who seems to be the virtual head of the Mystery Writers of America. I have to laugh at him because his attitude is so contrary to mine on almost everything, and he is so deeply shocked at my attitude of regarding writing as a business, whereas he regards it as an art. However, he can reconcile our viewpoints because he thinks my stuff stinks. He is one hell of a nice chap, entirely different from most of the crackpots. . . . But I think his ideas of merchandising are all cockeyed. . . .

"I criticized the organization as undemocratic, and he brushed that criticism aside as being unworthy of discussion. Then I asked him how they awarded their Edgars, if they sent out a ballot to each member in the organization. He said, 'Certainly not.' The Executive Committe handled that. I asked him how many that included on the awards and he said, 'About five.' "

It was the radio award that annoyed Gardner; it had been given in duplicate to the *Ellery Queen* and the *Mr. and Mrs. North* shows, the authors of each being prominent on MWA committees. He told Ray, "There is something humorous in this idea of five people setting themselves up to speak for a couple of hundred writers as far as preferences are concerned."

Ray answered this with "Sometime ago I had a letter telling me I had been awarded an Edgar and plans to present would be communicated to me later. I didn't even answer, mostly because I expected a quick follow-up. I think by now they may have changed their minds."

Somewhere along the way, Chandler received his Edgar. Almost twenty years later, in 1960, in spite of his earlier reaction, Gardner accepted his Edgar, awarded to him as a Grand Master of the Mystery Writers of America.

Charles Morton's article in the *Atlantic Monthly*, mentioned previously, is in the opinion of many of his friends the best article ever written about Gardner. During the preceding interviews, Morton and Gardner became good friends, as did Gardner and Ted Weeks, editor in chief of the magazine. This led to Gardner's writing, on order, a number of articles for it. In time it was suggested that he write a history of the pulps but this he refused, informing Willis Wing, his agent, that he hadn't time for such a venture and the research it would impose. He did offer to do an article about the pulp days, with "a few interesting anecdotes" about some of his friends of those days.

The *Atlantic* countered with the suggestion that he write one about modern mystery literature, mentioning, in particular, authors Mickey Spillane and Ian Fleming. Gardner had personal likes and dislikes but he had a tenacious feeling of solidarity with all his fellow writers. He would not permit himself to be put into a position of casting aspersions on them.

"I just don't want to comment on the work of Mickey Spillane or Ian Fleming," Gardner wrote for Wing's eyes only. "Mickey Spillane 'borrowed' Carroll John Daly's character, Race Williams, or the twin brother of Race Williams, introduced sex and created a formula by which the first girl who took her clothes off in the story always wound up getting shot in the belly with a .45 automatic at the end.

"Ian Fleming has a very expert touch. He somehow manages to take the reader along with him. His impossible situations become convincing. I have a feeling that if he didn't drag the reader in between sheets with a few gals, his stories might have been just as popular.

"You'll probably have to be tactful about this," he continued to Wing, "because Ted Weeks and Charles Morton have evidently decided they very definitely want an article from me along the lines mentioned, and I just don't want to write it. On the other hand, I love those two guys and don't want to hurt their feelings." While in this discussion period, Gardner said he was "quite willing to comment about Raymond Chandler and tell a few stories about him, some intimate anecdotes that probably haven't been told before. I can tell a little stuff about Dashiell Hammett."

Concerning Chandler, he wrote: "Charles Morton did a wonderful job for Chandler, because I think it was Morton who inspired Chandler's article about the mystery story, about the sordid backgrounds and the hero who stood out against these sordid backgrounds because, while he would plunge into the moral cesspool of his environment, he somehow always managed to be the knight on a white charger who came to the rescue. His lance may have been sullied but his shield never was. Chandler was innately clean, and somehow the moral cleanliness of the guy cropped out in his stories. Even when he tried to have his heroes be a little tough and sadistic, they never got dirty."

Eventually Gardner's idea for an article about the early pulp days must have prevailed, for in the January 1965 issue of the *Atlantic*, "Getting Away With Murder" appeared under his byline. In a brief introduction, the editors pointed out that Mr. Gardner broke into print as a contemporary of Dashiell Hammett and Carroll John Daly, "and at our urging, he has written this amusing account of their early days."

Erle's article opened with two introductory paragraphs about the sex and violence of current literature and what effects these might possibly be having on the younger generation. It continued:

"Life was seemingly more innocent and certainly more secure in the early days when Carroll John Daly, Dashiell Hammett, and I began writing for *Black Mask*, edited first by a man named Sutton. . . . Carroll John Daly helped to originate the hard-boiled school of detective writers when, some forty-odd years ago, he created the character of Race Williams.

"Race Williams could well have been the parent of Mike Hammer. In fact there are such startling resemblances that one can certainly suspect a family relationship. The big difference between Daly's stories and the adventures of Mike Hammer is that Race Williams was too busy for sex. Race Williams would draw his gun and would ask the reader 'Was I bluffing?' The other man in the story evidently thought he was, because he would keep coming.

"But Race Williams never hesitated. Daly would tell of how he tightened the trigger, how the round hole appeared in the man's forehead, and of the look of surprise on the man's face before the eyes started to glaze. Then the hole, which had been purple around the edges, would turn red and the man would pitch forward."

The last line of one of Daly's stories was one Gardner never forgot: "I sent him crashing the gates of hell with my bullet in his brain."

Daly was tough in spirit but slender in physical build. He once said to Gardner, "You think I don't get enough exercise and that I'm not an outdoor man. I want you to know that on some sunshiny days I think nothing of going out and walking the full width of this lot on the sidewalk—and this is a fifty-foot lot!"

Daly lived in White Plains in one of a row of identical houses and always found his difficult to identify. On one occasion, he rang the bell of one of the houses on his block and asked the lady if she could tell him where Carroll John Daly lived. She started to reply and then said, "Why *you're* Carroll John Daly."

As Gardner told the story: "Daly bowed. 'I know who I am, Madam. I am only trying to find out where I live.' "

In some of his early letters, Gardner may have given the impression of attacking Dashiell Hammett. This was not true. It wasn't Hammett he was attacking; it was the editors and critics who were, he felt, destroying Hammett as a writer by turning him into a sacred cow.

Of their early pulp days, Gardner wrote, "Dashiell Hammett was one of the few writers I have known who had all the earmarks of genius and the temperament which goes with it." He was "a fast hand with a dictionary of criminalese and had a vast knowledge of editorial psychology." As a former Pinkerton man, his "criminalese" was taken as gospel by editors.

He introduced the word "shamus" into his stories, and it appeared later in the American Underworld Dictionary as "a Jewish-American word meaning a policeman or prison guard," and in the Slang Dictionary as meaning "a policeman, informer, or stool pigeon." During his Court of Last Resort years, Erle would inquire of detectives and prisoners as to the meaning of "shamus." No one he met had ever heard it used. But finally he found a Jewish haberdasher's assistant who knew the word. It meant "a phony."

Another of Hammett's jokes, Erle decided. Just as "gunsel" was one of Hammett's jokes. "Hammett became enraged over a rejection by Shaw and quit writing for *Black Mask*. I was in New York at the time and after conferring with Shaw, wrote Hammett a letter pleading with him to return to the fold." Which Hammett did. "Later on, of course, after the fame of *The Maltese Falcon*, Hammett could do no wrong. Captain Shaw not only went all out for Hammett but tried to get writers to follow the Hammett syle. One of my big differences with Shaw came when I accused him of trying to 'Hammettize' the magazine."

However, before the rift between Hammett and Shaw healed, Hammett used an expression in a story to which Shaw reacted with a letter saying that *Black Mask* would never publish such vulgarity. Thereupon Hammett wrote a story in which he set a deliberate trap for Shaw. One of the characters spoke shamefacedly of being "on the gooseberry lay." It meant only that he stole clothes from clotheslines. In the same story, Hammett had another character proudly say he was now a "gunsel." The editor reacted as Hammett expected. He wrote Hammett that he was deleting the gooseberry expression. But he never touched the "gunsel."

"It has been at least thirty-five years since Dashiell Hammett played his little joke on Captain Joseph T. Shaw," Gardner wrote, "but the aftereffects of that joke are still seen in American murder stories." Actually "gunsel," or in its pure German form "gänzel," has no relation to what it sounds like.

Chapter Twenty-two

Of all Erle's friendships, certainly the most unusual was with Marlene Dietrich. Reporters who hadn't done their homework were inclined to turn this into a romantic episode, but the truth is that he never met the lady. For close to twenty years, they were that pleasant sort of twosome, "pen pals." Erle spoke of another close "pen pal" he had, the writer Gene Fowler. But he had met Fowler once.

The Dietrich affair began in September 1944. In the August 15 issue of *Vogue*, she had included him in her list of "most interesting men." Gardner wrote a thank-you letter to her in Hollywood. In this, he spoke commendingly of her war work. It was known that while many other actresses had made a trip or so to the front lines, Marlene Dietrich had enlisted for the duration. In the *Vogue* article, she had mentioned that it was while working "in that miserable Army hospital in Bari" that she had come across Gardner's books and read all that were in the hospital library.

Erle sent her some books, including his first Baja book, *Land of Shorter Shadows*, and the Alva Johnston reportorial story, *The Case of Erle Stanley Gardner*. He also told her of an incident reported to him by the Red Cross of an amputee who in his depression wouldn't even read a book. Until someone brought him a Gardner. He then read every one of the Gardners and when he had finished he was back to normal, willing to cooperate in therapy and to learn a trade.

The books arrived just as Dietrich was leaving for the East. She wired Gardner from La Junta to thank him for sending them and for the personal expressions he had written in them. This was still the day of train journeys. She had waited to open the package until she was on board. She was certainly a true reader, one who doesn't stop as long as there is something to read, for she concluded the wire, "I still have two more days to New York and no more books to read. Love and admiration, Marlene."

Letters dwindled when she returned to Europe. But in 1959, when she was considering going into television, she wrote asking if he had forgotten her. She wanted some advice from him.

His response was, "Have I forgotten you? Are you kidding?" He told her then of how he had wanted her legs for the book jacket of his third Perry Mason, *The Case of the Lucky Legs*. But after discussing it with Paramount, his publisher had learned that her legs were too expensive, and therefore they settled on some less beautiful which they could afford. Whether she knows it or not, he added, she is "one of the family and an Honorary Member of the Gardner Fiction Factory." And, mentioning her earlier comments about him as an interesting man, he said he had been "coasting on that reputation ever since."

In 1962, after another long lapse in correspondence, Gardner was quoted in a magazine interview as saying of Dietrich, "I don't talk her language and she doesn't talk mine." He was so angry over this garbled quotation that he wrote to her, apologizing, saying that she, too, must know that one is at the mercy of an interviewer and cannot correct what is said. Hers was one of his most prized friendships. Actually, when the reporter asked him why he had never looked up Dietrich, "what I told him was that I was an old man, living in an entirely different world, where people talked an entirely different language."

The letter reached her in Paris, in September of 1962. She had just returned from two months in Switzerland, taking care of her daughter's baby, "and not caring if anybody hit the moon." (This was a year of moon exploration.) She had not seen the article. But even if he had been quoted as not wanting to meet her, "I wouldn't worry. I admire you—and that's enough for me." But, she wrote, what she thought strange was that he quoted himself as saying she was "a glamorous Film Star. You don't think that, do you? Please don't!"

This ended the correspondence between a lovely lady and one of her ten most interesting men. A grandmother and a grandfather. Who had never met.

Part Six

THE
BIG TIME

Chapter Twenty-three

In the thirties no book was selling in multimillion figures and few, if any, in the hundred-thousands. It was a time of major economic depression. And depression or no depression, books had always been considered a luxury, gifts to be bought for Christmas or a birthday.

General readers depended on public libraries for most of their novels, and mystery readers depended largely on rental libraries. Public libraries, with their limited budgets, could not afford to buy many mysteries. Rental libraries bought most that were published, since they rented the book (ten cents for three days was the common price) and were soon repaid the initial cost, making a small profit as well.

It was in 1939 that the first successful twentieth-century paperback venture was started in the United States. It revolutionized the publishing business. The idea came from Robert Fair "Bob" de Graff, who received backing from the owners of Simon and Schuster, Dick Simon and Max Schuster. The idea was to publish reprints that would literally fit into one's pocket and be bound not in cloth but in paper. They would sell for twenty-five cents a copy and be marketed principally through department and drug stores and newsstands. Later on they also became an important part of bookstore sales. The field mushroomed after the war and the name of de Graff's creation, *pocketbooks*, became generic for all small paperback reprints.

The paperback book was not new in publishing, as Freeman Lewis, executive vice-president of Pocket Books for many years and one of Gardner's closest friends, has pointed out. Rather, it was a return to nineteenth-century publishing when the paperback was as general as the hardbound.

When *The Case of the Velvet Claws* was published by Morrow in the early thirties, there were two well-known reprint houses, Grosset and Dunlap, and A. L. Burt Company. These companies reprinted from the original plates and used the original jackets. The books were hardbound and sold for seventy-five cents, except for Grosset's "Novels of Distinction" line priced at one dollar, and were marketed for the most part in department stores. Not long after, the Garden City division of Doubleday and Company entered the field with Triangle Books. These were also hardcover, selling for thirty-nine and forty-nine cents, primarily in Woolworth's five-and-ten-cent stores.

Pocket Books was something else again, in price, size, and format. An experimental list of ten titles was launched in June of 1939. Mysteries were represented on this first list only by Agatha Christie's *The Murder of Roger Ackroyd*. But mystery fiction rapidly became so important to the Pocket Books line that in the first five years more than one third of all titles were in the genre. Simon and Schuster had put their outstanding mystery editor, Lee Wright, in as Pocket Books' mystery editor. She was already moonlighting as crime editor of WOR's *Inner Sanctum*, and had had correspondence with Erle about doing some of his work on radio. She brought Gardner to the list in September 1940 with *The Case of the Velvet Claws*. It was Pocket Books' fifteenth mystery title, and Erle was the twelfth mystery author to be reprinted by the new company. In Lee's opinion he was "a brilliant plotter and a fantastically hard worker." Within five years, eight of the ten best-selling Pocket Books were Perry Masons.

Freeman Lewis, called "Doc" by his good friends, had come to Pocket Books in 1945. He had earlier been associated with Blue Ribbon books, and had moved from there to Doubleday's Triangle Books. Although the two men had never met, among the titles he handled at Triangle were those of Erle Stanley Gardner. Lewis, through the reprint field, had been good friends with Hobson for a considerable period. According to Lewis, when he came to Pocket Books, the Perry Mason titles were already star performers.

"Gardner led the boom in paperbacks," Lewis states, and "no other author has yet come anywhere near his total of sales." In large part this was because of a unique contract put together by Thayer Hobson, representing the original book publisher; Freeman Lewis, representing the paperback house; and Erle Stanley Gardner, the businessman-author. Where the original idea came from none of

Doc Lewis

them seemed to know; doubtless a part came from each of the three men. What it amounted to was the consideration of Gardner titles as a "property" rather than as individual books, and the decision, as Lewis explains it, "to go for high and continuing total annual sales rather than trying to get maximum mileage out of any single title."

Not many authors wrote the volume of work which would make possible such a treatment. According to the contract, Pocket Books guaranteed Gardner $100,000 a year from royalty earnings, with an eventual total of $1,800,000. Excess earnings were put into a fund to cover the possibility that some year sales would not come up to the one-hundred-thousand-dollar level. During the contract's life, only once was it necessary to go to the holding fund. Using this merchandising philosophy, "no individual titles were ever beaten to death by promotion and oversupply," says Mr. Lewis, "yet there was always a plentiful list of titles available through a constant stream of reissues."

As sales mounted, Gardner's Pocket Books contract was the largest single source of Gardner's book earnings. In 1944, on Pocket Books' fifth birthday, he was awarded the "Gertrude," a replica of the publisher's kangaroo colophon. This made him a member of the Million Copy Club. The book which had sold the million was *The Case of the Curious Bride.*

A few years later he received a larger gold Gertrude as a member

of the Five Million Copy Club. And by the mid-fifties he had passed
the fifty million mark in sales with *The Case of the Lonely Heiress.*
On that occasion he was given a framed copy of the title with a
scroll of his record. The publisher Bennett Cerf, president of Random
House, wrote in his widely syndicated column, "The Cerf-
board": "WHEN DOES CRIME PAY? Answer: when Erle Stanley Gardner
writes about it. Sales are growing at over seven million each year.
Makes him a national institution. Gardner takes it in stride. At sixty-
two he is a hale and hearty extrovert, cocky and unconventional. He
can bellow an entire Perry Mason detective saga into his Dictaphone
in four mornings flat and then decamp for an extended fishing or
hunting trip without a worry in the world. 'When I die,' he boasts,
'it won't be from ulcers!' Nor does he share the reticence to talk
about himself or his work that grips most writers in public." Cerf
went on to tell about a recent gathering where in addition to Gardner there were present "a three star general, an ambassador, the
head of an international airline, the owner of a group of magazines,
an editor of *This Week,* and a bevy of high-powered society gals.
Twenty minutes later all of them were meekly listening to Gardner."

In 1960, Leslie Hanscom, an associate editor of *Newsweek,* wrote
in "Man of Mystery," a feature article on Gardner, "Yet if sales are
the measure of a man, Gardner tops Shakespeare, dwarfs Homer—
even surpasses Mickey Spillane. . . . A total of fifty-one Gardner
books have gone over the million sales mark. Thirteen titles have
sold more than two million copies each. . . . By popular suffrage,
Erle Stanley Gardner, at seventy, is incomparably America's greatest
living writer. The most popular fictioneer of this century, he is
probably the most widely read novelist who ever lived. One reason
is that there is so much Gardner to read."

Gardner also made history—he had a habit of history-making—
with Walter Black's Detective Book Club, which reprints current
mystery novels in hardcover omnibus form. So much in demand
were the Gardner books that a spin-off was developed, The Gardner
Mystery Library.

In 1962 Gardner had surpassed one hundred million copies in
Pocket Books sales. He was presented with a large double plaque
of silver, with his record engraved on one side, his name on the
other. Since as soon as a figure is released it is out of date, it has
never been possible to keep up with the number of Gardner books
sold by Pocket Books. Suffice it to say that no other author ever came
close to the record of Erle Stanley Gardner.

Chapter Twenty-four

ONLY THOSE who lived through the period know how important radio was as an entertainment medium before the advent of television. For the first time, live entertainment was brought into the home. That it was an audio medium only was no deprivation. In fact, when television was being introduced, everyone believed that its drawback was that you had to sit there and watch it, that you couldn't be about other things as you could when you only had to listen to a show.

Erle's first personal experience with radio was in 1935 when Joseph Henry Jackson asked him to appear on the book show which Jackson hosted. *Radio Readers' Guide* was such an admirable book show that it ran for ten years on NBC out of San Francisco. For twenty-five years, Jackson, one of the top book critics of the country, was literary editor of the San Francisco *Chronicle*.

He and Erle had met long before. As Jackson said in introducing Gardner on the program, "About ten years ago, I was sitting at an editorial desk at the old *Sunset* magazine. In those days, as a good many of you will remember, *Sunset* devoted itself in a great measure to articles about the West, particularly the outdoor West. One spring morning Gardner was announced. He had an idea. His occupation was the law, but he had a hobby. His hobby was exactly the thing that *Sunset* was interested in—the West outdoors."

His idea was a series of articles on typical two-week vacations in the West. In this way his vacations would pay for themselves. Jackson ran about a half dozen of the articles in the next year, and the two became lasting friends.

Radio entertainment was at its height in the thirties and forties. There was enormous demand for stories and the money was big, perhaps not as big as selling to the movies, but close to it if an author had the good fortune to make it with a series.

Gardner had his usual ups and downs before *Perry Mason* went on the air. In the early forties, it was off again, on again, with a radio deal. He wanted one, for the money, because with his expenses, money was important. He also wanted it as advertisement for his books; he was always watching out for Perry Mason. He knew that the *Ellery Queen* radio show, which preceded *Perry Mason* on the air, was of great advertising value for the Queen mysteries.

He also wanted a radio show for prestige, not prestige as such, but he was a competitor, and if one of his competitors in mystery had a show, he too would have a show. With all of the reasons for wanting to sell radio rights, he was firm about not letting his characters be falsified, as he contended they had been by the movies.

He was determined to keep control of the radio show. In the end he wasn't able to; it wasn't the way things were done. But he did better his position in that he had some veto rights. He would not get full control of his books in another medium until television, when he would form his own company to produce the *Perry Mason* show.

When Gardner began looking for a Hollywood agent, he talked it over with his friend, Ruth Waterbury, editor of *Photoplay*, for whom he was writing some stories. She passed the word about this "good mystery story writer" to Cornwell Jackson, who was head of the motion picture and radio division of Berg Allenberg, saying that if Gardner liked him, Corney could probably sign the author.

Jackson wasn't interested and told her so. He had at least eight highly successful mystery authors on his list and neither wanted nor needed more. But to save Ruth embarrassment, as she had already set up a meeting, he agreed to go with her to the Hollywood Knickerbocker Hotel where Erle was staying.

When they entered the room, Erle walked quickly across to them, put out his hand, and said, "Well, they tell me you're the greatest agent in Hollywood."

Corney was, to say the least, taken aback. In his own words, he'd never considered himself Hollywood's top agent and "God knows no one had ever called me that." He learned in time that it was characteristic of Gardner to catch a newcomer off base. Erle continued in the same manner. "How do you know which books will sell and which will not?" he demanded.

As Erle recalled it, Corney answered him just as straight. "I don't. I have had horrible stories that have brought great sums of money. I have had good stories that no one seems to want."

Erle pressed on. "How can you tell which books they are going to like?"

And Corney answered, "I can't. They can't. I don't think they know any more about it than I do. I don't know how their minds work and I don't think they do either. They usually just want something—anything—they think somebody else wants more."

At this, Erle stuck out his hand again and said, "You're my agent. Now, let's have dinner."

Gardner said he knew a place that had good wine and good cocktails, and Corney, accustomed to Hollywood mores, thought he had run into "one of *those* drinkers" and that they were going to booze it up. This was far from the case, of course. They had no more than two cocktails, no wine, and returned after dinner as "sober as judges sometimes are."

The two became friends that day, a special friendship that was to continue unabated throughout Erle's lifetime. Corney has written that Erle was "the most understanding and generous person I ever met, and although we had many a long and violent argument," his respect for and admiration of Gardner never diminished.

Erle said over and again that if Donald Lam, "that cocky little bastard," had a model, it was Corney. When Erle and Corney got together, a good example of what would ensue is their experience with a producer who wanted to buy a Perry Mason book for motion pictures. Corney had had dealings with the man before, none of them pleasant. Therefore, he asked Erle to go along with him so that they could dish out to the producer some of his own kind of treatment. The producer kept raising his bid; they kept turning it down. Finally he demanded to know why they wouldn't discuss it. Corney told him, "You just don't have enough talent to handle Perry Mason." And Erle added, "Besides, we have a taxi waiting outside and the meter is running."

Jackson worked hard for Gardner and his properties. He thought there were excellent opportunities for a radio show. He took at least five of the top advertising executives to Temecula to talk with Erle.

"The first genuine appreciation of Erle came from Hubbell Robinson," Jackson recalls. "Hubbell immediately sensed the enormous potential in Erle's genius." Robinson was a New York agency man at the time; when TV arrived, he became a top executive at CBS. He and Corney worked together and came up with what looked like genuine pay dirt with a show for Bromo-Seltzer. They were confident and elated until, like many a deal before and since, it fell through. Where most authors would have been screaming for his scalp, Corney says, Gardner never uttered one word of recrimination. Later on, when hopes for yet another show were dashed and plans for a conference by all concerned had been arranged, called off, rearranged, and called off again, Gardner was inspired to write a letter to Corney which began: "You know about these radio guys. Their grandmothers *always* die. Everything was in the bag when this guy's grandmother died and he had to go to the funeral." He predicted that was exactly what would happen to Hub Robinson who, having put off the Temecula trip because of urgent business elsewhere, would no doubt avoid coming at all by killing off grandma all over again. He continued:

> Well, anyway, to break it to you all at once, a guy wants Jean and me to join him in Montana or some such place for a pack trip. But we couldn't get Pullman reservations. Then it seems when Louie Roripaugh (the cattleman you met) came over early this morning to help us chase out city slickers who were hunting doves on New Deal gasoline, which we can't get, but which the slickers get, that he is about to leave this evening on a cattle buying trip which is going to take him to Twin Falls, and after consulting maps and wondering if we could hitch-hike, and could we make it, and what have you, and how about going on to New York so it really will be a business trip, because, after all, we should go to New York . . . well, how about Hub Robinson? "We can't run away and leave him." "Why not?" "Oh, Erle, it wouldn't be right." . . . "Tell you what, Jean, we'll write Corney and explain that Grandmaw passed away in Billings, Montana, which happens to be where we meet the pack train, and then we'll start tonight with Louie and get as far as we can, and then stand in line for busses and hitch-hike and get to Grandmaw's funeral."
>
> She was a grand old lady, Corney. . . . Just to show you how she loved me, at the end, when she learned we wanted to go to Billings, Montana, and that we'd waited long enough for this radio outfit, the grand old lady up with her gun and blew her darling brains out. . . . The first goddam time my grandmother dies before the other guy's. Hub's grandmaw may be a good egg all right, but she can't hold a candle to the woman who was my grandmaw until she blew her brains out an hour ago. My grandmaw is an opportunist.

In 1942 there were two pending Gardner radio deals. One was in Hollywood with Walter Pidgeon playing Perry Mason. On this Gardner would receive three hundred and fifty to five hundred dollars a week "without having to do anything." The other was one in which Erle had collaborated with Jack Simpson, a New Orleans

Jack Simpson and Gardner

radio man. This deal was an audience participation crime show which they called *Life in Your Hands.*

Erle's first meeting with Simpson was back in 1938. That winter, Erle, Jean, and Nonie Bibler were working in New Orleans. He needed some service on his Dictaphone and called the local office. Simpson at the time was selling Dictaphones by day, and writing at nights and on weekends in his attic apartment in the French Quarter. The short stories he poured out were sent out to magazines, both pulp and slick. Mostly they were rejected, but that autumn he had one printed in *Detective Magazine.*

The serviceman who came to repair Gardner's machine was so proud of Simpson that he carried around a copy of the magazine to show to people. He told Gardner all about Dictaphone's own writer, and on his return to the office, informed Simpson that Gardner would like to meet him.

Simpson found this hard to believe but he telephoned Gardner, who said, in effect, as Simpson recalls, "Sure, kid, come on up." They became good friends and Simpson spent quite a bit of time with Erle during his stay in New Orleans. "I had never met a man with more dedication and consideration for his fellow man than I found in Erle. Corny as it is to say, he had a true milk of human kindness in his soul."

A year or so later, when Gardner returned to New Orleans, he found Simpson had taken a job with an advertising agency and was handling the writing, production, announcing, and sales connected with radio work. They saw a lot of each other after working hours. Bourbon House was their favorite hangout, and they would often play the pinball machine until the "wee small hours."

One night, after some good-natured rivalry as to who was the better man, the owner bet Erle he could drink him under the table. Gardner won hands down, but in relating the incident Simpson concluded, "I never saw Erle take more than one drink an evening after that." And this was true of everyone who knew him. Surrounded by the hard-drinking publishing and radio crowd, Gardner would nurse one highball, then switch to ginger ale or water for the remainder of the occasion.

It wasn't all play that winter of 1941–42. Gardner and Simpson talked shop for long hours, especially on the plotting and developing of stories. Erle was working on *The Case of the Drowning Duck.* He had written his archer-physicist friend, Paul Klopsteg, to see if it was possible to drown a duck. Dr. Klopsteg was at the time helping to develop detergent. He sent Erle a sample and told him there was only one way to find out, and that was to try it. As if Erle would drown a duck! Another problem Erle had posed was that if you put the detergent into a fish tank, would it also kill the goldfish? Simpson, like Klopsteg, thought there was only one way to find out. He bought a small fishbowl and some goldfish, unaware of the outrage killing innocent creatures would arouse in Jean and Erle. Simpson lived with the fishbowl and fish for many years.

In their discussions on plot development, one of Erle's favorite subjects was the unreliability of eyewitness reports. This idea was turned into a radio show by Simpson. He sold it to the local Seven-Up bottler; it was therefore called *The Seven-Up Show.*

Gardner spent many hours that same winter planning a Perry Mason show. When it was time to return to Temecula, he asked Simpson to take a leave of absence from the agency and come out to the ranch to work more on the proposed program. He would pay Simpson the same salary he was receiving from the agency and also pay his expenses for the trip. Jack and his wife, Mary Alyce, thereupon accompanied Erle, Jean, and Nonie on the homeward journey. After a week or so at the ranch, Gardner took an apartment for the Simpsons in Hollywood, and loaned them a car to enable Simpson to keep in closer touch with the networks. He also introduced Simpson to Corney Jackson.

Meanwhile, Willis Wing had reminded Gardner of the attitude of the *Saturday Evening Post* and *Ladies' Home Journal* regarding commercial radio use of characters in their stories. At this time publishers felt that radio competed with magazine sales. "Thayer and I both feel future prospects for Mason and the *Post* are very bright," Wing wrote. "Nothing should be done to impair that future. So it amounts to this: if you want to carry Mason on with the *Post* in the future, you can't permit any radio dramatization of him." Temporarily this put an end to the Perry Mason negotiations.

Gardner and Simpson moved at once into redeveloping the old *Seven-Up Show*, which they retitled *A Life in Your Hands*. When it wasn't bought, Erle, Corney, and a friend of theirs each put up seventy-five dollars for an audition record. Later Erle bought out the other man and it was agreed that when and if the show sold, Corney and Simpson would share the profits. In 1943, on the strength of his direction of this audition, Simpson got a job as a director with NBC in Chicago. From there he went to head up the broadcast department of a national agency. When a summer replacement for the Hildegarde program was needed—Hildegarde was a star singer of the day—he played the record for the president of the Brown and Williamson Tobacco Corporation, who bought the show for an initial thirteen weeks and kept it for two years. It played a third year for the H. J. Heinz Company.

In May of 1942, Wing wrote Erle that "six of us agents have just succeeded in a battle with Curtis about their new purchase form . . . in which they were grabbing everything in sight." At the same time the agents' committee clarified the Curtis attitude on radio rights: "They will now permit exercise of radio and TV rights, ninety days after publication. No ifs, ands, or buts." Perry Mason was activated again.

In January 1942, Corney Jackson left Berg Allenberg for the duration of the war to set up the radio bureau in Hollywood for the Office of War Information. Wayne Griffin was named to head the radio department of the agency in his place. Erle wrote Wing that he didn't know Griffin and asked Wing to take over radio and motion picture rights while Corney was away. Gardner wanted

Corney in on everything, particularly financial arrangements, and if Corney could help, he asked Wing to work with him. Wing took over.

In one of his sudden enthusiasms, Gardner had signed with a promoter full of big ideas for a Perry Mason radio show. This man had discussed it with Procter and Gamble, who refused to deal with him. Wing arranged to pay off the promoter for Gardner. Procter and Gamble were interested again and the Perry Mason radio show began to move.

Corney's parting words of advice to Erle had been, "Now, don't let them persuade you to put this on as a daytime soap opera. Perry Mason should be a half-hour or an hour show in prime time." The Perry Mason show went on the air in October 1943—*as a daytime soap opera!* By January 30, 1944, it had national coverage, in those days over fifty-seven stations.

In the early years it was nothing but trouble, with scripts, casts, agencies, production—the works—and there is a voluminous Gardner correspondence file to prove it. Some quotations in a typical vein are: "What the hell difference does it make to me if the problems of a script writer call for a Della Street who is constantly asking dumb questions in order to make Mason talk?" "To hell with letters! I heard the Goddam broadcast on the air." "Completely fed up with the manner in which my objections to character portrayals are ignored." "This Perry Mason situation is absolutely impossible and it's got to stop and stop right now." He even had something to say about the funereal tone of the commercials. But when the writer Irving Vendig was discovered, everything suddenly became right, or close to right. Gardner kept Vendig on the show throughout and beyond, even into television.

In the twelve years Mason was on radio, Gardner never let down his monitoring of the show. At the ranch, no matter what else was going on, he would retire alone to his study for that half hour, to listen and make notes.

There were frequent radio conferences, held from California to Florida and points between. They are remembered by the Temecula gang as one remembers good parties. Of them all, the most memorable was a Florida meeting on the beach, when Erle convinced a reporter that the group was a sand-castling organization, and had come to that particular strand because the guano content made it the best sand in the United States for building castles. Later his conscience got the better of him, and before the story could be turned in he called the reporter and apologized for the joke. The editor ran the story anyway, it being such a good yarn.

The first Corney knew that the show was on the air was when he began receiving large weekly checks. He called the ranch to find out why and learned that Erle was in the Bahamas covering the Sir Harry Oakes trial. He cabled Erle at once that he had had nothing to do with the radio deal and was returning the payments. Erle cabled back: CASH THOSE CHECKS AND SHUT YOUR TRAP. Said Corney: "I did. For twelve years." The final Mason radio show was aired December 30, 1955.

Chapter Twenty-five

IN THE THIRTIES AND FORTIES the big city newspapers, in particular the Hearst papers, used "trained seals" for color stories of important trials. Erle Stanley Gardner was a natural, since he was a lawyer as well as a mystery writer.

Erle had no idea he was about to become a trained seal when he went to New York in 1943 to handle last-minute problems before the launching of the Perry Mason radio program. Because of wartime restrictions on travel, instead of taking his usual two or three secretaries, he had brought only Jean with him.

Thayer Hobson met them at the train. Erle told him at once, "I can't stay for more than forty-eight hours. I only want to get certain things wound up in connection with the radio program and then I'm on my way."

Thayer's reply, as related by Erle, was, "You don't know anything. You're going to the Bahamas to cover the trial of Alfred de Marigny for the murder of Sir Harry Oakes."

Gardner stated he was too busy for that. Instead of listening to him argue, Hobson sent him over to his agent's. Willis Wing informed Gardner that it was a fact, the Hearst papers had decided they wanted a trained seal whose name meant something in the field of mystery writing. Two or three names had been considered but Gardner had the inside track.

"I simply told Willis Wing I couldn't go, and didn't think too much about it.

"The next day Willis Wing called me and told me that things were definite. Hearst wanted me to go over to the Bahamas.

" 'I can't do it,' I said. 'Tell him to go jump in the lake.'

"Willis Wing said dryly, 'One does not tell William Randolph Hearst to jump in the lake.'

" 'What does one tell him?' I asked.

" 'Well,' he said, 'if one really doesn't want to go, one makes a counter offer that is so exorbitant in its terms that Hearst tells *you* to go jump in the lake. So you are the one to jump in the lake and somebody else goes to the Bahamas.'

" 'I don't give a damn who jumps in what lake,' I said, 'just so I don't have to go over there at this time. So make the counter offer.'

"That was Friday. I was planning to leave for home on Saturday.

"Friday night was quite a night. The radio show was getting ready to open with a fanfare of trumpets, and representatives of the advertising agency gave us quite a party.

"Ordinarily I can't sleep in the morning. I waken around six o'clock no matter how late I've been up. But this Saturday morning was an exception. I was still sleeping at eight-thirty when the phone rang.

"I fumbled for the instrument, said hello, and a hard-boiled voice said, 'Is this Erle Stanley Gardner?'

"I said it was.

" 'This is Paul Schoenstein, the city editor of the New York *Journal-American*. Get up here. You're working for me.'

" 'What do you mean I'm working for you?'

" 'You're working for me,' he said impatiently, 'and I don't want my reporters in bed at this hour of the morning. Get up here.'

" 'What do you mean I'm working for you?'

" 'Didn't your agent submit Hearst a proposition to cover the de Marigny case?'

"I gulped a couple of times and said, 'I don't know.'

" 'Well, he did,' Schoenstein said, 'and I want you up here. It's twenty-five minutes from your hotel to this office. I'll expect you here in half an hour.'

"He slammed up the phone.

"Later on, I learned that Schoenstein had quite a sense of humor but I didn't know it at the time. Overlaying this sense of humor is a very, very hard-boiled exterior.

"Being city editor of a paper like the New York *Journal-American* is not a soft job. A man has to reach instantaneous decisions and put those instantaneous decisions into split-second action. He doesn't have time to beat around the bush. He requires action, he gives action and he gets action.

"Schoenstein got action. I was up there in half an hour.

"Schoenstein looked me over, told me that he wanted a first article to be ready on Monday morning.

"I had never even heard of the Oakes-de Marigny case. Schoenstein gave me a big envelope from the newspaper morgue and told me to get familiar with every phase of it."

This case had as many or more fictionlike aspects than any ever devised by a mystery writer. Alfred de Marigny was on trial for the murder of Sir Harry Oakes, father of his wife, Nancy. In efforts to clear her husband she had sent to the States for a prominent detective, Raymond Schindler. The Duke of Windsor, who was governor of the Bahamas at the time of the murder, had also sent to the States for an investigative officer, a Florida police captain he had become acquainted with when visiting there. The crime itself involved bizarre suggestions of voodoo, feathers and fire, blood running uphill, and featured a mysterious small handprint on the wall.

The case finally collapsed when Schindler proved the fingerprint in the master bedroom, presumed to have been left by the accused, had been forged, and lifted and repositioned on the wooden screen near Sir Harry's bed. But the case was never solved. That is, officially solved.

Schoenstein not only told Erle to have twelve hundred words in by Monday morning but also told him to be prepared to leave Monday night for the Bahamas; they would start pulling wires to get him a passport. He also wanted some pictures which he could use from time to time in the paper, so Gardner put in an hour or so posing for pictures showing him pounding the typewriter, pictures of him reading typescripts, pictures of him doing just about everything.

"Then," according to Erle, "I took the morgue file and Jean and I went out to Thayer Hobson's place in Connecticut to spend the weekend and work on the story.

"I was still in something of a daze. My agent embarrassedly explained to me that he had made a proposition which certainly should have been rejected. I was to receive a guarantee, a per diem, a flat rate of expenses. I was to have the expenses of two secretaries. Wing hadn't even bothered to tell me about it because it was a foregone conclusion the offer would be rejected.

"So I was working for a newspaper.

"We sat out at Thayer Hobson's that Sunday afternoon and I wondered what I was going to do about getting another secretary; what with travel restrictions such as they were, and working against a time limit, there was no time to get one from my California office.

"I was literally snowed under with work. In the first place, I was having to prepare radio plots, I was behind on a book I was writing, and the idea of covering the de Marigny case in the Bahamas kept appealing to me less and less the more I thought of it."

Thayer offered Hennie Trilling Gelber, his personal secretary, to go along. "She knows Jean, she knows you, and you'll all get along together."

"So we rang up Thayer Hobson's personal secretary, who had spent ninety-nine and ninety-nine one-hundredths percent of her life within the confines of metropolitan New York, and explained to her that she was to rush in an application for a passport because she was going to the Bahamas.

"I took the story in Monday morning. Schoenstein glanced at it, tossed it on the desk, paused a moment, thoughtfully picked the story up, started reading it again, then slowly and thoughtfully turned it face down on his desk and looked me over.

"During the war it was difficult to get clearance for the Bahamas. He instructed me to get on the plane that night and to get as far as Miami, Florida. . . . The average professional newspaperman has but little use for a trained seal, particularly a high-priced one . . . he left no doubt in my mind as to how he felt or where I stood.

" 'Don't try to cover news,' he warned. 'You couldn't write newspaper stuff anyway.' Schoenstein went on to inform me that if I didn't send in around twelve hundred words a day of the sort of background copy that would interest newspaper readers and which, because of my legal experience, wouldn't be noticed by the news reporters who were on the job, I'd be fired."

Without the girls, Erle took off for Florida, where he met Raymond Schindler, also awaiting transportation. They flew together to the Bahamas. It was the start of another longtime friendship.

"My two secretaries finally got their passports and plane reservations and arrived two or three days after I had started sending my stuff from the Bahamas. At the time they arrived they found I was being waited on by an official delegation that was pointing out to me the British law of libel and furthermore indicating the danger of contempt proceedings because of my violation of the rules of British journalistic procedure. The delegation was not in a friendly mood.

"The British law of libel does not simply protect a man against the publication of something which is false and defamatory, it protects him against the publication of anything that is defamatory. After my first two or three stories it became quite apparent that there were people in Nassau who didn't like the type of stuff I was sending in.

"Things eventually became so heated against the American press that for some period of time whenever I would leave my hotel for court, my secretaries would see that everything was packed up in our rooms and loaded into a taxicab which waited out behind the hotel, ready for instant departure. I also took steps to see that we could get out on the first available plane despite the red tape of wartime restrictions."

As the trial was nearing an end, Gardner managed to corral an official witness and ask him an explosive question, which, Erle believed, if asked in court would have blown up the case. He also believed that it gave him the identity of the true murderer. Erle never revealed either the question or the name of the murderer. The information was, he knew, too hot to cable to New York. It had to be delivered in person. He was certain that the final defense witness would be de Marigny's wife.

"Eventually Nancy Oakes de Marigny was called to the stand. I listened to her testimony. The court took a recess. I left the courtroom without my hat and without even saying goodbye to anyone. I strolled casually out through the grounds of the courthouse and ten minutes later was on my way to the airport." The girls were waiting with the luggage.

"I got to Miami Beach and then started a mad scramble trying to get to New York. It was the day before Armistice Day, priorities were in effect, and even high officials were being bumped off the planes. I explained the circumstances to a young woman in charge of reservations at the airline company . . . and I walked into the office of the New York *Journal-American* the next morning imbued with enthusiasm and feeling I had uncovered a key clue. I outlined it to Schoenstein. By that time the case had been submitted to the jury and a verdict was expected momentarily. It was then I learned something about running a newspaper and about public interest.

"Schoenstein pointed out . . . that with the verdict the case was officially finished. . . . They would play up the story of the verdict . . . then turn the spotlight on a new headline crime.

"The newspaper wasn't faced with the responsibility of solving the murder of Sir Harry Oakes particularly. It didn't care about having a lot more of my theories, comments, analyses, and speculations. The newspaper was there to print news. . . . If I would wait until the verdict came in and then write a comment on the verdict, I could get on a plane for California, submit a bill covering my expenses, and draw my compensation.

"My function as a trained seal in the murder trial of Alfred de Marigny was over."

Gardner covered some other spectacular cases, one of which, the murder of a coed in Denver, introduced him to Gene Lowall, then city editor of the Denver *Post*. Later Lowall became an important investigative member of the Court of Last Resort.

It was the Abbott case in Oakland, a child rape-murder case, which Erle covered for the San Francisco *Examiner*, which was his final performance as a trained seal. He realized at that time that the expense of transporting his secretaries, of his office staff, of meals, lodging, and miscellany, was too much for a newspaper to swallow. He had priced himself out of the market.

But not out of the magazine market. A member of the staff of *Look* magazine rang up Thayer Hobson to see if he could persuade Gardner to do an article on the trial of Willie "The Actor" Sutton. Hobson named a price based on Erle's fiction scale rather than that of a magazine article.

"The representative of *Look* hit the ceiling and hung up," Erle records. But the next day the magazine again called Hobson. They would make a price of exactly one half what Hobson had asked. Hobson told them he wouldn't even bother to call Gardner to the telephone for that and hung up. A couple of hours later they phoned to accept Hobson's figure and he phoned Erle.

Willie Sutton was a character criminal. He was a bank robber and an escape artist of reputation, dubbed "The Actor" because he used disguises and could and did act his way out of tight spots. Before the start of the trial, newsmen were permitted a "pooled" picture of Sutton, with police officers in attendance. After that cameras were not allowed in the courthouse. Daily, detectives were stationed at each end of the spectator benches before the doors were opened. A cordon of officers escorted Sutton into the courtroom and were seated behind him and his codefendants at all times. The tight security was because the man who had alerted the police, after recognizing Sutton, was gunned down on the street prior to the trial.

Since *Look* was primarily a picture magazine, and since it had a weekly schedule, it was bound to be scooped by the daily newspapers. Therefore, decided Erle, it was up to him to come up with something special in a picture.

Erle got the picture. What a picture! Of it he said, "How I managed to get the only photograph of Willie Sutton flanked by his counsel and shaking hands with me is a story in itself. I really shouldn't have done it. However, *Look* was paying me what it considered a perfectly fabulous lump sum to cover the trial, and quite naturally expected something fabulous in return."

Not in any of his notes, or in any other of his personal reminiscences, does Gardner tell the story of how he managed the scoop. This, Jean remembers, was to protect the girl reporter he had persuaded to smuggle a camera into the courtroom and at his prearranged signal, snap the picture.

Chapter Twenty-six

BEFORE PERRY MASON took his final bow on radio, after starring five days a week for twelve years, there was little or no doubt that he would be stepping onstage in TV. In those twelve years there had been 3,221 scripts and at least a half dozen Perrys, Dellas, Traggs, and Drakes—fewer Hamilton Burgers, as he was not too important in the radio scripts. The year 1955 marked the beginning of the end for radio dramatic shows. Gardner could have had a new contract; however, it would not have been for first-rate terms, and in his words, "I refused to cheapen the product." The big money was going to TV. Statistics were proving that the returns from TV were astronomically greater than those from radio.

The bids on Perry Mason were in before the radio show folded but Gardner turned them all down. He'd been burned more than once, and he was not a man to forget. First of all, there had been the ill-fated movie contract. This he never got over. "Warners proceeded to ruin Perry," Gardner said, not once but every time he thought about it in the ensuing forty years. Dwight Whitney, chief of *TV Guide*'s Hollywood bureau and one of the best of personality interviewers, in the sixties wrote a two-part profile of Gardner, "The Case of the Indestructible Hero," in which he quoted Gardner on Mason's introduction into motion pictures: "It seemed to me he had about an acre of office and Della was so dazzling I couldn't see her for diamonds. Everybody drank a lot." Although the suave Warren William, for whom Warner Brothers had purchased *The Case of the Howling Dog*, was, in Gardner's opinion, the best who played the role, he was "distinctly not Perry Mason." William had been cast because of William Powell's terrific success in *The Thin Man* at Metro, and William was as close to Powell in looks and sophisticated acting as a rival company could come up with.

Warren William, Peggy Shannon, and Gardner

It is hard to disagree with Gardner's opinion of his motion picture experience when one "great genius" wanted him to write something to be called *Perry Mason in the Painted Desert* because of the success of *The Petrified Forest*. And when they cast Ricardo Cortez as Mason, than whom no one could have been further from the image, the roars could easily be heard from the camp wagon to Burbank. Donald Woods would have improved the image, Gardner believed, but he was too low-keyed for the author's idea of a fighting lawyer. The final payoff came when *The Case of the Dangerous Dowager* was released as *Granny Get Your Gun*, a Western. It continues a puzzlement why the motion picture company would buy a best-seller with its built-in advertising value, then destroy all vestige of identification.

Once burned, twice shy. Gardner had never been able to get the deal he wanted on a radio contract and had settled for less. Yet, in each contract he made in radio, there were certain safeguards to protect the character of Mason. Where TV was concerned, Gardner intended to hold on to all of his rights. More or less what he did, under Corney Jackson's direction, was to conduct trials. Certain leading advertising companies, production companies, independent producers, and the networks were informed that "if they could produce talent capable of putting Mason on television we would enter into a contract." One leading ad agency, making an exception to policy, invested three thousand dollars of its own money trying to find writers who could deliver suitable scripts. They gave up. In Gardner's opinion, "writers simply didn't know the characters well enough to get the spirit across to an audience."

It was during this period that Jackson lunched with two Very Important Persons from a leading agency, in the course of which they asked him if Gardner would take a million dollars for the TV rights to Perry Mason. Jackson didn't bother to consult Erle; he turned it down, informing them, "Not a chance. It's worth much more." When he told Gardner, his decision was given unqualified approval. In fact, turning down a million dollars became one of Gardner's pet stories.

"All of these things are matters of record," he stated in a memo dictated in January 1957, at the time the Perry Mason show was being prepared for its debut on television later that year. As was the decision to form his own company to produce the show.

The decision to form Paisano Productions came because he simply did not have the time or the experience to try to supervise production—"and we were therefore in the position of having a potential gold mine which we couldn't develop." Gardner was a "we" rather than an "I" man, as is evident in his one-sentence account of how the company was formed: "It was suggested that we organize a partnership consisting of the secretaries who had been with me for thirty-five years and who knew the characters intimately, and Mr. and Mrs. Cornwell Jackson, who also knew the characters over a period of some fifteen or twenty years." Deane Johnson of the Hollywood law firm of O'Melveny and Myers, and also a good friend of Gardner's, was the attorney who set up the partnership.

The idea, Gardner explained, was that the partnership could negotiate a producing arrangement and offer personalized supervision. Not long after the partnership was formed, he wrote, "Results have abundantly justified this line of reasoning. What at first threatened to be a completely mediocre presentation turned into a very attractive show which has now been filmed and is ready to be offered to sponsors."

In another statement Gardner credited Corney Jackson with organizing Paisano Productions. At the time, Jackson was a vice-president of the J. Walter Thompson advertising agency in charge of the Hollywood offices. He had married Gail Patrick, a motion picture star, and she too had become a member of Uncle Erle's family.

Gail Patrick and Corney Jackson

According to Gardner's report on the beginnings of Paisano, Jackson turned its working mechanics over to his wife. From that, her job "just growed," as was the norm for Gardner projects. She recalls very well how on one matter after another, Gardner would tell her, "You take care of it, Gail. I don't know anything about Hollywood and you do."

Jackson and Gardner had picked a winner in Gail Patrick. She was a dynamic young woman who not only knew Hollywood inside out, but who had purpose, energy, charm, and as indefatigable a devotion to work as Gardner himself.

Gail Patrick had not planned an acting career. In fact, she wanted to be a lawyer. At the junior college level in her home town in Alabama, she had been preparing for entrance to the University of Alabama law school. It was by chance that she made a trip to Hollywood.

Paramount was conducting a talent test across the country that year, and as one of the student leaders at her college, she had signed up four of her classmates for the test. She shepherded them to California. She herself did not intend to enter the contest but the other girls urged her to join them, and at the last minute she did, in a dress belonging to Kay Francis, an established star, borrowed from wardrobe. Unlike the way it was in the movie musicals of the days, she didn't win. However, she was offered a stock contract at seventy-five dollars a week. She had a scholarship to the University of Alabama and the extra money would be valuable for additional expenses there, but she turned down the offer, then reconsidered and accepted a twenty-week contract. She never went back to Alabama.

Throughout 1956, preparations were in high gear for the Mason show. The production had been turned over entirely to Gail, but no script was going to be produced without Gardner's okay. And he was a perfectionist.

While he was reading scripts, she was working on casting. For one entire year she tested, in New York as well as in Hollywood. By the first of April, 1956, it looked as if Fred MacMurray would be Perry Mason. In a memo from Gardner to the Jacksons and to Honey Moore on April 9, he wrote, "Apparently Fred MacMurray is the person who will probably be selected." Gardner knew so little about show biz, movies, or TV, that he had never seen MacMurray, an important motion picture actor, and didn't know who he was. Gardner wanted to know if any of his movies were currently showing so that he could look him over.

In another memo he was to say: "Actually I think actors don't do as much acting as they are supposed to do. I think it is largely a question of casting and then using enough direction to bring out some of the natural talents of the actor. However, this is something I know nothing about." He went on to say, "Pierre Salinger, a hell of a good newspaperman, told Sam that we should consider Richard Egan for the Perry Mason part." Later in April in a business letter to Gail, Honey added the note, "I see references to the Perry Mason show in the paper and in *TV Guide* and get a big thrill. I'm dying to know who will play the parts."

At last the time came for Miss Patrick to run tests on the actors and actresses. With the exception of the latter, of course, all had applied for the Mason role. But as millions of TV viewers know, Bill Hopper became Paul Drake, Perry's detective friend and fellow worker, and William Talman became Hamilton Burger, the district attorney. Raymond Burr had been asked to read for the D.A., Corney remembering him from his highly praised portrayal of a similar part in the motion picture *A Place in the Sun*. Burr agreed, but only if he could also test for Mason. According to production memories, he was asked to lose weight and return. Gardner happened to be on the set the day Burr came back, and announced, "That's Perry Mason." Some five years later, Gardner was to say in the already

Gail Patrick, Gardner, Jean, Erd Brandt, and Raymond Burr

quoted Dwight Whitney article, "Burr is still my choice. Of course, I said granite-hard and he is cow-eyed. But you've got to hand it to Raymond. He got to be a pretty damn good lawyer. Bill Talman is really a wonder. He actually looks as if he expects to win a case."

Barbara Hale became a major asset in her portrayal of Della Street. She not only conveyed Della's astuteness as well as her charm, but she projected Gardner's own interpretation of the efficient, loyal, and devoted secretary. And Ray Collins's wry imperturbability made him a memorable Lieutenant Tragg.

The cast was decided on long before Gardner had okayed any scripts. At one time there were eighteen in the works, accepted but not good enough to film. Gardner himself could only suggest what he wanted done because he would not rewrite another's script. He had learned in radio days that he could not create dramatic scripts; he was a narrative writer. The emergence from the tunnel more or less came about when a onetime lawyer, Ben Brady, was hired by Gail as a producer.

From Temecula to Hollywood the memos concerning *Perry Mason* were unending. Most of the memos were concerned not with plot and not with dramatic values, but with how Perry should be presented. For example, "Perry Mason has to be the equivalent of the knight on the white charger riding to rescue damsels in distress." Another long memo said in part: "Mason is clever. He is quick. He is ingenious—but he is not a smart aleck. The minute Perry Mason starts wisecracking, the audience feels that after all the situation isn't very serious. . . . [The situation] is robbed of its suspense and the show simply becomes the smart aleck type of murder comedy which has been so done to death. The more I see of what is being done, the more I think that this is perhaps the keynote to so many of our troubles. Writers feel that they should be clever in presenting Perry Mason, so they start writing clever dialogue, and pretty quick the whole situation becomes an Alice-in-Wonderland farce out of Never-Never land."

There was another memo on TV plot problems: "It is impossible to have a good mystery show without an element of suspense . . . The reader knows Mason is not going to be disbarred; he knows Mason's client is not going to get convicted. I use many tricks in the books to build suspense . . . It is my feeling that our shows should be scripted, directed, and acted so that we have our Perry Mason more worried, more apprehensive, less smug and not giving so much the impression of a conquering hero about to engage in a one-sided battle. I think this is necessary to get proper suspense."

Paisano Productions was not set up for the Perry Mason show alone, but for the presentation of all the Gardner characters, with early work being initiated on a Bertha Cool-Donald Lam series. "The Bigger They Come," a single Cool-Lam show produced by Walden Productions, had been presented in January 1955 on the CBS *Climax* show, with Jane Darwell as Bertha and Art Carney as Donald. The first big recorded disagreement between Gardner and Gail Patrick came in regard to a Donald Lam script not long after Paisano Productions was formed in 1956. Gardner said that it was written "around a character who was a pansy. He had the characteristics of a pansy . . . a distinct feminine touch to everything he said and did. The writer was thinking about a little guy in the terms of a pantywaist."

Gail was no pantywaist and wasn't about to take trouble lying down. She had too much good fighting Irish blood for that. After a heated exchange of words, on August 31 Gardner addressed Gail, in part: "No one is going to fall in love with a pansy unless it be a

violet." He added, "I get violent, I erupt, I emote, I shout. Please
get used to me. But please, oh please, don't discount what I say about
the characters. I think I know something about what the public
wants and a hell of a lot about what the public doesn't want."

And: "On the other hand, a great deal of our future is tied up
in this thing. If it goes sour and becomes a flop it will hurt you professionally, it will raise hell with me financially. Therefore, as I
see it, it is going to be a thousand times better to go down fighting,
rather than to approve of something that we know isn't good, in
order to promote harmony."

In September a long letter arrived from Erle to Gail about the
show, which brings with it the feeling of "this is where I came in."
With variations he had written this letter many, many times before:
"Gosh, girl, cheer up. Maybe it isn't half as bad as I think, and
maybe my letter to you being hurriedly written emphasized only the
feeling of uneasiness I had. I certainly didn't take time to list the
good points. —This is a damn good show. There is no question about
that. *BUT* is it going to hold an audience for an hour and make
the audience turn back next week?"

If there is in anyone's mind the supposition that Gardner was not
a worrywart, which his nearest and dearest called him over and
again, this letter should dispel it. Not only had he been agitating
over the Mason show but, "the last Donald Lam book that I did,
I put away feeling that it was too lousy to revise and send on to
my publisher until I could get a new slant on it. The last Perry
Mason book I had done seems to be just good enough to pass and
I don't think it is at all up to the standard of the last three or four
stories I have done."

In a rather back door apology, he stated that Gail's producing
job had kept her "battling with all sorts of people who are arrogant
and conceited, using tact, ingenuity and stamina . . . carrying all
the responsibility of getting Perry Mason on the air . . . For God's
sake don't feel you are fighting me or that I am fighting you," he
wrote. "At any time you feel we have this problem licked, I am
completely content to abide by your judgment and shoot the works."
This letter was written one full year before Mason made his TV
debut.

He advised her to reach the point where she would "have to say to
Erle Gardner, 'I'm sorry but I don't think we can ever get a script
that will satisfy you while we're dealing with the present Guild rules
and the present writing situation as it exists in the industry to date.'

I'll keep calling the turns the way I see them," Gardner stated, "but you *must* remember that I am making suggestions to you of how I feel. I am not going to lie about it just because of the affection I have for you. —You have seen these actors, you have talked with the directors and producers. You feel enthusiastic about the shows. If you think they are going to make the grade, that's good enough for me."

After many vicissitudes and plenty of hard work all around, the *Perry Mason* show made its first appearance on television on September 21, 1957. It was an immediate success, and would continue to be one of the top-ranking television shows for close to nine years, until May 22, 1966. Reruns are still going strong. There was a built-in Perry Mason-Erle Stanley Gardner audience, to be sure, but it wouldn't have been around for half a dozen shows if there hadn't been all the qualities in the production which made for high-caliber entertainment.

After the second show, Erle wrote Gail, "I don't think I have ever seen a better show at any time on television than 'Sleepwalker's Niece' last Saturday night. I was so darned excited at how perfect it was I just couldn't settle down afterwards. —It had the suspense, intrigue and everything else one looks for and doesn't find in most plays and I kept wondering how on earth you ever chose every single actor so they were perfectly cast. —I saw the first one so imperfectly on a motel TV set that this is really my first one and I'm still thrilled whenever I think of it, and mentally say, 'Thank you, Gail, for everything you've done.' "

The success of the early Mason shows did not end Gardner's watchdog tactics concerning scripts. The *Perry Mason* show was never easy to write for, as any TV writer who tried it admitted freely. Yet many of the top TV names wrote for it: Jackson Gillis, John Meredyth Lucas, Leo Townsend, Malvin Wald, Philip MacDonald, Stirling Silliphant, Sam Newman, Arthur Orloff, Robert Dennis—the list seems endless. Eugene Wang, another lawyer-writer, later became a story editor whose taste upgraded submissions.

For as long as the show was in production, Gardner passed on every story from original presentation to final script. There was one writer, Seeleg Lester, whom he considered "to have tremendous abilities . . . I feel that Lester could be given the job of creating original plots and . . . could turn in first draft scripts which could be used with very little rewriting."

Sarcasm in his business letters is scarce, but in this following one he laid it on, a sure sign that he was burned up by the script-writing situation and getting more burned up by it as he wrote. "While it is true that I have only written a hundred books in the last twenty-five years, I am not unaware of the problems facing a writer who must work under pressure and at high speed." He then proceeded to relate his own records for speed.

In part of a memo to Gail that summer, Gardner said: "It is also necessary to face cold, hard facts. If we become too critical in our attitude and too demanding we are going to cause the good script writers to turn elsewhere and leave ourselves faced with the necessity of getting the show put together by script writers who aren't in the first string. . . . Of course, as you know, I don't know who writes a script when I comment on it, and I like to have things that way."

It wasn't that Gardner felt that the Mason books should be preserved in amber. In February 1961 he entertained the idea of putting a young assistant in Mason's office, to appeal to the younger generation, and also to bring in a love interest, which he continued to reject for Della and Perry. Obviously he had second thoughts on the addition because in October, in a memo regarding novelty in scripts, he pointed out that as early as the first two or three Perry Mason books, Hobson and his editors were writing that the characters were doing the same thing in the same way in the same environment and he wasn't going to keep his audience unless he changed. He refused to change, and it became obvious that the public didn't want a change. "Now, after nearly seventy Perry Mason books, when I even talk about an element of novelty, the publishers have kittens. —Tell a kid the story of the 'Three Bears' and the child wants to hear it over and over again. Try to change it and the kid has a fit."

From the earliest days of the TV show, there were those who wanted to change the basic premise of Perry Mason and his associates. For example, there were the critics who insisted Mason shouldn't win all of his cases. To which Gardner replied simply, if Mason loses a case, then the client is guilty, and we detract from Perry Mason's invincibility. The complaint that District Attorney Burger always lost was answered once and for all by Gail Patrick who stated flatly that Hamilton Burger won all his cases on Monday, Tuesday, Wednesday, Thursday, and Friday; only on Saturday (the night of the *Perry Mason* show) did he lose. Gardner had the final and conclusive word: "People haven't tired of that basic approach in a period of some twenty-five years."

Script difficulties did not abate. In August 1961, *Writer's Digest* in its television market list said of the *Perry Mason* show: "This show has the reputation among writers as being the hardest one in Hollywood to work for; for this reason there are fewer writers trying for it, since the money is as good as any other hour show."

By spring of 1962, the actors were adding to an already difficult situation. Burr criticized scripts publicly and continued to do so through the rest of the year. Gardner was low-key in protesting Burr's comments although he felt it poor public relations to attack one's own show in the public press.

By the next year, William Talman was joining in; his criticism was not of the scripts but of the characters. He compounded his poor judgment by quoting Gardner, who had never said, and never would say, the things attributed to him. This attack, although a mild one, was particularly hard to swallow, as Gardner had not only always praised Talman as an actor, but had stood foursquare against firing him after he was involved in a front-page scandal. Without Gardner's advising Paisano Productions to stand behind Talman, it is almost certain that he would have been summarily fired. Gardner's most telling comment on the Talman remarks was "when it comes to the field of public relations, that guy needs a guardian."

Gardner's concern with television scripts in these years had increased his workload to an onerous extent. Before taking off for Baja in 1960 to gather material for another travel book, he told Gail, "I want to do some adventuring and it is quite apparent that one of several things is going to have to happen." Number one: he'd have to give it up to edit scripts "at any hour of every day. This I don't like," he said, "first because I don't like it; second, because it is not good business. As my publishers realize, the more I can surround myself with glamour and adventure, particularly as I reach a statistical age * where people are going to regard me as an old fuddy-duddy, the more I can sell books and build up my publicity."

The alternative was to insist on scripts far enough ahead, which was "theoretically difficult and perhaps practically impossible." There were other points but nothing came of his tally except that the scripts were sent to him even in the wilderness.

With all its troubles, the Mason show continued to ride serene above its competitors until May 1966. Gardner's integrity had paid off. While other top-ranking shows faded and died from lack of good scripts, by his fussing and fuming and refusing to budge for poor material, Gardner kept the Mason show from becoming stale. At

* He was seventy-one that year.

its close, the show went immediately and with incredible success into syndication. After ten years of reruns, the public continued to echo the statement of one station manager: "Do you know what I want for the fall? I want another one hundred and ninety-five episodes of *Perry Mason*, this time in color."

Gardner expressed his opinions of the show in an article he wrote for *TV Guide* in 1959. These opinions are as pertinent now as then: "I am proud to be associated with the mystery story on television. Perry Mason represents a member of the legal profession who is fighting for human rights and liberties. I am proud of the fact that he has endeared himself to such a large audience and I am hoping that the people who see him will learn to appreciate the importance of the law and the necessity for fearless, intelligent lawyers who are, above all, primarily loyal to their clients. I don't claim television is perfect . . . but as I see the awakening of creative imagination, I suggest that we look at the *whole* picture of television, not just at the dark corners."

Part Seven

DIVERSITIES

Chapter Twenty-seven

THE COURT OF LAST RESORT was not a premeditated goal of Erle Stanley Gardner's; it evolved unexpectedly from a three-part article, "The Case of Erle Stanley Gardner," by Alva Johnston, published in the *Saturday Evening Post* in 1946 and in book form by Morrow the following year. While being interviewed, Gardner talked at length about one of his favorite subjects, his days as a lawyer defending the Chinese people of Oxnard, and as a result the finished piece devoted considerable space to Gardner as a champion of the underdog.

In his own unpublished autobiographical material, Gardner commented: "A person who hasn't had the actual experience can never visualize what happens when many millions of people see something in print." At the time, the *Saturday Evening Post* had a circulation of five or six million. This did not include all their readers, as the *Post*, being a family magazine, could have anywhere from two to ten per family. "All I know for sure," said Erle, "is that many, many million people read that I was the champion of the underdog. I was therefore literally deluged with underdogs who needed championing."

Although many appeals were what Gardner dubbed "the bum beef," a considerable number were seemingly valid. One of these was a case in which the lawyer, Al Matthews, had, in Erle's words, "picked an underdog for himself." Matthews was later to become widely known as a trial attorney, but at this time he was a young Los Angeles lawyer, trying to save from the death chamber a man convicted of rape-murder whom he believed to be innocent.

The convicted man, William Marvin Lindley, was a nobody, penniless, not mentally stable, who, in Gardner's words, had been "arrested for a sex murder, adjudged insane, sent to a state hospital

for the insane, and then, after a year or so, pronounced sane again.
. . . He had then been sent back to the county where the crime was
committed, tried, convicted of first degree, sentenced to death," and
the case had been affirmed on appeal by the state supreme court.

When Erle received the transcript, the date of execution was at
hand. The governor of California, Earl Warren, out of state at the
time, had left directions with the lieutenant governor, Frederick F.
Houser, that no more reprieves or stays were to be granted.

This was early in 1947 and also at hand were the February 3 deadline for a Perry Mason radio script, the February 5 deadline for a
Perry Mason mystery novel, and the February 8 deadline for launching his first full-scale exploration of Baja California. But as Gardner
said, "Of all deadlines, there is none more inexorable than that of
a death sentence."

In reading the transcript, Gardner realized that Al Matthews had
found evidence not only indicating that the wrong man had been
convicted, but also had quite probably put his finger on the actual
murderer. Against this was the seemingly insurmountable fact that
identification of Lindley had been positive, that circumstantial evidence was against him, and that the dying victim had, apparently,
accused him.

Gardner wrote, "I reconstructed the crime, not according to the
hands of a watch, but according to what must have been done by
certain people in order to fit into a pattern of continuity." And suddenly he found "the evidence in the case not only failed to prove
the defendant guilty beyond all reasonable doubt, but did prove
that it was a physical impossibility for him to have committed the
crime unless he could have been in two places at the same time. . .
The State of California was about to execute an innocent man."

Gardner at once wrote the governor's office and each member of
the state supreme court, and he sent to the attorney general copies
of the letters. There was no time for him to make a formal appearance, and it would scarcely have done any good, for every legal
channel had been explored thoroughly, and formally closed to the
defendant.

"Later, one of my friends who was a Justice of the California
Supreme Court told me that my letter created something of a sensa-
tion." Lieutenant Governor Houser granted a reprieve at once. And
when Governor Warren returned, he commuted the sentence to life
imprisonment in order to give opportunity for another investigation
to be made. Lindley was, in due time, found innocent.

Harry Steeger

Of all the friends in the book and magazine world, it would seem that Harry Steeger, publisher of *Argosy* and other magazines, was the one most compatible with Gardner when it came to adventuring in the wilds. He was at home around a campfire.

So when Gardner made a flying trip to New York early in 1948, he dropped in after hours on the offices of *Argosy* to see his old friend Harry Steeger. At the time Steeger was experimenting with a change in the magazine and was not very pleased with developments. In discussing the problems concerned, Erle mentioned that no magazine had ever done anything really to improve the administration of justice, that it was a wide open field. He then proceeded to draw a general outline of the idea of the Court of Last Resort. Steeger became enthusiastic and brought his partner over to Gardner's hotel later the same evening to discuss it further. The partner turned down the idea.

It was probably at this time that Steeger expressed interest in traveling to Baja over the route Erle had taken the preceding year. Steeger was a great camper and his wife, Shirley, a member of the New York Botanical Society, was deeply interested in the flora of new places. Gardner immediately began making plans to repeat the twelve-hundred-mile drive for their benefit.

In March they started off, Jean and Erle driving jeeps, accompanied by their guests, Sam driving a Dodge Power Wagon loaded with camping gear. And inevitably, one evening the Lindley case came into their talk around the campfire. It was then that Steeger, partner or no partner, decided to go ahead with the Court.

Night after night in Baja, Gardner and Steeger discussed pros and cons. What was often not understood, although Gardner stressed it in all of his writing, was that the actual "Court of Last Resort" was the people. "It is customary in legal circles to refer to the highest tribunal in any jurisdiction as 'the court of last resort.' In a democratic government, public sentiment is the ultimate authority."

They talked over how a case could be presented to the people and what the reactions might be, and what effect these reactions might have on the government. As they talked about it, Gardner, the lawyer, posed problems. What could be done for the better administration of justice? What was the percentage of guilty men who were wrongfully acquitted? What was the percentage of innocent men who were wrongfully convicted? The very freedom of camping in the wilderness under the stars gave Gardner an extra perception of what it must mean to be an innocent man locked away in a cell. He would lie awake in the night cogitating, knowing what it would do to him to be wrongfully deprived of freedom. One morning he spoke of this, only to find that Steeger had the same thoughts at night.

They had made some firm decisions before their return from Mexico. Steeger would give space in *Argosy* to publicize the cases of innocent men who had been wrongfully convicted. Gardner would write up the cases. Both men realized they'd get nowhere if the magazine were to say, in effect: "We think John Doe has been wrongfully convicted because Erle Stanley Gardner says he has; therefore, you readers should demand that John Doe be pardoned."

"We needed to have evidence," Gardner said. "We needed to have facts and figures, and we needed to have a group of experts who would be willing to donate their services in the interests of justice; men who were well known in their fields, who were expert as criminal investigators; men who had no particular need of personal publicity. We needed men who would be willing to donate their services because something of this sort must necessarily be put across on a basis of real public interest and not as a means of boosting personal incomes."

In the give and take of their discussion, the idea came of a Board of Investigators. They thought at once of Dr. LeMoyne Snyder.

Members of the Court of Last Resort: from left to right,
Marshall Houts, Alex Gregory, Dr. LeMoyne Snyder,
Harry Steeger, Raymond Schindler, Park Street, Gardner

Dr. Snyder was both an attorney and a physician. In the field of
forensic medicine, he was a noted expert. He was author of *Homicide Investigation*, still considered the authority on this subject.

Gardner lined up other experts, the best man in each field. The
detective, Raymond Schindler, with whom Gardner had become
acquainted on the Oakes case, was asked to head detection, and
Dr. Leonarde Keeler to be in charge of the polygraph. Keeler, a
pioneer in the field, died shortly thereafter, and was replaced by
Alex Gregory, a past president of the Academy of Scientific Interrogation, and an outstanding authority on the use of the polygraph.
Clark Sellers, internationally known handwriting expert, volunteered to help whenever there was anything needed from his field.
In all respects, a noteworthy group was put together.

Only a few weeks after Gardner and Steeger returned from Baja,
and before they had time to put it into action, the Court was presented with its first case, that of Clarence Boggie, an Oregon lumberjack, serving a life term for murder. It was brought to Gardner's attention by the Reverend W. A. (Bill) Gilbert, rector of St. Paul's
Episcopal Church in Ventura, California, and part-time voluntary
chaplain at the state penitentiary in Walla Walla, Washington. He
became another of Erle's closest friends as well as an enthusiastic
working member of the Court's organization. Also as a result of this

The Reverend Bill Gilbert and Gardner

case, the Court added two more surprising members, Tom Smith, warden of the Walla Walla penitentiary, a man characterized by Gardner as an idealist with a passionate desire for justice, and his assistant, Bob Rhay. When they left their positions at the prison, they became valuable members of the Court's investigative team.

Unusually important help came to the Court less than two years after its formation. Henry Franklin, a young New Hampshire attorney who had been a member of the FBI, asked and was given permission to organize an auxiliary committee of lawyers who, like himself, had had experience with the FBI. The subcommittee he formed included E. Cage Brewer, Jr., of Clarksdale, Mississippi; Philip V. Christenson of Provo, Utah; John C. Firmin of Findlay, Ohio; Thomas E. Heffernan of Corona del Mar, California; W. Logan Huiskamp of Keokuk, Iowa; Paul F. Kelly of San Francisco; Donald A. Rosen of Los Angeles; and Marshall W. Houts of Tulsa, Oklahoma.

When he was in Oklahoma City to speak before the Oklahoma Bar Association in 1952, Gardner met Marshall Houts personally. Recalling the meeting, Houts has said that Gardner was a vigorous, hearty, robust man, although he was then in his mid-sixties, and never in better form than addressing the meeting. Gardner took to

Houts at once, believed he had great potential, and initiated steps to get him on the Court team. He was able to have Houts named General Counsel for the Court, in which position he traveled over the country to investigate cases and compile the results. According to the initial agreement in setting up the Court, Gardner arranged that Houts's salary would be paid by *Argosy*. When internal trouble struck in 1953 and Houts was let go with only two days' warning, Gardner put Houts on his own payroll until Houts was relocated in medicolegal work in California.

Erle did not neglect his writing for his work with the Court, he simply added on the extra hours. How, only he could explain. But for some ten years, according to his own figuring, the activities of the Court took up approximately eighty percent of his time. It led to many "interrelated activities" concerning justice and law enforcement, led him to speaking dates throughout the country before law organizations and law enforcement officials, and to receiving many honors in the legal field.

Perhaps nothing in his entire career meant as much to Gardner as the Court. He explains it in detail, and tells of many of the cases handled, in his book *The Court of Last Resort*, published by William Sloane Associates in 1952 and reprinted in an augmented edition by Pocket Books in 1954. *Atlantic Monthly*'s Charles W. Morton, commenting on the book in his magazine, wrote, "a remarkable handbook on criminal jurisprudence and penology . . . full of extraordinary insights on the part of the author into human behavior, the ennobling as well as the destructive."

Gardner dedicated the Court book to Steeger, writing, "I have known Steeger for some twenty-five years, during which time there has been a close, friendly association which I value as one of my most cherished relationships. . . . And now, on behalf of my associates and myself, I want to make public thanks to him for the steadfastness of purpose which made The Court of Last Resort possible. . . ."

That the Court was an important feature in *Argosy* was attested by the many letters received from readers concerning its activities. Perhaps the largest response concerned the Sheppard case when readers believed the Court had withdrawn from it. This was only in part true, as Gardner explained in the magazine: "The Court did not withdraw from the Sheppard case, it withdrew from Ohio when its hands were tied. We did not start to investigate the Sheppard case as such, but undertook preliminary steps leading towards that investigation." In this case, Dr. Samuel H. Sheppard of Cleveland had been convicted of the murder of his wife. He had never ceased protesting his innocence. When the Court of Last Resort considered the case, it was agreed in advance that if lie detector tests given members of the Sheppard family showed that they had no connection with the crime, the Court investigators would try for a polygraph examination of Dr. Sheppard. If this test showed him innocent, the CLR would try to bring about his release. When the Court group returned to Ohio from negative tests of the family in Florida, the permission to examine Dr. Sheppard was withdrawn. There was thus no alternative but for the Court to withdraw.

At about this time, the Court began to have internal problems. Whether by coincidence or for other reasons, the fortunes of *Argosy* had taken an upward spiral with the introduction of the CLR feature. Some of the editors weren't happy about it, according to Gardner. With his usual objectivity, seeing all sides as well as the top and bottom of a problem, he agreed, "You can see the thing from the viewpoint of an editor. He was charged with the responsibility of the magazine yet he had nothing to do with the Court of Last Resort. That was handled by Steeger and Gardner. If the magazine was a flop, the editor was responsible. If it increased in circulation, the Court of Last Resort got a good amount of the credit. Naturally no editor liked this. After four or five years when things began to level off, there was a great deal of editorial hostility, which I heard about from time to time."

This led to a breach between the old friends. Gardner resigned from the Court and quit writing for the magazine. Later, when Steeger learned some of the background which had caused the breach, he asked Gardner to return to active participation.

Erle returned and was permitted to publish in the March 1955 issue of *Argosy* a RESTATEMENT OF PURPOSE. It began: "Harry Steeger has promised me I can have space in this issue to talk to you readers, and that what I have to say won't be edited, condensed, changed or revised. . . . I want to find out how you feel, and I want to tell you how I feel."

Reviewing the purpose and activity of the Court until then, he wrote that it seemed to have lost sight of the fact that its purpose was to improve the administration of justice, but gradually had come to be devoted solely to investigating cases of men who claimed to be innocent and wrongfully convicted. Once jockeyed into that position, the organization had been buried under an avalanche of cases, eight thousand of which had had preliminary investigation. He, Gardner, felt money had been thrown away for months just trying to sift the wheat from the chaff.

In summing up, he stated his belief that "the Court has reached a critical stage in its development. It has to know where it's going from here. I'd certainly like to have you readers write in and tell the magazine just how you feel. I'm personally willing to make great sacrifices if I can feel these sacrifices will help improve the administration of justice. I'm far too busy to run around trying to pick up all the grains of sand on the seashore. . . .

"So what do you want done?"

The letters came in, and for a while there was a rejuvenation of the Court. However, the need for single-handedly selecting cases, investigating and writing about them, along with handling his own involved literary affairs became too much of a strain on Gardner. There were times, he admitted, when the articles he wrote were "pretty thin as far as factual content was concerned."

Editorial hostility was renewed. It was demonstrated in part by playing down Gardner's articles. Before long he had heard "from sources which I couldn't discount, the fact that some of the employees of *Argosy* were stating that Gardner might be a good mystery writer but that his articles didn't amount to much as far as reader interest was concerned. . . ."

Gardner the businessman came to the fore, as always whenever anything threatened his writing stature. Being the producer, it was up to him to keep the product always salable, and not just salable, but salable at a high price. On April 28, 1960, he stated: "I simply couldn't afford to have a condition of this sort exist and this time I retired from the Court of Last Resort and simply quit writing [for *Argosy*]." This did not end his friendship with Harry Steeger. He said in the same discourse, "I feel very close to Harry. I enjoy being out with him. I value his friendship."

Gardner recommended Gene Lowall of the Denver *Post*, with whom he had worked as a trained seal, to take his place on the Court. He hoped that the organization would continue. Unfortunately there was a change of viewpoint with Gardner's withdrawal. Instead of cases being undertaken "with the idea of putting on a slow, steady, continual pressure to effect the release of innocent men," they seemed to be undertaken for "the purpose of making a spectacular appeal to the reader—or at least, so it seemed to me. The big point was that after the journalistic cream had been skimmed off, they were virtually dropped."

It wasn't easy for Gardner to forsake something which had meant so much to him. With the Court, he was what he wanted to be, a crusading lawyer again, fighting for the rights of the innocent man. He *was* Perry Mason, investigating, and by uncovering the truth, freeing the wrongly accused person. But on July 3, "which was a Sunday," he dictated a memo to his former Court colleagues, "in which I virtually dissolved partnership with Steeger and severed my connections with the Court of Last Resort. I tried to do it without rancor and . . . from a broad-minded viewpoint . . ."

The immediate cause of the break was the Chessman case, which was controversial from its inception. Caryl Chessman, having been convicted on seventeen counts and under the death sentence for kidnapping Mary Meja and Regina Johnson, had managed from death row to have his own story of his crimes published. The movement for his release was instigated by the far, far left, but managed to involve many more persons, and became world-publicized. The attitude of *Argosy* magazine in the Chessman affair was too much for Gardner to take.

Simultaneously, in New York, Steeger was dissolving the partnership with Gardner. A few days earlier he had, in fact, sent a tape recording to Temecula stating this. Because of the Fourth of July holiday, it was delayed, but it finally arrived. Gardner reported, "Steeger calls a spade a spade. He takes me to task because he says the Court of Last Resort is petered out, that it's a disgrace to both of us, that he doesn't want to be connected with anything that's a failure and wants me to quit writing letters and get on the job, call a meeting and get things started again . . ."

In justification of his own stand, Gardner said concerning the Court, "I had built it up during the past few years to a point where governors were attentive to what we had to say, where parole boards were very, very friendly; in fact, I've had several parole boards suggest that they were glad to have us look into cases. We had police looking at us, not quite so cordially, but understanding what we were trying to do. This article on the Chessman case lambastes the police and gives the authorities hell and announces that *Argosy* has taken on the mantle in order to go ahead and give a posthumous vindication for Caryl Chessman."

He states his opinion quite clearly: "I didn't believe Caryl Chessman should have been executed, largely because of the effect on international prestige as far as the administration of American justice is concerned, and also because I didn't think sex crimes should be punishable by death. But as far as Caryl Chessman himself is concerned, he was a criminal psychopath, an egomaniac and very definitely opposed to law, and I don't think myself there was any question about his guilt, although I never really made a study of the evidence in the case. To try and come out and make that fellow a sanctified hero, and lambaste the police and intimate that they let him go to his death by withholding information and so forth, runs directly contrary to the dignity and prestige I have been trying to build up for the Court of Last Resort."

In his final word on the subject, or almost final because Gardner did not ever speak a final word on a subject about which he had decided opinions, he said, "Steeger may be right in stating that the Court of Last Resort didn't hold the readers of the magazine, but it sure as hell made the Court of Last Resort a household word throughout the United States and if *Argosy* had been able to keep up with the Court of Last Resort, or rather, the concept of the Court of Last Resort, it would have elevated *Argosy* in dignity and prestige no end."

It was an unhappy end to a project started and fostered with high ideals. It had meant more than ten years' demanding work for Gardner. It had also meant the devoting of a considerable amount of his income yearly to further the work, for with all his hardheaded business sense, he more often than not paid his own out-of-pocket expenses. It had brought to him greater honor than he received in any other of his ventures. There was a widespread recognition of what he had accomplished, not only by lawmakers in the United States but also by those in other nations.

In one of his last books, written when he was in his eightieth year, Gardner named some of his prized honors: "I am an Honorary Texas Ranger with the rank of captain. I am a deputy in several counties in Texas. I have a diamond-studded star presented to me by the Texas Sheriffs' Association. The city trustees of Wichita, Kansas, appointed me an honorary chief of police of Wichita. I am a life member of the Kansas Peace Officers' Association. I am one of the one hundred Gold Star Deputies of Alameda County, California, and a deputy sheriff of Butte and of Riverside counties in California. I am an honorary member of the Fraternal Order of Police. I have spent a great deal of time patrolling with officers in radio cars. I have twice been invited to and attended Captain Frances G. Lee's seminars in homicide investigation at Harvard University. I am an honorary lifetime member of the American Polygraph Association, and I have a backlog of twenty-five years courtroom experience as a trial lawyer. . . . For the past thirty years I have been interested in homicide investigation and in police science. Some twenty-two years ago I helped organize the so-called Court of Last Resort, and from my experience with that organization, learned a lot about the investigation of crime."

Because of his work with the Court, he had made himself a lay expert in scientific methods of detection. He had studied forensic medicine, polygraph work, and criminal psychology to hold his own in discussions of the subjects with professionals in the field. His "Ten Steps to Justice," published untitled as the final chapter of the Pocket Books edition of *The Court of Last Resort*, was the format for what he hoped would be achieved through the Court. These "Ten Steps" were to become an important study in law enforcement and legal circles.

The last of his non-fiction works, *Cops on Campus and Crime in the Streets*, was published by William Morrow on January 30, 1970, only slightly over a month before he died. It was written at a time of great national ferment, when the student revolutionists seemingly had gained control, not only over their campuses, but over those who would enforce the law. As his own grandson was a college student at the time, Gardner had more than a cursory interest in what was happening. In the opinion of many lawyers, there has not been a more reasoned, just, and honest statement of all sides of late-twentieth-century law enforcement problems than in this work. It would seem destined to be a classic statement.

Marshall Houts, who worked more closely than any other person with Gardner on the legal matters of the Court, and who, furthermore, was associated with him in seminars at the UCLA law school, says that the impact Gardner made on the administration of justice cannot be overemphasized. In 1948, when the Court was formed, "no one in law cared two hoots about criminal law and criminal justice." What Gardner and the investigative committee found out about the state of criminal justice in the United States was shocking, and Gardner went around saying so. There had never been an overall study of the entire crime picture. There were few police training programs. In some cities, the police had never been on a firing range, because there was no firing range, and no money for one. In many places the police were paid no more than fifty dollars a month, and had to buy their own uniforms and side arms. As late as 1954, in one large midwestern city, police received only ninety dollars a month.

But it was not alone the police and the judges and attorneys who benefited from Gardner's crusade. What he accomplished in the area of prison reform was notable. For thirty years he had been pressing against inequities in this area, in cooperation with Jim Bennett, director of the United States Bureau of Prisons. The publicity he could give through the Court cases made some important changes.

For reforms in trial procedure, Gardner went all the way to the top, the United States Supreme Court. He can be credited with helping bring about the Supreme Court ruling that a man on trial, and without funds for legal help, is entitled to a lawyer paid for by the state. And that the accused is also entitled to expert witnesses and to independent experts, and to study the prosecution's pathology and fingerprint reports. All at the expense of the state.

As early as 1951, the American Bar Association, aware of what Gardner was striving for, appointed a committee on criminal justice to work with the Court of Last Resort. And in the late fifties, the ABA went to the Ford Foundation for funds with which to inaugurate the first full-scale investigation of American justice. Out of this investigation came President Lyndon Johnson's establishment of a crime commission, the first in the United States.

Everyone who knew him well has said it: In his heart, Erle Stanley Gardner was always the lawyer. No matter his success as an author, no matter the world fame, he thought of himself always as a lawyer who had left the law to write stories. Not because he was a failure in law. On the contrary, it was his success, and rapidly growing greater success as an attorney, that made him quit the profession.

"I had sense enough to realize that the more successful I became as an attorney," he wrote in the June 1965 *Atlantic Monthly*, "the more I would be chained to one office, one desk, one chair, and one county seat." But like the country and the boy, he could take Gardner out of the law but could never take the lawyer out of Gardner.

When the Court of Last Resort was finally dissolved, Gardner arranged to pass its work to the American Polygraph Association. For various legal reasons, the name had to be changed, and the board of directors of the association took the new name Case Review Committee. It is still active.

While working with the Court, Gardner had become exceedingly interested in the polygraph, or as it is popularly called, "the lie detector." He learned of the research program in the field of scientific interrogation which C. B. "Chick" Hanscom was working on at the University of Minnesota. He immediately arranged a meeting with Hanscom in Chicago. They became close personal friends.

With his usual whole-bodied enthusiasm for a program in which he believed, Gardner, whenever possible, loaned himself to further the program of the organization, a part of which was university training and a degree required of all examiners. He arranged to appear at the polygraph conventions, usually as the main speaker, and never accepted an honorarium, not even expenses for himself. He gave innumerable press interviews and made radio and TV appearances to promote the cause. His final appearance at an association meeting was in Houston in late August 1969. He was scheduled as guest speaker, but three weeks beforehand he called Hanscom to say that he was ill and would be unable to attend. Hanscom informed the association president, who without telling Hanscom called Gardner to say how much they needed him, since the association had recently received much adverse publicity from a member of the United States Senate. Erle got out of bed and went, Jean and Sam accompanying him.

Hanscom was shocked at Gardner's appearance when he arrived, he was so pale and wan. After taking Gardner to his hotel, Hanscom went on to a board meeting where he severely criticized the president for urging a man as ill as Gardner to come to the meeting. Gardner heard of this and admonished Hanscom, saying that if the APA needed his help, he was proud and happy to give it. He gave press, radio, and TV interviews as he lay on the couch in his suite. Yet he appeared on his feet to speak with wit and humor at the banquet, and from there took part in an hour-long TV show.

It wasn't the first first time that Gardner had changed his program to appear for the benefit of the APA. There was one occasion when, because of a heavy workload, he had refused an invitation to speak to a convocation at the University of Minnesota. The invitation was a signal honor; among celebrities who had spoken there were Haile Selassie and Admiral Halsey. Two vice-presidents of the university, knowing of the Gardner-Hanscom friendship, asked Hanscom to see if he could get Gardner to come. Erle's answer to

Gardner and Jean with C. B. "Chick" Hanscom at American Polygraph Association
annual seminar in Houston, Texas, 1969

Hanscom was, "If my coming will in any way help you, then I will come."

"It was during the middle of winter," Hanscom recalls, "and Minnesota was experiencing one of its most severe winters in many years, twenty-five to thirty degrees below zero, and serious blizzards. Yet he came, 'just to help a friend.'"

Despite the rigors of the trip, he did his usual job of charming all who heard him. Not only that, he visited the state penitentiary, forty-five miles away on icy roads, because the prisoners had invited him to come. When Hanscom took him to the airport after the festivities, "he was happy as a young boy. I went home and went to bed; I was bushed, and a much younger man than Uncle Erle."

Chapter Twenty-eight

GARDNER HAD BEEN a visitor to Tijuana and Ensenada as far back as 1910. In his Ventura days, a friend had invited him to join a sailing party to the tip of Baja California, called Cabo San Lucas, and to San José del Cabo. This holiday ended in manic abruptness when en route the boat tilted over and marooned itself in the shallows off the coast, and the guests disembarked to return home by other transportation. The long-term result of that particular experience was the friendship of Anita Haskell Jones, who was a member of the party on board.

Gardner had made one trip from Tijuana to Ensenada "when the roads were mere washed-out car tracks." Somewhat later, he traveled by automobile to the sportsmen's haven, Hamilton Ranch, below Ensenada, when the road was "a nightmare."

Why, first the interest in exploring Baja, and later his love affair with Baja? It isn't too difficult to figure; Baja was at hand. In a bit over an hour's drive from his ranch, he could be in Mexico. No tickets, no time wasted sitting around airports or railway stations or harbors.

But his interest in Baja went back beyond his Rancho days: ". . . The lure of Lower California was originally implanted in my mind by a geography which I studied in grammar school. This geography showed the sea coast of Lower California as a thin green border, interspersed with the names of one or two cities. The entire interior of the peninsula was depicted in blank, marked with the word 'unexplored.' This, of course, was far from being the case. The worthy Spanish Fathers had explored the interior of Baja California a hundred and fifty years before the geography had been compiled. Baja California had missions for almost a hundred years before the first mission was built in Alta California at San Diego. Doubtless the geographers, confronted with the fact that no accurate maps were in existence, simply tossed the whole thing out of the window and let it go at that. After all, no one would care about the interior of Baja California."

It should be said here that Erle Stanley Gardner's affinity for the Mexican people was not something that was slowly developed. It was instant rapport. Everyone is aware of how certain peoples are simpatico to him, whereas others are not. It is a matter of style and spirit; or for those who insist, of chemistry. The Mexican people possessed the qualities Erle most admired. They were warm-natured and valued friendship; they had pride and dignity and self-respect. Certainly he also admired them for their courtesy, a good New England virtue which he valued, increasingly hard to find in a changing world. He gave them and they gave him love and friendship. They were easy together; perhaps that is the basis for likes and dislikes.

What gave his Baja "air castle" a real foundation seems to have been a map published in the late forties by the Automobile Club of Southern California. Two hardy explorers had been sent down to cover the ground of Baja for the purpose of making the map. Gardner acquired it on publication. He studied "the long dirt road, eleven hundred and eighty-seven miles of it, winding down the peninsula, threading its way across mountains and dry lakes, up sandy washes and across the rock-strewn beds of dry streams, inching its way around the precipitous sides of tall mountain ranges, dipping alternately into the Gulf on the east and the Pacific Ocean on the west," and began making plans to drive down it.

On February 8, 1947, Gardner launched his first expedition to the peninsula. On his return he began his series of thirteen travel books, which would cover not only Baja explorations but also his desert roaming and his forays into deeper Mexico. Later he would also write of his explorations of the Sacramento Delta.

The first Baja book, *The Land of Shorter Shadows*, was published in April 1948. In 1954 he combined four of his adventurelands in *Neighborhood Frontiers*, a book designed by Merle Armitage which features exquisite sepia photographs of his travels from Puget Sound to the Barranca country of Mexico, with stop-offs between. He returned to writing about Baja in 1960 with *Hunting the Desert Whale*, which for typical Gardner adventuring cannot be equaled. Everything that could happen happened: rain, wind, marooned boats, the necessity of flying back and forth across the border because of trouble at home with TV scripts on the Mason show—and Gardner was just past his seventieth year. He found the whales and he, Jean, and Sam photographed them. In 1961 came *Hovering Over Baja,* which tells of exploring by methods varying from the Pak Jak ("something of a cross between a motorcycle, a scooter, and an army tank"), invented by a Paradise, California, friend and fellow explorer, J. W. Black, to the first use of helicopters by him below the border.

The most incredible of his adventures, *The Hidden Heart of Baja,* was published in 1962. He had returned, again with helicopters, to explore further inaccessible places, and had made an important archaeological find of prehistoric cave paintings. He went back to the ranch after his first look at them in order to mount a full-scale expedition to study this discovery. This time he took with him Dr. Clement Meighan, a professor of archaeology at UCLA, who later wrote a detailed study of the caves, *Indian Art and History: The Testimony of Prehispanic Rock Paintings in Baja California.* This has been made a part of the Baja California Travel Series. At the time of Gardner's expedition, no Mexican archaeologist was free to accompany the Gardner party. On a second full-scale expedition sometime after, Dr. Carlos R. Margain of El Museo Nacional de Antropología in Mexico City, accompanied Erle and his party. Dr. Margain gave full credit to Gardner for uncovering this important prehistoric treasure.

Later Gardner wrote *Off the Beaten Track in Baja* and *Mexico's Magic Square,* the story of his blimp expedition, published in 1967 and 1968 respectively. All the travel books are more than just accounts of his traveling; they are documents of his friendships on both sides of the border. They are filled with campfire stories and anecdotes of his years of adventuring. His own photography, as well as that of Sam and Jean and a few others, illustrates them. In truth, the travel books are a major part of the autobiographical material that he never had time to put together into an autobiography.

Between *The Hidden Heart of Baja* in 1962, which told of the caves, and the retracing of the old byways and the discovering of new in *Off the Beaten Track in Baja* in 1967, Gardner wrote nothing concerning his favorite peninsula. In 1963 there was the Southwest desert book, *The Desert Is Yours,* and in 1965 *Hunting Lost Mines by Helicopter,* also about the Southwest. He had found the Delta in 1964 and wrote of it in *The World of Water.* But he wrote nothing more about Baja California.

Dr. Carlos Margain and Gardner

This was due not to disenchantment with its by now familiar beauties or with the tremendous secrets yet unexplored but to the most extraordinary circumstance of Gardner's being barred from Baja. If caught crossing the border, he would face being arrested and thrown in jail.

The strange affair began in 1964 with a letter from Señor César Osuna Peralta Delgado of Santiago, who wrote of other cave paintings and some fish-fossil beds found in his neighborhood. He invited Gardner to come view them. This Erle was eager to do; therefore with Jean and Sam, and with his good pilot, Captain Muñoz, flying them, they took off for La Paz.

On arrival, Erle went to the hotel to rest up a bit, as did Jean. Sam and Muñoz went down to the park on the bay and were enjoying a beer at a café when uniformed officials approached and informed them that they had been told Erle Stanley Gardner was in La Paz, and demanded to know where he was. They had a warrant for his arrest and displayed it for Sam and Muñoz to read.

The charges were the wholly unbelievable ones that Gardner had been stealing archaeological treasures from Baja and taking them back across the border to Alta California; and that he had used bulldozers to destroy valuable archaeological sites. Such obviously trumped-up accusations made it clear to Captain Muñoz that Gardner was being used as a pawn in some political squabble in Baja.

Both men denied that Gardner was in La Paz. Their story, ad-libbed, was that the captain had been flying down to La Paz for the day and that Sam had decided to accompany him. Whether the police official believed them, or whether he simply wanted to believe them and avoid arresting Gardner, he and his men departed.

When they felt it was safe, Sam and Muñoz made their way to the hotel. They told Jean what had happened. She was to pass the word along to Erle and make sure that he remained in his hotel room until night, when under cover of darkness they would transport him to the airport and all of them would take off for the border.

This they did, Muñoz flying them out at three o'clock in the morning. On their arrival in Tijuana, they learned from officials there, who were, of course, longtime friends of Gardner and his associates, that they had had a like warrant for some time. They hadn't said or done anything about it, because they knew it was just a political maneuver. In fact, they just laughed at it. There was no difficulty there in Gardner's getting back to California.

Gardner had no intention of going back again to Baja until the entire affair had been righted, both in Mexico and at the Mexican consulate in Los Angeles. His first step was to inform Gilberto González Muzquiz of Chihuahua. The Muzquiz family had been close friends from the time the late José Gandara had taken Gardner into the Barranca country, an adventure related in *Neighborhood Frontiers*. On that occasion, Señor Muzquiz had sent his son Gilberto along to help with the supplies and driving. Gardner did not know then how important this family was, with their hundreds of thousands of acres of timberland, their lumber business, and their cattle ranches.

After the senior Muzquiz's death, the sons took over the multiple business interests. One son, Mario González Muzquiz, was honored as Executive of the Year in Mexico in the late sixties. Another son was José G. González Muzquiz, a prominent attorney in Mexico City. Gardner's friendship with Gilberto was so close that he was invited to be a "sponsor" at the marriages of each of Gilberto's daughters, Blanquita and Natalia. He, Jean, and Sam attended both weddings in Chihuahua.

When Gardner told his friend of his La Paz experience, Gilberto immediately informed his brother, José, who in turn passed the information to Licenciado Miguel Alemán, then head of the tourist bureau in Mexico. Alemán immediately got in touch with Wulfrano Ruiz, who was a more or less unofficial member of the bureau, a troubleshooter for Alemán. When Alemán had been president of Mexico, Ruiz was one of the most important members of his diplomatic corps, being the official who set up the trade agreements between Mexico and France after World War II, and who continued to handle Mexican missions throughout Europe and northern Africa. Ruiz wears the French Legion of Honor rosette in his lapel and has received all of Mexico's highest awards.

Licenciado Alemán asked Ruiz to try to make amends for the insult to Gardner and to take the necessary steps to reinstate him as an honored visitor to Mexico. Ruiz called the ranch, but Erle wasn't there. After numerous calls, Ruiz appealed to Peggy, who was in charge of affairs in Erle's absence. Peggy managed to locate him on the Delta. When Erle received the message, he and Sam drove at once to Sacramento and caught a plane to San Diego. There David Hurtado met them and drove them to the ranch. The next day Ricardo Castillo, Gardner's camping friend, the Tijuana restaurateur, drove Señor Ruiz and a Ruiz son to Temecula to present Mexico's apologies. Later that week, Erle, Sam, and Peggy motored to Tijuana for lunch at the Ruiz home, where further apologies were offered. However, Gardner would not go again into Baja until all matters had also been cleared with the Mexican consulate in Los Angeles.

This was the beginning of Señor Ruiz's attempts, at the behest of Alemán, to arrange a trip to Mexico City where Gardner could be honored by the head of state. Erle kept turning down the invitation. He pled a minor heart condition, and said that plunging into such social activity without time for gradual acclimation to the altitude of Mexico City, more than seven thousand feet, seemed unwise.

He also turned down a motor trip because he did not have the time to spare for a journey of that length. And then Ruiz came up with the idea of traveling by train, a special private train, to Mexico City. There were no more excuses. Mr. and Mrs. Ruiz were the host couple on the journey. Jean and Sam were guests, of course, and among the others whom Gardner invited to go along were Corney Jackson, who found many tennis *compadres* in Mexico City, and young Doug Allen, who was at the time filming his documentary of Gardner.

The journey became the book *Host with the Big Hat*. It was preceded in publication by two other books in the genre: *Off the Beaten Track in Baja* in 1967, about an exploration into the interior of Baja and along its coastline augmented by the helicopters which found the more inaccessible corners, and *Mexico's Magic Square* in 1968, the account of one of the greatest adventures of them all, that of the Goodyear blimp. Sam and Erle had been driving home from San Diego one day, and noting the one method of transportation that they hadn't used in Baja, Erle decided to arrange a visit by blimp. This he did, and he and a party rode the blimp over the square from Tijuana to Mexicali to San Felipe to Rosario and return, with interim flights over the interior.

On their return Gardner learned that the then president of Mexico, Gustavo Díaz Ordaz, was coming the next week to Tijuana on an official visit. Gardner went into action. The Goodyear company and the Mexican officials were persuaded "to cut all red tape," and when El Presidente arrived, the blimp was "floating over the night sky with its illuminated messages of welcome—a remarkably impressive sight." That was the year Gardner reached his seventy-ninth birthday.

There was no rest after the blimp holiday. He scarcely had time to go back to the ranch before returning to Tijuana for a two-day celebration in his honor. And the following week he was honored at a banquet in Ensenada.

Host with the Big Hat was the last of his travel books. It was published in January 1970, just two months before his death. It was his farewell to Mexico, filled with his genuine affection for the country and the people, filled with the photographs he took, and expressing his appreciation for the royal reception he was given, not only in Mexico City but all along the route.

But this was not enough. When he wrote, he always had to give more than full value, and he decided to add the story of the Acámbaro mystery to the train story. In August he went to that little town, between Mexico City and Guadalajara, home of the astonishing Julsrud collection of some thirty-six thousand prehistoric figures dug from the surrounding earth. The collection had been in existence many years when Erle heard about it and was persuaded to look into its authenticity. There is still controversy as to whether the collection is authentic or a gigantic hoax. Gardner took no irrevocable stand on it; he simply presented the evidence. Even more than his discovery of the caves, the story of Acámbaro may be the crowning achievement of his archaeological investigations.

Part Eight

THE
FINAL YEARS

Chapter Twenty-nine

IN THE ACADEMIC CENTER at the University of Texas in Austin there is an Erle Stanley Gardner room in the center of which is his study, just as it was in the days when he worked in it. The outer walls of the study are replicas, but within, it is the real room. The walls are hung with Gardner trophies and mementos. His great desk is there, his oversized desk chair, his dictating machines and typewriters and his files. On the desk are the memorabilia he gathered from all over the world. The bookshelves are crowded with his books, each one where he placed it himself. The Navajo rugs, his gun collection and his lassos, his drums, many of his awards—his favorite things are all there. With the push of a button, you can hear Uncle Erle himself, on a tape he made for the purpose, telling about his treasures.

A short walk across a campus of green grass, tall trees, flowers, and fountains brings one to the handsome modern building of the Humanities Research Center. Here are housed some of the most important manuscript collections of modern writing. With the increase of vandalism in today's world, security is tight at the building. You must have permission to take the special elevator to the fourth floor library, where Gardner's books, manuscripts, and papers are housed, including certain files which are not to be opened until some as yet undivulged future date.

And how did the Gardner archives come to the University of Texas instead of to one of the great universities of his own state of California? The answer is that Texas asked. Not until Gardner had agreed to send his material to Texas did California make any overtures. It was then too late.

Actually it all started, as so many things did for Gardner, with the Court of Last Resort. If there had not been a Court, Park Street,

Dr. R. B. H. Gradwohl and Gardner in Temecula study

a prominent San Antonio lawyer, would not have met Gardner, worked with him, and become one of his good friends. And Park Street would not have introduced Gardner to Dr. Merton M. Minter, founder of the Minter Clinic in San Antonio, and a member of the Board of Regents of the University of Texas.

Dr. Minter first met Gardner when he was speaking at the annual Law Enforcement Conference, instituted by the then attorney general of Texas, John Ben Sheppard, who became another great Gardner friend. Later, when Gardner served as an advisory director to the Texas Law Enforcement Foundation, Dr. Minter worked with him and became one of his closest friends.

Dr. Minter was named a regent of the university in 1955 and served until 1961, later becoming chairman of the Board of Regents. While eating breakfast one morning (according to his account, he eats rather early), he had a telephone call from Dr. Harry Ransom, then chancellor of the University of Texas. The night before, Dr. Ransom had started to read Erle Stanley Gardner's *The Case of the Daring Decoy*. He noted with surprise and pleasure that the dedication was to Merton Melrose Minter, M.D.

Dr. Ransom was and is an authority on library collections, and a mystery buff as well. For some time he had realized that the university possessed the nucleus of one of the finest collections of mystery writers' works extant. There was an outstanding Poe collection, over twenty copies of the various states and issues of the famous 1845 edition, including the Ellery Queen copy of the earliest impression of the earliest issue, one of six known copies in original wrappers. There was Poe's own copy of the 1845 *Tales*, with his autograph additions to the texts of seven of the stories.

The library's Ellery Queen collection contained five thousand books and manuscripts, most of which were the stories which the Ellery Queen collaborators had gathered for their bibliography of the mystery short story and for *Queen's Quorum.*

The library also had many Conan Doyle manuscripts, including "A Scandal in Bohemia"; almost all of Graham Greene's manuscripts; and the Julian Symons papers for his history of crime stories, *Mortal Consequences.* They even had a ninety-nine-page mystery manuscript, handwritten by Mark Twain, and only printed privately; also Twain's personal notebook for 1892 and other non-mystery titles. In non-mystery also, the collection of Evelyn Waugh, another mystery buff, was there, including his personal library.

But, Dr. Ransom informed Dr. Minter, they had no Erle Stanley Gardner. He had long realized that if they could acquire the Gardner papers, they would possess, in one library, the greatest collection of mystery writers' works in the world.

Dr. Ransom had been keeping an eye open for someone interested in the university who also knew Mr. Gardner and would approach him about his papers. Last night, he told Dr. Minter, he'd found him in the pages of a book, right in his own quad.

As far as Dr. Minter knew, the Gardner collection had not been committed. He was certainly willing and happy to do what he could to have it come to Texas. Gardner was due in San Antonio in about two months. Dr. Minter would let Dr. Ransom know in advance the exact date, and plan to have him and Mrs. Ransom come to San Antonio to meet the author.

Dr. Minter had little or no hesitation in broaching the subject to Gardner. But he wanted help to sell the idea, and the logical person was Park Street. The difficulty was that Street was "a loyal alumnus of the University of Oklahoma." This may sound trivial, but not to those who have been in Austin for the annual football game between Texas and Oklahoma. It can only be equaled by the rivalry between UCLA and USC in Los Angeles, and in earlier days between Harvard and Yale. As a transplanted Texan, however, Park Street agreed to help.

In due time, Gardner came to town and Dr. Minter set up a meeting between him and Dr. Ransom, with Park Street and himself as backup men, to discuss the project. "Erle was primarily interested in knowing just how it could be made available to interested students, writers, and scholars, if, as he put it, 'anyone was really interested.'" Dr. Minter has said parenthetically, "It is my sincere opinion that he never really realized that he was the greatest writer of mystery fiction who ever lived, as demonstrated by the fact that his books have sold more copies worldwide than any book except the Bible."

In recollecting the meeting of Dr. Ransom and Gardner, Dr. Minter wrote: "After our conference was finished, I think that he was impressed by Dr. Ransom's imaginative plans. We left the hotel suite to go out to a club for lunch. Erle rode in my car, and we had time for some private conversation. The conversation ran something like this:

ERLE: Just what do you want from the materials I have?
MERTON: We just want all the manuscripts, corrected proofs, galley proofs, first editions, and correspondence between you and the publishers, your files of unpublished cases which you have investigated and have locked up and which may be kept sealed as long as you designate, the thousands of photographs you have taken, the articles published in *Argosy* for the Court of Last Resort . . .

"And by that time we had reached the club."

Nothing was decided on this visit. Gardner would go home and let Dr. Minter know what he decided. He said he must talk it over with the girls. Without the approval of Jean, Peggy, and Honey, he would not take this step.

Shortly thereafter, Dr. Minter had a message from Gardner which said in effect that he had told the girls what was being asked for and they wanted to know if the university did not want the contents of the study too. It was Jean's suggestion and from it came the idea of taking the knotty-pine office from the ranch, shooting many pictures of the interior first, and then rebuilding it at the university exactly as it had been in Temecula. Dr. Minter told Erle that they all thought this would be an inspiration for scholars.

Dr. Minter and Dr. Ransom planned an advance trip to the ranch. The night before their arrival, Gardner spoke to a group at the University of California at Berkeley. After the lecture, the president and some of the regents of the university invited him to come by their hotel suite, ". . . for a little talk." Erle had a hunch what was coming. When they asked for his collection, his reply was, as he told it to Dr. Minter, "Gentlemen, I am sorry. You are two weeks late. I have just given my collection to the University of Texas." He said they almost jumped out the window.

Details were worked out for the removal of the study's contents to Texas. Gardner added two prized possessions to the collection, the movie of the "desert" whales in Scammon's Lagoon, and the document telling of his method of developing plots, which for years many had wanted to see, but few had been so privileged. In a short time, all the papers were signed and the work of transferring the study began.

At Dr. Minter's request, Gardner agreed to put him in touch with Thayer Hobson, in the hope of obtaining his voluminous Gardner files for the collection. About three days later, Gardner called Dr. Minter to say he had talked with Hobson, who was living in San Antonio. Not only did Hobson include his material in the collection but he was also instrumental in helping the university acquire the papers of some other noted authors. Gardner put Dr. Minter in touch with Ben Hibbs, who gave magazine material and correspondence, including some illustrations of a Gardner story then appearing in the *Saturday Evening Post*. With only a few exceptions, everyone who was asked contributed his Gardner material to the university.

Dr. Carl Eckhardt and scholars from Austin came to the ranch and made a diagram, noting the location of everything in the study, "foot by foot and object by object, all two thousand of them." Dr. F. Warren Roberts of the Humanities Research Center worked very closely with Gardner and the girls in arranging the many artifacts of Gardner's career.

There was only one slipup, caused inadvertently at the ranch. When Erle used the study, the floor was waxed wood with Navajo rugs on it. After the study contents had been transferred to Austin, Jean carpeted the floor and refurnished the room so that Erle could continue to have a place to work. When an architect from Austin came to make final measurements to reproduce the room, he noted the carpet, and unbeknownst to Temecula, took a sample of it. He had it reproduced and laid in the Austin study, placing the Navajo rugs on top of it. No one had told him it was a new acquisition.

The only other difference in the study at Austin, as Jean says, is that it was never that neat when Erle was working in it.

Chapter Thirty

In April of 1963, when Gardner was in Baja, his three-wheel Butterfly turned over, pinning him underneath. He broke three ribs where they were attached to the spine and it was this that necessitated his finding, for a time at least, a quieter form of adventuring.

He found it in the Sacramento Delta, a thousand miles of inland waterways as it is described in those parts. He fell in love with it and established headquarters on Bethel Island. With characteristic enthusiasm he moved up five housetrailers, which were kept in readiness for him and full entourage whenever he decided to visit, and in short time had amassed a flotilla of two houseboats, one cruiser, and three smaller boats, the fastest used to scoot for the mail when he was exploring the sloughs.

In *Gypsy Days on the Delta*, published in 1967 and the most high-spirited of his three books on the subject, he wrote:

"On my father's side I am descended from hardy New England stock. My forebears were the captains of windjammers, whalers which went out of Nantucket and remained for many months, clippers which raced to China and sailed the Seven Seas. My dad always loved the water. The more it stormed, the better he liked it. He loved to feel a good stout deck quiver and shake beneath his feet as some heavy ocean roller shook the boat from stem to stern . . . he would stand braced against the wind, the salt spray hurtling past him, a look of keen enjoyment in his eyes.

"My mother always got seasick.

"I take after my mother."

Actually, he was a combination of mother and father. He loved the water, loved adventure, loved sailing to strange lands, coming in to foreign ports, "But when the ship starts creaking and groaning 'I chicken out.'"

Gardner trying out the Butterfly

No wonder he fell in love with the Delta. There was water, boats, but no chance of getting seasick. Gardner's story of foreign ports and seasickness can be read in full in *Gypsy Days*, and should be. Most Gardner readers don't know that he excelled as a homespun humorist.

"Because I have a steady stream of book royalties coming in, as well as an interest in television, I am financially able to live as I would like to live in the Delta country," he confessed in *Gypsy Days*. He even had television, radio, and the convenience of walkie-talkies from boat to boat.

The best part of having his flotilla on the river was that this was another place to enjoy with his friends. And as always, wherever he went, he added a host of them. There were Moyne and Dick De Shazer from whom he learned about houseboats, and of whom he wrote extensively in his Delta books. There was Constance "Connie" King and all her family of the Chinese village of Locke, she who had on first seeing Erle, "hung with cameras and visors," thought him just another tourist, until he began to speak in Cantonese. There were the Perrys, at whose marina was an aviary of exotic birds, including a pet quail who "talked" to Mr. Perry. And there was the Giusti family, whose dining place on the river probably

The happy yachtsman. Dick De Shazer in background

went back to Gold Rush days, according to Erle, who called it "my favorite of all." There were, of course, many others who became friends, all written about in the three Delta books, *The World of Water, Gypsy Days,* and *Drifting Down the Delta.*

It was Erle's idea to put the men on one house cruiser and the women on the other. The women were always sweeping and tidying up their houseboat while "we kept ours in a state of masculine informality which was a joy to behold. I have always loved disorder. That is, I am really a landlubber, and while the trained seaman has a place for everything and everything in its place, I have progressed to a point where I have a place for everything and everything someplace else."

The year before, 1962, had been upsetting in several ways. Gardner had been in and out of the hospital, and Grace's husband had died after a series of heart attacks. Whether or not this was the reason, around this time Erle gave his daughter half interest in the book rights to future A. A. Fair's, starting "when the manuscript begins, not when the book is published." And because of bad times falling on the magazine industry, the *Saturday Evening Post* had changed its policy regarding serialization. They were holding a couple of Perry Masons and talking of making them into one-shots or two-part serials.

He did not want the novels to be cut to either extent, but the *Post* money was a sizable part of his income and it would be pretty hard to get along without it.

In early January of 1963, Gardner sent Grace a present of a thousand dollars with a covering letter which said in part, "Thank heavens I was smart enough to get by New Year's without killing myself. I told everyone I wasn't going to be here. We went over to Palm Springs, had four or five people in for the evening . . . I love New Year's Eve. I like to have people come in and sit and talk and visit, but by ten-thirty I wish New Year's would _____ up and come. We sit around and wait for midnight, then we _____ refreshments, then people start going home, and then there's _____ a few people who decide to start all over again, start lappin _____ ampagne and about three-thirty in the morning decide it's time to go home. Since I always wake up around six or seven o'clock, no matter what time I go to bed, I'm glad I've reached such antiquity I can look at them with tired eyes and say in a quavering voice, 'You young folks can do whatever you want to but old man Gardner is going to go to bed at nine-thirty.' "

From 1960 to 1970, with the exception of 1964 and 1965, he published at least one travel book a year. In the same decade, he wrote and published twenty Perry Mason and ten A. A. Fair mystery novels, and sixty-two articles for such varied magazines as: *Sports Afield, Popular Photography, Popular Science, Desert Magazine, Boys' Life, Life, Atlantic Monthly.* He also contributed articles to various newspapers. In 1967 he wrote the final chapter of the Prentice-Hall book, *The President's Mystery Plot,* whose first chapter was written by Franklin Delano Roosevelt.

This final decade of his life brought deep personal sorrow as well as many honors and the happiness of a second marriage. A totally unexpected recognition, which pleased him enormously, came from *The Camellia Journal* with the announcement in its July 1965 issue of the Erle Stanley Gardner camellia. The flower, shown on the cover, was described as a deep pink, of a salmon-rose color with a blue cast, and it measured five inches in diameter "without gib." It had been developed by Blanding V. Drinkard of Mobile, long an admirer of Mr. Gardner. With permission, Mr. Drinkard named the flower for him, the "author of numerous mystery novels and a distinguished humanitarian."

Thayer Hobson had been in declining health for several years and by 1966 was spending more time in the hospital than out of it.

Thayer Hobson as Texas rancher

Gardner and Jean made a number of trips to San Antonio to see him and kept in constant touch by letter and phone.

Gardner was seventy-seven that year and hieing off as usual on Baja explorations and desert adventures. Also in May, the Perry Mason television series closed after a nine-year run. In the last show Gardner was persuaded to play the role of the judge, where his acting ability could be viewed by millions, not just the family circle. He had been well-pleased with the series, as with any and all of Perry Mason's successes, but it was something of a relief to be out from under such a heavy workload.

In December, Erle wrote his customary Christmas letter to Thayer: "As you know, I don't give and don't want to accept presents at Christmas. But along at the last minute I sometimes get swept along on the tide of goodwill and the acids in my system get mellowed into eggnog." He repeated his favorite holiday joke, "Abercrombie and Fitch have as yet failed to open a branch office in Temecula, which means that Jean, who tries to take all the responsibility off my shoulders, is a very busy woman and a very tired woman. And we are all getting to the point where we shouldn't be so tired."

He went on to talk of his animals. "We have always had certain

Gardner in role of judge in last Perry Mason TV show

hostages to civilization—dogs and horses which need to be cared for with a tender, loving hand." Every time he went on a long trip and had to leave the animals to strangers, he regretted it. "They have their spirits subdued, their personalities warped, and their attitudes changed. After all, when you raise a dog to feel that man is put on earth for canine convenience, it comes as a shock to a dog to encounter some individual who thinks otherwise and who is—at least temporarily—master of the situation."

He didn't know the answer or if there was any answer. He did know that "the Hobsons and the Fiction Factory have got to start taking life a lot easier." They should work out a gigantic combine with horses and dogs. ". . . We could make sort of a Disneyland with televised conversations between publisher and author for the amusement of the tourists." He sent his best to the nurses whom Thayer hadn't fought with by the time of this letter.

Gardner went up north for Christmas with the family, then returned to the ranch. On the last day of the year, he informed Morrow that the frontispiece color picture for his new Baja book is "just too namby-pamby . . . I still look like a pot-bellied Bo-Peep who has lost her sheep." But he agreed it was the best they could dig up of him in Baja.

The next year, 1967, was Gardner's busiest of the decade. The early months had been devoted to his work. He had his usual Baja and desert trips, and by spring was on a travel schedule that would have tested the stamina of a man half his age.

Thayer was in the hospital in San Antonio again, but he was able to write to Erle on March 2 from inside his oxygen tent, advising him to hang on to his D.A. stories, not sell rights to them.

Gardner kept in touch by phone and by mail as he had to be in Chihuahua City in Mexico on the sixth of April and back by the seventeenth for the famous blimp trip to Baja. He stayed home and worked in May, and on the second of June, he had a letter from Larry Hughes that Thayer had taken a turn for the worse. From June 11 to 16, Gardner, Jean, and Sam were in Las Cruces, New Mexico, for a seminar on the investigation of homicide in which Dr. LeMoyne Snyder and Marshall Houts took part. From there they returned to the ranch for a short breathing spell.

Natalie wrote Erle on the first of July, stating what both knew, that she would be eighty-two years old on July 16, and he, seventy-eight on July 17. "I can't expect to be young and gay now," she wrote, although she was feeling much better, with no heart or muscular pains. In April she had given up her beloved car as she no longer was strong enough to drive it. Before the letter arrived, Erle had already taken off on his Lost Blue Bucket Mine trip in the southeastern Oregon desert. He returned to Oakland for the birthday celebration on July 17, before going home to the ranch.

On August 9, Thayer telephoned Erle, who reported that he "sounded wonderful. Full of pep, no shortness of breath, and really his old self." Gardner had the meeting of the American Polygraph Association that month, and coming up a big event on October 4, when he was to be one of the stars of the program at New Mexico State University in Las Cruces, and across the border of Mexico in Juarez, for Miguel Alemán Day. On his return to the ranch after that celebration, Gardner had definitely decided to make another trip to the South Seas. He planned a six-week cruise, sailing on October 23 on the SS *Mariposa*. He had invited his Tijuana friends, Alicia and Wulfrano Ruiz, to join the party. Jean would go and also Anita Haskell Jones. Peggy couldn't make it, since she was just back from a trip and her desk was stacked too high. Honey couldn't get away. He wrote Helen King that he was sorry she couldn't be along as she could have learned how to dance the hula South-Sea-Island-style. He concluded the letter with, "Actually I'm going to try to get as much of a rest as possible, and see that Jean takes it as easy as she can. We have been working too hard, too long, too frequently, over too many years."

On October 12, Thayer had come down with, of all things, a ruptured appendix. He got through the operation but was not able to pull through and on October 19, 1967, he died.

Honey wrote to Hennie for all of them, "Just a tiny note to let you know we here in the office have just had the news about Thayer, and somehow it seems like the end of a lot of things for us here, as I know it does for you. . . . Erle is in San Francisco but is flying down tonight, I think . . . this will hit him harder than anything could. . . . Jean and Peg and I link Thayer and Erle together in their careers and felt almost the same about Thayer as we do Erle."

She wrote again next day that Jean and Erle would depart on the South Seas trip that weekend. "We're so glad he's getting away for many reasons (as he needs a rest, that's for sure), and for the fact that he will have time to adjust to Thayer's leaving us before he gets back, as this has hit him very hard."

After her return from the funeral in Texas, Hennie wrote to Honey, "I too keep thinking it's the end of an era—and nothing will ever be as vital or interesting or as much fun as Thayer was able to make it. But how very lucky I was to have had so many years close to him. . . . And of course I know how he and Erle felt about each other. I was glad for Erle's sake that he was about to take off and couldn't make the services."

On the twenty-sixth of February, 1968, Natalie Gardner died of a heart attack. Erle had written her on that very day, enclosing her membership card in the Automobile Club of Southern California, with the notation, "Despite the fact that you aren't driving anymore, you will find this Automobile Club card is a handy thing to have."

His epitaph to her memory is in a letter to an old friend of Natalie's: "Her passing was a great shock. I realized, of course, that both she and I were no longer young . . . While we had been separated for some thirty-odd years, we remained good friends, and I was very, very fond of her."

Thayer was gone and now Nat was gone. Gardner was old but he wasn't to be put to pasture yet. In March came the fabulous honoring of him by the Mexican government, sixteen days in all, the railroad trip written up in *Host with the Big Hat*. Later, in a May letter to Hennie from Temecula, Jean said, "The past couple of months have been the worst yet, and we no sooner get here than we take off again. My room is always a cyclone spot with unpacked bags standing around and no time to unpack them before the next trip. I hope after the New Mexico trip we can settle down to simple things like writing books. Erle's life includes so many other activities that it seems we never get time to write books any more—at least not Perry Mason books."

In a letter to Helen King concerning the constant traveling, Jean wrote, "Clothes! I wear them out dragging them around because I never know how long we'll be or where we may have to head for during the trip, so I go pretty well prepared for whatever direction may call. Sam has become resigned to laying a load of clothes on top of the heap in the trunk or in the back seat. I refuse to pack them all in suitcases unless we go by air."

The New Mexico trip was a return to Las Cruces on the first of June, where Gardner received a Doctor of Laws degree from the university. After this, Jean was evidently able to slow him down for a brief time because on July 31, a few weeks after his seventy-ninth birthday, he wrote a letter jointly to Helen and Larry: "Dear Both of you: I told you I was going to write the next Perry Mason book before I wrote up the Mexican trip. For the first time in my life I am having really serious trouble with a Mason book. Of course, each book becomes progressively harder to write because of the necessity of getting entirely away from the things Mason has done before. Also I would *like* to have each succeeding book sufficiently ingenious so the trade can't say I am riding on my reputation.

"I had this Perry Mason book about a third finished. I have ripped it to pieces three times, completely revised the plot and still I am not entirely satisfied, but I'm getting it." He was planning a quick trip to Acámbaro.

"I'm going to let the Mason book cool off and pick it up four or five weeks later. I have a horror of finishing my Mason stories with a book that will be considered mediocre. I want each book I write to be better than the others." A few days later he sent another letter, saying, "After I wrote you that I was having trouble with the Perry Mason book, I ripped the whole thing to pieces, went back to the ground roots, and am fitting it together as a brand new plot so that the thing isn't quite as pedestrian as it was. I'm beginning to get some explosive situations together but I still need the spark to set them off."

He says nothing in this letter of marriage plans, nor does he in a letter to his grandson, Corky, on August 2. It is one of his typical grandfather letters: "You are going to get entirely out of patience with your old grandfather, but your old grandfather is entirely out of patience with himself." He had lost some photos Corky took of the study. "Your poor, old, senile, decrepit, doddering grandad took these god damn pictures and put them somewhere where they would be safe where I wouldn't lose them. . . ." But at the same time the study was being moved to Texas, the carpet torn out and a new one laid, "and making a long story short, I can't find those pictures. I found my checkbook, however, so I decided it was easier to get new pictures with a checkbook than by tearing things to pieces and finding a lot more stuff I don't know what to do with.

"So how about cashing this check for fifty bucks, jogging down to the camera store, getting the camera store to make me two more duplicates of each transparency and then making a five by seven print of each transparency. If this amounts to less than fifty bucks, you have made yourself a little profit. If it amounts to more than fifty bucks, you will call on me to make up the difference. . . ."

On August 7, 1968, Erle and Jean were married in Carson City, Nevada. The ceremony was at the home of their dear friends, Naomi and Art Bernard, and they took off immediately afterward for Mexico.

Erle's brother, Dr. Kenneth, heard the news of the wedding on car radio on August 8. When the Gardners returned from Mexico, they found his note: "You finally made Herb Caen." Caen's famed San Francisco column said in part, "The Case of the Missing Bridegroom, age seventy-nine, honeymooning somewhere in Mexico with longtime secretary Jean Bethell (over twenty-one), married a few days ago in Carson City."

On September 6, after their return from Acámbaro, Jean added in a business letter to Hennie, "But I really want to thank you for your nice letter about our marriage, and if you think things have been hectic in the past, you should have been following us around the past few weeks. The week we were married, we were on the telephone constantly arranging the trip to see the Acámbaro figurines, about which he will be doing a book. At the same time, I had to go to Riverside to get my rings; I had two hours to shop in La Jolla for a wedding dress, it was between seasons and they were showing only heavy wool suits with heavy fur on sleeves, etc. I wound up with a suit, which after I got there found was much too hot so wore a Pucci print I'd had for some time. By main force and human strength, Naomi Bernard and I had the wedding in her house instead of at a Justice of the Peace and it was very nice . . . and after that our wild man settled down a bit. We took about ten people on our honeymoon to Mexico to see the figurines, had a rush trip, but an interesting one. . . ."

On his return from Acámbaro, Erle was ill, purportedly with a bug picked up in Mexico. After a checkup with his brother, Dr. Kenneth, in San Francisco, Erle, Jean, and Sam headed for home by car. They stayed the first night in Bakersfield. Erle later wrote: "I got up at night on wobbly legs, started to stagger, grabbed for a doorknob to steady myself, the door came open, I fell over the rim of a wastebasket, fractured two ribs, one in two places." It wouldn't have been a minor accident in a young person; at Erle's age of seventy-nine, it was far from that. "I have had to take so much dope for pain I'm having a lot of trouble with my sleep pattern."

In addition, the mockup on *Drifting Down the Delta* had to be handled and sent back to Morrow quickly, and in addition to that, he was "frantically engaged in getting out photographs and copy" on the Mexican trip, as he thought he had a sale to *Life*. He did.

Jean wrote Hennie a month later, "We've been sticking around the ranch for about a month now and it's HURTING. Something tells me we'll be off somewhere one of these days." And just one week later, she was writing, "We're in a lather of activity around here getting books to the proper Mexican bigwigs. What a mess. Erle and Sam have been dashing back and forth to Tijuana to get the right people lined up. It can never be done simply because we don't work that way so everyone gets nervous and upset and a good time is had by all. If Erle didn't have so much fun getting the material for these books, I'd wish he'd never write another. He *says* he's not doing any more and will go back to Perry Mason. Life would be simple then."

In November, Jean wrote to Hennie again. They were going with friends to Mexico for Christmas. "He thinks it will mean no Christmas but it really means that I have to go like mad to get it all done by the fifteenth of December."

It was 1969 when they returned to the ranch. Speaking of what a vicious thing the flu was that year, Jean wrote Hennie, "While in Mexico we went down like tenpins. Anita is still holed up. We should be but we struggle on. Everyone is dragging his heels everywhere, sort of pushing to get through the daily chores. Erle didn't have it too badly down there but yesterday came down with an intestinal thing which I hope is a short flu. He always thinks the worst, he's falling apart, etc., but I still think it's a flu. . . ."

He came out of it soon enough, for he went with the members of the American Cetacean Society on a Goodyear Blimp whale watch on the tenth. Returning from that adventure, he and Jean took off for the Palm Springs house, expecting to escape the storms headed Temecula way. Erle wrote Larry of their experiences at the Springs. "You've guessed it. We got right in the middle of everything. I had to lift sandbags to keep water out of the house and we had terrific windstorms which tore awnings off the place, slammed the garage door shut and wedged it so I couldn't get it open, etc., etc., etc. . . . Out at the ranch the road washed out. The roof blew off the room where we store our camping stuff. A few hundred dollars worth of sleeping bags got ruined but I guess we'll survive all right."

By February 14, Erle was writing Larry that *The Case of the Careless Corpse* was dictated and transcribed but needed revising. It would be on Larry's desk in about three weeks. He wasn't sure of the title, it may have been used, but he "just wanted you to know the damn story was finished." He sent it in as *The Case of the Falsified Client* but eventually it was retitled *The Case of the Fabulous*

Larry Hughes

Fake. It was his last Perry Mason novel. Two more were published posthumously, *The Case of the Fenced-In Woman* and *The Case of the Postponed Murder,* but both had been written before *Fabulous Fake.*

For several years Gardner had known he had cancer and for many reasons, primarily professional, it was a closely guarded secret. And in fact, he kept to his rigorous schedule unimpeded by serious discomfort until approximately six months before his death. Certainly in April of 1969 he was on top of business affairs. He didn't like the jacket cover prepared for *Host with the Big Hat* and objected strenuously. It was a handsome one in sepia with a sombrero hanging from two decorative lanterns against the corner of a brick wall but he felt it should have some action; actually what he wanted was to get on the cover a picture of the train. "I have a feeling that readers of travel books want action, excitement, and adventure, and they are going to fight shy of books with a still-life picture on the jacket." He finally was talked out of changing it.

On the second of May, after a bout in the hospital, Erle wrote Larry from Palm Springs, "I had clean plumb forgotten all about the dedication on that last Mason book until Helen remembered it, after the book had gone to press." He went on to say, "I am still a little groggy from all the dope I had to take. I came over here to do a little work. The pain kept getting worse, then a fever came up and I wound up by getting my first ride in an ambulance. I was in the hospital with special nurses around the clock and it wasn't a pleasant experience."

In May, Gardner had decided to write the police book that had been under discussion for some time, a book to bear a double title, *Cops on Campus and Crime in the Streets.* Larry Hughes and Doc Lewis had arranged for its publication simultaneously by Morrow and Pocket Books. Larry Hughes and Helen King had sent ideas on how Gardner might take it easy on writing the book, to which Gardner on May 12 replied: "You should know Gardner better than that. When I get enthusiastic about something, I put the whole machinery into operation. . . . The book is about two-thirds finished in rough draft at the present time and I am terribly afraid you and Helen are not going to like it." He and Doc Lewis were to have some battles about part of the book, but all came to a meeting of minds before publication.

Gardner had returned to his Palm Springs hideout to work and Sam brought over the galleys of the Mexican book which Betty

Burke had already read and compared with the manuscript. "Now this catches me right in the middle of everything," Gardner complained to Larry. "I am working on this police book with such white-hot enthusiasm that I can't take time out without throwing the mental train off the track." On top of all else, he had been sent a television script "to be read, analyzed, and commented on."

On the twenty-second of May, he wrote Larry that he was going to have to slow up on *Cops and Crime*. He had to leave on the twenty-sixth for Stockton, as he had a speaking date there the twenty-seventh. He would be delayed four or five days in Oakland on his return.

His daughter had remarried some years before and was now Mrs. Anthony Naso. She and her husband had just bought a home in Bishop, California, to which they would soon be moving. His granddaughter was married at the time to Edward Jensen and they too lived in the Bay Area. His grandson, Corky, was graduating from high school in Oakland that spring, and would go East in the autumn, having been accepted at Boston University. Erle's congratulations to him included also the dictum, "Just don't let your hair grow long, grow sideburns and a beard or I'll personally kick you all the way out of Miles Standish Hall and into the middle of Boston Harbor. Take care of yourself and keep your hair cut."

In answer to a family letter asking him to stop over longer in Oakland after the Stockton engagement, he wrote, "I am eighty years old, have been making trips to the hospital and am probably going to keep on making trips to the hospital . . . I can't stand and I can't sit. I'm doing all my work these days lying down. I have a golf cart to take me from my study to the kitchen and am making very slow progress." He was fulfilling his commitment in Stockton, having made it some time ago. "I can go up lying on the back seat of an automobile," but regarding staying over longer in Oakland, he planned to see Grace for "a brief visit . . . I can't climb the stairs to your place . . . Your old man just wants you to know that he loves you but things are pretty tough and this hip gives me a LOT of pain."

On June 14 he was at home, sputtering again to Larry and Helen. "This business of trying to write books in the midst of twenty-thousand interruptions . . . Mail comes pouring in in a steady stream, the telephone is ringing and everybody wants something." In spite of conditions, he sent the new A. A. Fair book to Larry on July 7 with the tentative title, *Some Fish Won't Bite*. It was the last Fair book, and although in the publisher's hands in 1969 was published posthumously under the title *All Grass Isn't Green*. Like the last Perry Mason, it was as sharp and spunky as if it were the first of the series.

His eightieth birthday was on July 17. Because of his precarious health, no big celebration was planned, just the Temecula family and neighbors. It turned out to be a gala. Rose and Larry Hughes flew from New York bearing a magnificent gift from Morrow, a leatherbound copy of every Gardner nonfiction book published by the firm. With these was a set of Tiffany silver book ends engraved with the signature of every member of the Morrow family. Also from New York came Doc Lewis bearing gifts. With no advance planning, more and more old friends kept turning up.

Corney Jackson remembers how much Erle enjoyed his unexpected party. Corney hadn't intended to go down to Temecula but that morning Doug Allen, the photographer of Gardner's documentary, flew into Burbank in his plane, accompanied by Bob de Roos, the writer who had written the commentary for the documentary. Doug invited Corney to fly down with them. On the way Corney reminded the others that Erle was not much for celebrations, and even though it was his eightieth birthday, if they made a big fuss over it, they should "be prepared for a frosty reception." He was mistaken this time around.

At the ranch Erle greeted them with "the abrazo, the customary Paisano welcome." And the party continued to grow. As Erle later wrote of it to Gail Jackson, who was in Hawaii, "It turned out to be some shindig."

Corney had unfinished business in Hollywood, and Doug had to return for business appointments. So in mid-afternoon, they went to say their farewells. Erle urged so strongly that they not leave, that Corney felt sad about it, and finally said simply, "I have to," and they took off. They were no sooner on their way to the airfield, Sam driving them, than Corney felt impelled to call out, "Stop the car." To the others he said, "What the hell am I doing this for? Erle doesn't want me to go, you could tell by the look on his face. Over the years, he's given me a lot, but he has never asked for anything. I am going back." They all went back.

"The look on Erle's face gave me a present I shall cherish forever," Corney has said. The party became a "houseful of happy,

carefree people. We could not have had a more enjoyable get-to-
gether if we had planned it for months. We didn't know then that
it was Erle's farewell birthday celebration."

The morning after, Erle was up early and dictating letters to Jean.
Neither the years nor the celebration had dulled his wit. Answering
a police chief's query as to Gardner's definition of a "blunt instrument," his reply was in so many words: "Since the purpose of a blunt
instrument is to render the victim unconscious, the best definition
that I can think of for a blunt instrument is an after-dinner speaker."
Larry Hughes recalls it was a spur-of-the-moment phrasing, showing
how active Gardner's mind was throughout his lifetime. After the
Easterners had returned, in his thank-yous Erle wrote, "After all, an
eightieth birthday is something of a milestone—They don't happen
every day. . . . God bless all of you and thanks, thanks, thanks."

In spite of his health, Erle was well enough by August to fulfill
a speaking engagement in Houston before the American Polygraph
Association. From there he went to Dallas to speak before the Dallas
County Criminal Bar Association. On their return August 22, Jean
wrote to Hennie saying, "Everyone loved him and appreciated our
coming in August. . . . The humidity must be one hundred per
cent. I stuck my head out of our hotel room door and my glasses
steamed up! If you want a steam bath one minute and to freeze to
death the next, go to Texas. It is literally steaming and their air
conditioning is so cold you freeze."

On his return from Texas, he found it necessary to take steps
concerning an Israeli piracy case which had been going on for some
time. Throughout the years, he had almost constant difficulties concerning the pirating of his books by foreign publishers. In this instance, he made a personal visit to the Israeli consulate in Los
Angeles and was able to settle the matter.

By late August he was in Palm Springs again, writing to his "dear,
dear Brother" that he had stood the trip to Texas better than he
expected. He had found a new doctor, Peter Lewis, in Riverside;
it was too far for him to come to San Francisco for treatments any
longer. He also had a doctor in Palm Springs, Dr. Fitzmorris, who
had attended Eisenhower. He was being given the medication that
he needed. He signed off saying:

"I am no longer a young man.

"I like Dr. Lewis tremendously.

"I have the honor, Dr. Gardner, to remain your devoted brother, deteriorating rapidly in physical condition but firm in his affections."

His favorite sign-off to Kenneth over the years had been "The Black Sheep of the family." This time he varied it, "I remain the source of black wool to the family."

In September, he had a visit from Jack and Mary Alyce Simpson, his New Orleans friends of more than thirty years. It was the last time they would see Erle, and all must have known it. His last words to them were typical joking ones. The Simpsons had stayed overnight in Arizona on the drive out and had not remembered that the state didn't have daylight saving time and was thus on the same time as California. They therefore were up and away far too early the next morning. On Sunday, as they were leaving Palm Springs, Erle's good-bye to Jack was, "Kid, when you get to Arizona, call me and let me know what time it is."

In early October, Erle was building his last air castle. "I want to get down to Baja California for one more trip. . . ." But when *The Case of the Fabulous Fake* was published later that month, he was back in the hospital. It was during this stay that they began giving the debilitating cobalt treatments, with hope of slowing the progress of the cancer. Not in any of his letters did he give any hint of this. He wrote to Helen in November, "I'm still in durance vile in the hospital taking treatments designed to head off an arthritic condition before it gets any worse, the idea being to nip this stuff in the bud."

Helen's letter crossed. She was writing, "So you like all that hospital attention so much you've decided to stay awhile. Well, you didn't reckon on your old Simone Legree." She was sending him two sets of galleys on *All Grass Isn't Green*, and he was to be sure to return one set. She added, "It's a lovely Fair, bless you."

He was back at the ranch on November 26. Jean wrote to Hennie two days later that he was "a bit shaky yesterday but seems much better today and talking of going back to work (not that he hadn't been doing quite a bit all along)." She was trying to get him to finish his autobiography.

Erle was able to write to Helen again on the second of December. "I am just back from the hospital with a trained nurse around the clock. I ran into all sorts of complications and I am bothered at the moment with weakness due to a change in life from roaming around the wilds of Baja California to spending four weeks in a hospital with special nursing around the clock, and food that I simply couldn't gag down, meat that was like shoe leather, etc. etc." He then turned to points raised in the galleys she had sent and remembered that "Thayer Hobson used to quote his mother who said, 'After all, on a trotting horse who is going to see the difference?' The main thing is to keep the horse trotting and the pace fast and furious."

It was Christmastime again. The year before he and Jean and their friends had taken off for their simple Christmas in Baja. This year he was too ill to go. Christmas was at the ranch.

But he was still keenly protecting Gardner interests. On December 23 he wrote to Larry about the current issue of *True*, which reported that Simenon was the world's best-selling author, having sold fifty million copies of his books. Erle did not want this to go unchallenged. He himself couldn't challenge, a matter of good taste, but Morrow could refute the statement. Erle referred to Alice Payne Hackett's book, *Seventy Years of Best Sellers*, covering the period from 1895 to 1965. Only one hundred and fifty-one mystery books were best sellers in that period, best seller being defined as a book selling a million or more copies. Of these one hundred and fifty-one mystery best sellers, ninety-one had been written by Gardner, either under his name or as A. A. Fair.

The year turned, and on January 12 he was again taken to the hospital. By then, all knew that his days were running out. Jean remained in Riverside, at first at a hotel; later she was permitted by the hospital to move into a room near his. Peggy took over at the ranch as she had taken over for him through the years whenever he was away. She came into Riverside weekly to stay a day or two with Erle while Jean attended to necessary affairs. Honey traveled between the ranch and the hospital daily, handling and transporting the mail and taking care of other important business matters. Some of his last words, painfully spoken, were to her: "How are you, Kiddie?" And so like him, thinking of her, not himself: "Are you happy?" To him she was always the little sister.

Family and friends were constant visitors at the hospital. Gail Patrick drove down from Hollywood daily. She knew there was nothing she could do to help, "but I just felt better being there." Grace and her family came down from Oakland. Dr. Ken and his wife Dorothy were frequently there.

On one of the days when Dr. Ken went into Erle's room, Erle was reciting to himself the twenty-third Psalm, "The Lord is my

Sam Hicks stacking works of Erle
Stanley Gardner as latter looks on

shepherd, I shall not want, He maketh me to lie down in green pastures . . ." All of his life, in moments of stress, he would recite this Psalm. He could and often did recite many different passages from the Scriptures, a memory from his boyhood of the Methodist Sunday school he and his brothers had attended.

There were few who were permitted to see him; he was under sedation most of the time. Yet in his waking periods, he had the spirit of the old Erle.

On one of the final days at the hospital, Erle was sleeping when Corney went into the room. He came awake, and, recognizing his visitor, he asked, "What are you doing down here?"

Corney replied, "I just came down to see how you are feeling."

"He looked at me a long time," Corney relates, "then said in that slow, deliberate manner that must have shaken many a witness, "You drove all the way down here from Los Angeles just to see how I am feeling?"

Corney retorted, "Yes! How *are* you feeling?"

And the old Erle took over. "Well, for Christ's sake, for a smart bastard you can be the most stupid son of a bitch I have ever known. If you wanted to know how I was feeling, why didn't you pick up a phone in Hollywood and call me here and ask me? You didn't have to drive ninety miles to get a simple answer to a simple question. Jesus, when in the hell are you going to learn how to get organized, conserve your time and energy and do things the simple way instead of the hard way?" He went on like this for quite a time. But when the nurse edged Corney to the door, Erle said, "Thanks for coming down, Corney." It was the last time Corney was to see him.

By February 25, there was nothing further to be done medically, and Gardner was taken back home to the ranch. Jean was in constant attendance as she had been for most of his life. Peggy and her daughter, Meg, were also there to give the extra nursing and comfort he needed. Honey spent her days at the ranch, not only taking over the office but also sharing the needs of the sickroom. She, with Jean, was with him, and she was holding his hand when he died on March 11 of that year, 1970.

Services were held on Friday the thirteenth at the Garden of Prayer Chapel in Riverside. The eulogy was spoken by Marshall Houts, his devoted friend from the Court of Last Resort, who had in 1956 dedicated a book to Erle with these words: "To Erle Stanley Gardner, lawyer, author, citizen, friend, who has contributed more to the cause of justice than any man of his generation." This he used as his text.

At Jean's suggestion, his ashes were scattered by Sam over his much-loved Baja California. They were flown by Francisco Muñoz, who had offered his plane, and were accompanied by J. W. and Lois Black, Alicia and Wulfrano Ruiz, and Ricardo Castillo.

Erle called his autobiographical notes "The Color of Life," and he wrote: "My life is filled with color and always has been. I want adventure. I want variety. I want something to look forward to . . . Looking back, I recall various adventures, both at home and in foreign lands. Looking forward, I find that there are seeds, which properly nourished can sprout into new adventures . . ."

And his closing words in the notes were, "The one dividend we are sure of is the opportunity to have beautiful daydreams. . . . This is as it should be. This is the color of life. I love it."

EPILOGUE

ON THE DEATH of Erle Stanley Gardner tributes poured in. Only a few are included here to round out the picture of a most unusual man.

Larry Hughes's April memo "To Everyone at Morrow" tells much of the Gardner his publishing family knew. In part, he wrote:

> All of you know the statistics. That at the time of his death Morrow had published 141 books by Erle Stanley Gardner, including 80 Perry Mason stories and 29 works under the A. A. Fair pseudonym. That these titles in various editions had sold more than one hundred and seventy million copies in the United States alone and perhaps an equal number throughout the rest of the world. (We believe that this is the greatest sales record of any fiction writer in the English language.) . . . You knew all these facts before, but very few of you presently at Morrow knew Erle Stanley Gardner himself.
>
> In the days since Erle's death, many of you have asked me questions about him. . . . What kind of man was he? Why did we call him "Uncle" Erle? But even if you hadn't asked me I would have wanted to tell you what I knew about Erle Stanley Gardner, because I believe the relationship between him and us is a unique publishing story. . . .
>
> In 1933 Morrow published *The Case of the Velvet Claws*, which was the very first Perry Mason novel. Mr. Thayer Hobson, who was then President and owner of Morrow, urged Mr. Gardner, who was already a prolific and very successful magazine story writer, to concentrate on this character and develop a series of books about the lawyer. The rest, as the saying goes, is history, except that Erle Stanley Gardner never forgot the debt he owed Hobson for the suggestion and help in launching the series and Thayer Hobson never forgot how much he owed the author for the accomplishment. Helen King, Hennie Gelber, Richard Rostron, Frances Phillips (who recently retired) and others here at Morrow can tell you a lot more about the relationship between Hobson and Gardner than I possibly can. For example, for many years Helen, as editor of Mr. Gardner's books, was "the man in the middle" between the opinions of Thayer Hobson and the opinions of E.S.G. And let me assure you that those two men were never lacking in opinions, and not always the same ones either. But from 1949 to 1960 I worked for Pocket Books, Inc., who are the paperback reprinters of

the Perry Mason books. I can guarantee that we at Pocket Books were constantly aware of Thayer Hobson's attentions on behalf of Erle Stanley Gardner. Mr. Hobson did such a thorough job making sure that Gardner works were properly sold and promoted in hard cover and paperback editions as well as book clubs (all his mysteries have been used by the Detective Book Club) that Mr. Gardner turned over foreign and other rights to him too. This eventually led to the formation of Thayer Hobson & Company, an organization devoted almost exclusively to the worldwide selling of the book rights on Gardner's works. That company today is managed by myself and Hennie Gelber and at the specific wish of Erle includes as its partners Mr. Hobson's children and Mr. Donald Stevenson, who succeeded Hobson to the Presidency of Morrow and is now retired. . . .

Frankly, one of the reasons we promoted the hell out of Perry Mason books at Pocket Books was because they were highly profitable books to sell. The mathematics worked out that if, for example, we sold one thousand Gardner titles we made more profit than if we sold one thousand books by author X. If you had been the publisher, whose books would you have promoted? . . .

Mr. Gardner was perfectly capable of raising the roof with his publishers. Robert de Roos had an article in the *San Francisco Examiner-Chronicle* which concluded: "I hope Gardner likes heaven. Otherwise some surprised angels are catching merry hell about now." However, over the years the personal relationship with many here at Morrow grew so strong that the term "Uncle" just came naturally. We really do feel part of Erle's family. . . .

To me the real loss of Erle Stanley Gardner is the man himself and the relationship we as publishers had with him as human being and author.

A few days after Erle's death we made a commemorative announcement in *The New York Times*. We could have said so much, but I think we were right in simply saying: "Erle Stanley Gardner, 1889–1970. No publisher ever had a more loyal author or a better friend."

The tribute from a fellow writer, Ellery Queen, came before Gardner's death but is included because it presents a facet of the man not otherwise described here. It appeared in the "unorthodox postscript" which concluded the "unorthodox introduction" to an Ellery Queen paperback quarterly devoted to Gardner's work. Queen had written Erle in the summer of 1951, in connection with awards to be given by *Ellery Queen's Mystery Magazine*, asking him to nominate ten best active mystery writers. In reply, Erle explained why he could not nominate the ten best, concluding, "If I should select a list of ten people whom I considered the best mystery writers, I would always be haunted by the feeling that I had done an injustice to the eleventh, twelfth, fifteenth and seventy-fifth . . ."

"Now that, dear reader," Ellery Queen wrote, "tells much more about Erle Stanley Gardner, about his sensitivity and conscientiousness and deep-rooted sense of fair play, than any biographical sketch or even any critical appraisal—not about Erle Stanley Gardner, the best-selling American mystery writer of all time, but about Erle Stanley Gardner, the man, the human being."

The late Ben Hibbs wrote to Jean, "You know how Edie and I felt about Erle. So far as we are concerned, he was a wonderful human being in just about every way there is to be wonderful. Actually, Jean, I have always been a little puzzled as to why Erle and I hit it off so well, because, as you know, we were about as opposite by nature as a couple of guys could be. Erle had that blessed spirit of good cheer and a certain devilish gaiety that everyone loved, while I have always been the too-solemn introvert who found it hard to make friends. Yet between the two of us there was a deep friendship and understanding that I treasured more than I can say.—Erle brought great pleasure to untold millions of people through his books, but to me he brought the pleasure of his own sunny, lusty, sweet, hell-raising nature. Damn, how I will miss the guy!"

Of all the writings about Erle Stanley Gardner throughout the years, and they were many and many were fine, the most perceptive is "Footnotes for an Obituary" by Freeman Lewis. It needs no introductory words, it needs only to be read and remembered, even in this shortened version:

> In the New York *Times* of March 12, 1970 there appeared an obituary of writer Erle Stanley Gardner by Albin Krebs. It was an exceptionally fine report. Even for a Gardner aficionado, which I am after over thirty years as friend and the publisher of reprints of his many books. But it necessarily did leave some matters unmentioned and I send this letter, hoping it will be published, as added data and commentary about the most widely read author of this century.
>
> Erle delighted in self-denigration, hence the headline of Albin Krebs's obituary: "The Fiction Factory" and the quotation from the author that he was "not really a writer at all." But while Erle delighted in such phrases, he had a very fierce pride about his skills as a writer. He was not as complacent as he seemed and always hoped that someone would contradict his own pronouncements.
>
> But he was not an easy man to contradict. He had a great capacity for ridicule and an almost brutal skill in verbally demolishing any opposition. As a frequently humbled opponent, I can testify to his

effectiveness in that regard. He coupled this with a curious selectivity. He attacked most fiercely those he liked best. So, after a while, you came to regard his destructive attacks as a sort of reverse compliment. And it became a matter of pride to observe how meekly he treated those he didn't like or felt to be unworthy. He spent his best efforts on Thayer Hobson, his publisher, his publishing mentor and probably his most respected friend. In due course I came to consider it a privilege to be something like a close friend. In his later years he mellowed and would, I believe, have liked to have been less successful in having people take him at his word as a "fiction factory."

Erle had a right to be proud of his skills as a writer. They were real and hard-earned. It often seemed to me that he operated as a professional in an area inhabited largely by amateurs. And it also often seemed to me that his books should have been reviewed by sports columnists rather than bookish people, for Erle had the kinds of learned and applied skills that sports fans understand and cherish but which book reviewers often are too pretentious to appreciate. (The late Anthony Boucher is wholly excluded from the above remarks.)

A concern with "soul" or "self" or "depravity" or "anger" or "social problems," etc., Erle had as a person. Much of his most recent book, *Cops on Campus and Crime in the Streets,* shows such concerns. But they were not in his opinion proper subject matters for his fiction. Nor did he think, as so many people do, that stories written out of such concerns are more likely to carry the hallmark of genius. Perhaps that was because he had a greater genius. He was a born story-teller. In over forty years as a publisher, I never met a writer so generously endowed with that quality. In an evening's conversation (perhaps monologue would be a better word) he would produce more ideas and plots for books than most writers come by in a lifetime. And the truly remarkable thing is that he never thought that remarkable.

He was mostly given bad marks or simply overlooked by "literary" critics and he resented it, though he seldom said so. But once, in a drive from Palm Springs to Temecula, he gave the most lucid lecture on how to write readable stories, how to plot, how to select and depict believable characters, etc., that I have ever heard. He was a very serious student of the craft of writing fiction and many of those who dismissed his talents would benefit from a serious study of his practices.

He learned his skills in the "pulps" of the 1920's and that obviously conditioned his observations. But he started with the proposition that the reader is King. And he had concluded that in-depth characterization did two adverse things to a story: it slowed the action and it deprived the reader of the opportunity to form his own images. . . .

Such regard for his readers may also have come out of his work as a "pulp" writer in terms of style. He learned to write simple declarative sentences because he found that any obscurantism or pronounced mannerisms turned his readers off. And in the "pulps" there was no cultural or reviewer-directed reading. Either the customers liked your story and the way it was told or they didn't. I argued with Erle to the very end about single sentence paragraphs, etc. He never budged an inch.

Most everyone admits that he did the drama of the courtroom better than any other writer. And it is clear enough that he constructed his stories with a view to leading the reader to the courtroom, that arena in which his skills were best displayed. But almost no one seems to realize the variety and veracity of the work that went into providing his readers with that highway.

Erle put in a prodigious quantity of study. He became an expert on guns and cameras and mining and "desert rats" and polygraph machines. He learned police procedures and prison management and the details of such oddities as the importation of works of art. He became quite expert in forensic medicine. He studied Chinese philosophy. He explored cave paintings in Baja and the breeding habits of the California gray whale. And most of this assorted knowledge ended up in his fiction as build-up for the eventual courtroom scene and the capacity to be expert in cross-examination whether the hero was Perry Mason or Doug Selby or Donald Lam.

To some extent I believe it was that devotion to giving his readers reliable data both before and during the big moment that made Erle so durable a writer. Certainly no one during the past forty years has written books which, to such a degree, go on and on being bought and read. He was a publisher's dream author. Even during the past half-dozen years when the number of his new titles fell off, sales figures held up because people kept buying his older books. They're still doing it and the record-breaking figures he has already set will grow larger. . . .

I doubt that anyone has ever lived the essentially simple life so expensively. Partly this was because he couldn't resist buying in multiples. This was understandable for his gun collection or his vast photographic equipment. But it applied also to shoes and suits and shirts and sports jackets and refrigerators and trailers and boats. And to his affections for his fellows. He made his large circle of friends, drawn from every walk of life, feel part of a big and loving family. As a result, many more people than his staff at Rancho del Paisano called him "Uncle Erle." I was one of them.

The final words seem to belong to Pinky Brier, who wrote, ". . . and while it may have been said of others, I believe it can be more sincerely said of Erle Stanley Gardner, that no matter what age he died, Erle Stanley Gardner died young."

BIBLIOGRAPHY

OF

ERLE STANLEY GARDNER

COMPILED BY

RUTH MOORE

1921

THE POLICE OF THE
HOUSE
Misc. short story.
Breezy Stories, June 1921.

NELLIE'S NAUGHTY
NIGHTIE
Misc. short story.
Breezy Stories, August
1921.

1923

THE SHRIEKING
SKELETON
(pen name, Charles M.
 Green)
Misc. short story.
Black Mask, December 15,
1923.

GAME OF THE BADGER
No publication informa-
tion. Approx. 1923.

IT WORKS PERFECTLY
(pen name, Charles M.
 Green)
Article.
Life Magazine (old),
approx. 1923.

NOTHING TO IT
(pen name, Charles M.
 Green)
Filler-article.
Droll Stories, approx. 1923.

SUSPENSE
No publication informa-
tion. Approx. 1923.

1924

THE SERPENT'S COILS
(pen name, Charles M.
 Green)
Misc. short story.
Black Mask, January 1,
1924.

THE POINT OF
INTERSECTION
(pen name, Charles M.
 Green)
Misc. short story.
Mystery Magazine, April
15, 1924.

A FAIR TRIAL
(Anonymous)
Misc. novelette.
Black Mask, June 1924.

PARTIES TO PROOF
Misc. novelette.
Top Notch, July 15, 1924.

ACCOMMODATIN' A
LADY
Bob Larkin short story.
Black Mask, September
1924.

A LANDLUBBER'S
CRUISE ON THE
YACHT "SPRAY"
Article.
Serialized in *Pacific Motor
Boat,* October–November,
1924.

WITHOUT NO
REINDEER
Bob Larkin novelette.
Black Mask, December
1924.

THE SEVENTH GLASS
(pen name, Charles M.
 Green)
Misc. short story.
Mystery Magazine, approx.
1924.

THE VERDICT
(pen name, Charles M.
 Green)
Misc. short story.
Black Mask, approx. 1924.

THE CAVE
(pen name, Charles M.
 Green)
Misc. short story.
Smart Set (?), approx.
1924.

THE TRAP
Misc. short story.
Chicago Ledger, approx.
1924.

BLOODY BILL
(pen name, Charles M.
 Green)
Misc. short story.
Chicago Ledger, approx.
1924.

JIM HURD'S WIFE
(pen name, Charles M.
 Green (?))
Misc. short story.
Smart Set, approx. 1924.

1925

BEYOND THE LAW
Ed Jenkins novelette.
Black Mask, January 1925.

THE FOG GHOST
Misc. novelette.
Top Notch, January 1,
1925.

THE CASE OF THE
MISPLACED THUMBS
Speed Dash novelette.
Top Notch, February 1,
1925.

HARD AS NAILS
Ed Jenkins novelette.
Black Mask, March 1925.

THE LAST WALLOP*
Western short story.
Short Stories, March 10,
1925.

TEN DAYS AFTER DATE
Speed Dash novelette.
Top Notch, March 15,
1925.

BEYOND THE LIMIT*
Misc. short story.
Sunset, April 1925.

EYES OF THE NIGHT
(pen name, Charles M.
 Green)
Misc. short story.
Triple-X, April 1925.

PAINLESS EXTRACTION
Bob Larkin novelette.
Black Mask, May 1925.

WITH FINGERS
OF STEEL
Speed Dash novelette.
Top Notch, May 15, 1925.

NOT SO DARN BAD*
Ed Jenkins novelette.
Black Mask, June 1925.

THREE O'CLOCK IN
THE MORNING*
Ed Jenkins novelette.
Black Mask, July 1925.

HAM, EGGS AND
COFFEE
Bob Larkin novelette.
Black Mask, August 1925.

TEMPERING FIRES
Misc. novelette.
Serialized in *The Farmer's
Wife,* August–September,
1925.

THE ROOM OF
FALLING FLIES
Speed Dash novelette.
Top Notch, September 15,
1925.

THE GIRL GOES WITH
ME
Black Barr novelette.
Black Mask, November
1925.

THE CASE OF THE
CANDIED DIAMONDS
Speed Dash novelette.
Top Notch, November 15,
1925.

A DESERT "SHEEK"
Western short story.
Brief Stories, December
1925.

THE TRIPLE CROSS
Ed Jenkins novelette.
Black Mask, December
1925.

THE LAW OF CACTUS
FLATS
Western novelette.
Argosy, approx. 1925.

ONE CHANCE TO LOVE
Misc. short story.
Dell Publications (no
magazine information),
approx. 1925.

THE WILL OF RICHARD
WARE
Misc. short story.
The Farmer's Wife,
approx. 1925.

THE JAZZ BABY
Misc. short story.
Macfadden Publications
(no magazine informa-
tion), approx. 1925.

THE THIRD DEGREE
Misc. short story.
No publication informa-
tion. Approx. 1925.

A BACHELOR AN'
A ORPHAN
Misc. short story.
Munsey Magazines group
(no magazine informa-
tion), approx. 1925.

1926

BEFORE DAWN
Western short story.
Brief Stories, January
1926.

PART MUSIC AND
PART TEARS
(Anonymous)
Misc. short story.
Smart Set, January 1926.

ACCORDING TO LAW
Ed Jenkins novelette.
Black Mask, January 1926.

ANY ONE NAMED
SMITH
Misc. novelette.
Flynn's Detective Fiction,
January 16, 1926.

TWISTED BARS
The Old Walrus short
story.
West, January 20, 1926.

GOIN' INTO ACTION
Bob Larkin short story.
Black Mask, February
1926.

THE SKELETON
ACCOMPLICE
Misc. novelette.
Top Notch, February 1,
1926.

"OPEN AND SHUT"
Misc. novelette.
Mystery Magazine,
February 15, 1926.

HOSS SENSE
Western short story.
Brief Stories, March 1926.

AN EYE FOR A TOOTH
The Old Walrus short
story.
West, March 20, 1926.

REGISTER RAGE
Ed Jenkins novelette.
Black Mask, April 1926.

WHEN A MAN'S ALONE
Misc. short story.
Smart Set, April 1926.

DOING IT UP BROWN
Western novelette.
Short Stories, April 10,
1926.

ACCORDING TO
SCHEDULE
The Old Walrus short
story.
West, April 20, 1926.

THISISSOSUDDEN!
Ed Jenkins novelette.
Black Mask, May 1926.

A FEATHER IN HIS CAP
Western novelette.
Top Notch, May 1, 1926.

SMILEY LANE'S WALL-
EYED JINX
Western short story.
Fighting Romances, June
1926.

FORGET 'EM ALL
Ed Jenkins novelette.
Black Mask, June 1926.

THE VEIL OF VERACITY
The Old Walrus short
story.
Cowboy Stories, June 1926.

NOW LISTEN!
Misc. short story.
Sunset, June 1926.

A MATE FOR EFFIE A
Misc. novelette.
Argosy, June 26, 1926.

ON THE POISON TRAIL
Western novelette.
Triple-X, July 1926.

MORE HUNTING LESS
KILLING
Article.
Outdoor Recreation, July
1926.

IN LOVE AND WAR
Misc. short story.
Argosy, July 24, 1926.

HAZEL OF THE MINING
CAMPS
Misc. short story.
Smart Set, August 1926.

THE LAW OF GLANC-
ING BULLETS
Fish Mouth McGinnis
short story.
Short Stories, August 25,
1926.

LAUGH THAT OFF
Ed Jenkins novelette.
Black Mask, September
1926.

A TIME-LOCK
TRIANGLE
Speed Dash novelette.
Top Notch, September 1,
1926.

THE MOB BUSTER
Western short story.
Argosy, September 4, 1926.

ON ALL SIX
Misc. short story.
Argosy, September 25, 1926.

THE ROUGH SHADOW
Misc. short story.
Clues, October 1926.

BUZZARD BAIT
Black Barr novelette.
Black Mask, October 1926.

MONEY, MARBLES AND CHALK
Ed Jenkins novelette.
Black Mask, November 1926.

MORE THAN SKIN DEEP
Western short story.
Top Notch, November 15, 1926.

DEAD MEN'S LETTERS
Ed Jenkins novelette.
Black Mask, December 1926.

THE MEANDERING TRAIL
Western short story.
Ace High, December 18, 1926.

STILL-HUNTING SMALL GAME
No publication information. Approx. 1926.

1927

WHISPERING SAND
Black Barr novelette.
Black Mask, January 1927.

THE GAME WINNER
The Old Walrus novelette.
Ace High, January 18, 1927.

THE CAT-WOMAN
Ed Jenkins novelette.
Black Mask, February 1927.

THREE DAYS TO MIDNIGHT
Speed Dash novelette.
Top Notch, February 1, 1927.

THIS WAY OUT
Ed Jenkins novelette.
Black Mask, March 1927.

THE CANYON OF THE CURSE
Western novelette.
Triple-X, March 1927.

THE CARDS OF DEATH*
Misc. novelette.
Clues, March 1927.

THE BACK TRAIL
Western short story.
Short Stories, March 10, 1927.

COME AND GET IT
Ed Jenkins novelette.
Black Mask, April 1927.

FOR HIGHER STAKES
Speed Dash novelette.
Top Notch, April 1, 1927.

ACES BACK TO BACK
Buck Riley novelette.
West, April 20, 1927.

FAIR WARNING
Misc. short story.
Clues, May 1927.

IN FULL OF ACCOUNT
Ed Jenkins novelette.
Black Mask, May 1927.

THE HOPE-SO HUNCH
Speed Dash novelette.
Top Notch, May 1, 1927.

A LOAD OF DYNAMITE
The Old Walrus short story.
West, May 5, 1927.

LANDLUBBING TO ALASKA
Article.
Sunset, June 1927.

THE RED SKULL*
Misc. novelette.
Clues, June 1927.

ON THE STROKE OF TWELVE
Speed Dash novelette.
Top Notch, June 15, 1927.

GETING AWAY FROM SCHEDULE
Article.
Field & Stream, August 1927.

RIBBONS OF LIGHT
Speed Dash novelette.
Top Notch, August 15, 1927.

WHERE THE BUZZARDS CIRCLE
Black Barr novelette.
Black Mask, September 1927.

ONE HUNDRED FEET OF ROPE
Buck Riley short story.
Brief Stories, October 1927.

THE WAX DRAGON
Ed Jenkins novelette.
Black Mask, November 1927.

THE LOG OF A LANDLUBBER*
Article.
Serialized in *Pacific Motor Boat*, November 1927–February 1928.

DOUBLE ACTION
Western novelette.
Short Stories, November 25, 1927.

THE TENTH POINT
Western novelette.
Outdoor Stories, December 1927.

GRINNING GODS
Ed Jenkins novelette.
Black Mask, December 1927.

THE CRIME TRAIL*
Sheriff Billy Bales short story.
Clues, approx. 1927.

THE GETAWAY
(pen name, Charles M. Green)
No publication information. Approx. 1927.

1928

THE RIGHT TRACK
Misc. novelette.
Complete Stories, January 1928.

THE BULLET GUIDE
Western short story.
Everybody's, January 1928.

WEST GOES EAST
Article.
Sunset, January 1928.

ADVENTURES IN ARCHERY
Article.
Outdoor Life, January 1928.

THE DEVIL'S THUMB
Buck Riley-Lost Mine novelette.
Brief Stories, February 1928.

YELLOW SHADOWS
Ed Jenkins novelette.
Black Mask, February 1928.

LORD OF THE HIGH
PLACES
Speed Dash novelette.
Top Notch, February 1,
1928.

THE DOOR OF DEATH
Misc. novelette.
Clues, February 25, 1928.

WHISPERING FEET
Ed Jenkins novelette.
Black Mask, March 1928.

SNOW BIRD
Ed Jenkins novelette.
Black Mask, April 1928.

CLAWS OF THE MAN-
BIRD
Speed Dash novelette.
Top Notch, April 1, 1928.

DEAD CENTER
Western novelette.
Serialized in *Three Star,*
April 12–May 24, 1928.

OUT OF THE SHADOWS
Ed Jenkins novelette.
Black Mask, May 1928.

THE GUILTY TRAIL
Sheriff Billy Bales short
story.
Clues, May 25, 1928.

GRUBSTAKE
Western short story.
Short Stories, May 25,
1928.

THE FUGITIVE MAN-
HUNTER
Western novelette.
Short Stories, June 10,
1928.

THE DEATH SHADOW
Sheriff Billy Bales short
story.
Clues, June 10, 1928.

GUN LANGUAGE
Western novelette.
Three Star, June 28, 1928.

THE LAW OF THE
LAWLESS
Western novelette.
Brief Stories, July 1928.

TRAPPED IN DARKNESS
Speed Dash novelette.
Top Notch, July 1, 1928.

THE FEMININE TOUCH
Misc. short story.
Clues, July 10, 1928.

THE DIAMOND OF
DESTINY
Misc. novelette.
Clues, July 25, 1928.

THE SKULL CRUSHER
Dave Barker novelette.
Three Star, July 26, 1928.

FANGS OF FATE
Black Barr novelette.
Black Mask, August 1928.

SKY PIRATES
Misc. novelette.
Three Star, August 9, 1928.

THE FALL GUY
Misc. short story.
Clues, August 10, 1928.

FINGERS OF FATE
Misc. novelette.
Three Star, August 23,
1928.

HARD-BOILED
Misc. short story.
Clues, August 25, 1928.

THE DEVIL'S DEPUTY
Black Barr novelette.
Black Mask, September
1928.

THE CASE OF THE
CRUSHED CARNATION
Speed Dash novelette.
Top Notch, September 1,
1928.

A BOLT FROM THE
BLUE
Misc. novelette.
Serialized in *Air Adven-
tures,* October 1928–
February 1929.

RAIN MAGIC*
Misc. novelette.
Argosy, October 20, 1928.

BROOD OF THE SEA
Misc. novelette.
Three Star, October 25,
1928.

RIPPLES OF DOOM
Dred Bart novelette.
Clues, October 25, 1928.

CURSE OF THE KILLERS
Black Barr novelette.
Black Mask, November
1928.

THE WEAK LINK
Misc. short story.
Detective Fiction Weekly,
November 10, 1928.

BARE HANDS
Western novelette.
Argosy, November 10,
1928.

A POINT OF HONOR
Misc. short story.
Clues, November 10, 1928.

THE NEXT STIFF
Ed Jenkins novelette.
Black Mask, December
1928.

CROOKED LIGHTNING*
Misc. short story.
Detective Fiction Weekly,
December 29, 1928.

1929

ONE CROOK TO
ANOTHER
Ed Jenkins novelette.
Black Mask, January 1929.

WHISPERING DEATH*
Misc. novelette.
Five Novels Monthly,
January 1929.

PHANTOM BULLETS
Speed Dash novelette.
Top Notch, January 1,
1929.

AN ARTISTIC JOB
Misc. short story.
Detective Fiction Weekly,
January 19, 1929.

BRACELETS FOR TWO
Ed Jenkins novelette.
Black Mask, February
1929.

ROUTINE STUFF
Misc. short story.
Mystery Stories, February
1929.

JUST A SUSPICION
Misc. short story.
Detective Fiction Weekly,
February 9, 1929.

THE PAINTED DECOY
Lester Leith novelette.
Detective Fiction Weekly,
February 23, 1929.

HOOKING THE CROOKS
Ed Jenkins novelette.
Black Mask, March 1929.

CLAWS OF CRIME
Speed Dash novelette.
Top Notch, March 1,
1929.

A TIP FROM SCUTTLE
Lester Leith novelette.
Detective Fiction Weekly,
March 2, 1929.

THE DUMMY MURDER
Lester Leith novelette.
Detective Fiction Weekly,
March 23, 1929.

NO QUESTIONS ASKED
Ed Jenkins novelette.
Black Mask, April 1929.

HAIRTRIGGER TRAILS THE HAWK
Western novelette.
Triple-X, April 1929.

THE CASE OF THE FUGITIVE CORPSE
Lester Leith novelette.
Detective Fiction Weekly, April 6, 1929.

THE PAY-OFF
Lester Leith novelette.
Detective Fiction Weekly, April 27, 1929.

A HOT TIP
Lester Leith novelette.
Detective Fiction Weekly, May 11, 1929.

WINGS OF DESTINY
Western novelette.
West, May 15, 1929.

ON THE UP AND UP
Misc. short story.
Clues, May 25, 1929.

SCUM OF THE BORDER
Bob Larkin novelette.
Black Mask, June 1929.

MANACLED VENGEANCE
Misc. short story.
Top Notch, June 1, 1929.

A CLEAN SLATE FOR SLIDER
Misc. novelette.
Detective Fiction Weekly, June 8, 1929.

KING OF THE EAGLE CLAN
Speed Dash novelette.
Top Notch, June 15, 1929.

ALL THE WAY
Bob Larkin novelette.
Black Mask, July 1929.

THE BETRAYING EMOTION
Dred Bart short story.
Detective Fiction Weekly, July 6, 1929.

A PEACH OF A SCHEME
Lester Leith novelette.
Detective Fiction Weekly, July 20, 1929.

STATE'S EVIDENCE
Misc. short story.
Clues, July 25, 1929.

MONKEY EYES
Misc. novelette.
Serialized in *Argosy*, July 27–August 3, 1929.

SPAWN OF THE NIGHT
Bob Larkin novelette.
Black Mask, August 1929.

EVEN MONEY
Lester Leith novelette.
Detective Fiction Weekly, August 3, 1929.

IT'S A PIPE!
Lester Leith novelette.
Detective Fiction Weekly, August 10, 1929.

THE HAND OF THE TONG
Misc. short story.
Clues, August 25, 1929.

FASTER THAN FORTY
Lester Leith novelette.
Detective Fiction Weekly, August 31, 1929.

HANGING FRIDAY
Bob Larkin novelette.
Black Mask, September 1929.

HAWKS OF THE MIDNIGHT SKY
Speed Dash novelette.
Top Notch, September 15, 1929.

DOUBLE SHADOWS
Lester Leith novelette.
Detective Fiction Weekly, September 21, 1929.

THE WINNING HAND
Misc. short story.
Clues, September 25, 1929.

STRAIGHT FROM THE SHOULDER
Ed Jenkins novelette.
Black Mask, October 1929.

THE ARTISTIC TOUCH
Lester Leith novelette.
Detective Fiction Weekly, October 26, 1929.

BRASS TACKS
Ed Jenkins novelette.
Black Mask, November 1929.

THE LETTER OF THE LAW
Misc. short story.
Clues, November 10, 1929.

LESTER TAKES THE CAKE
Lester Leith novelette.
Detective Fiction Weekly, November 23, 1929.

TRIPLE TREACHERY
Ed Jenkins novelette.
Black Mask, December 1929.

THE HARD-BOILED COMPANY
(pen name, Robert Parr (?))
Misc. novelette.
Prize Detective, December 1929.

THE DISAPPEARING WITNESSES
Misc. novelette.
Serialized in *Prize Detective*, December 1929 and February 1930.

THE SKY'S THE LIMIT
Misc. novelette.
Serialized in *Argosy*, December 7 and December 14, 1929.

THE SURPRISE PARTY
Misc. short story.
Clues, December 25, 1929.

FRAMED
Misc. short story.
Detective Fiction Weekly, December 28, 1929.

A SOCK ON THE JAW
Lester Leith novelette.
Detective Fiction Weekly, approx. 1929.

1930

DOUBLE OR QUITS
Ed Jenkins novelette.
Black Mask, January 1930.

BLUE FOR BLOOEY
Misc. short story.
Argosy, January 4, 1930.

THE DOUBTFUL EGG
Lester Leith novelette.
Detective Fiction Weekly, January 11, 1930.

ABOVE THE FOG
Misc. novelette.
Flyers, February 1930.

MIDNIGHT JUSTICE
Speed Dash novelette.
Top Notch, March 1, 1930.

THE HIGHER COURT*
Sidney Zoom short story.
Detective Fiction Weekly, March 8, 1930.

GOLD BLINDNESS
Whispering Story novelette.
Argosy, March 8, 1930.

FALL GUY
Whispering Story novelette.
Argosy, March 22, 1930.

THE GEMS OF TAI LEE
The Patent Leather Kid
short story.
Clues, March 25, 1930.

WILLIE THE WEEPER
Sidney Zoom short story.
Detective Fiction Weekly,
March 29, 1930.

THE GUY THAT
BUMPED GRIGSLEY
Misc. short story.
Short Stories, April 10,
1930.

"MY NAME IS ZOOM!"
Sidney Zoom novelette.
Detective Fiction Weekly,
April 12, 1930.

AN ADVENTURE
IN CRIME
Misc. novelette (?).
All Star Detective Stories,
May 1930.

THE CRIME CRUSHER
Ed Jenkins novelette.
Black Mask, May 1930.

BOTH ENDS AGAINST
THE MIDDLE
Lester Leith novelette.
Detective Fiction Weekly,
May 3, 1930.

THE PURPLE PLUME
Sidney Zoom novelette.
Detective Fiction Weekly,
May 24, 1930.

LOOSE THREADS OF
CRIME
Misc. short story.
Clues, May 25, 1930.

STONE FROGS
Whispering Story short
story.
Argosy, May 31, 1930.

HELL'S KETTLE
Ed Jenkins novelette.
Black Mask, June 1930.

GOLDEN BULLETS
Whispering Story
novelette.
Argosy, June 7, 1930.

PUT IT IN WRITING!
Lester Leith novelette.
Detective Fiction Weekly,
June 7, 1930.

GODS WHO FROWN
Yee Dooey Wah short
story.
Clues, June 15, 1930.

A FAIR REWARD
Misc. novelette.
Detective Fiction Weekly,
June 28, 1930.

BIG SHOT
Ed Jenkins novelette.
Black Mask, July 1930.

THE CHOICE OF
WEAPONS
Senor Lobo short story.
Detective Fiction Weekly,
July 12, 1930.

A SHORT CUT TO
ROME
Misc. novelette.
Complete Stories, July 15,
1930.

A YEAR IN A DAY
Misc. novelette.
Argosy, July 19, 1930.

STAINED
Misc. short story.
Clues, July 25, 1930.

HOT DOLLARS!
Lester Leith novelette.
Detective Fiction Weekly,
July 26, 1930.

THE CRIME WAFFLE
Misc. novelette.
Detective Fiction Weekly,
August 9, 1930.

IN ROUND FIGURES*
Lester Leith novelette.
Detective Fiction Weekly,
August 23, 1930.

THUMBS DOWN
Misc. novelette.
All Star Detective Stories,
September 1930.

TIME IN FOR TUCKER
Sidney Zoom novelette.
Detective Fiction Weekly,
September 13, 1930.

THE VALLEY OF
LITTLE FEARS*
Whispering Story short
story.
Argosy, September 13,
1930.

BLOOD-RED GOLD
Whispering Story
novelette.
Argosy, September 20,
1930.

THE MAN ON THE END
Lester Leith novelette.
Detective Fiction Weekly,
September 27, 1930.

THE CRIME JUGGLER
Paul Pry short story.
Gang World, October
1930.

THE KEY TO ROOM 537
Misc. novelette.
Detective Action, October
1930.

THE VOICE OF THE
ACCUSER
Yee Dooey Wah short
story.
Detective Fiction Weekly,
October 11, 1930.

WRITTEN IN SAND
Whispering Story short
story.
Argosy, October 25, 1930.

THE FAST WORKER
Misc. short story.
Swift Story, November
1930.

THE MURDER
MASQUERADE
Misc. novelette.
Detective Action Stories,
November 1930.

THE RACKET BUSTER
Paul Pry short story.
Gang World, November
1930.

WALRUS
Western short story. (Not
the Old Walrus series.)
Western Adventures,
November 1930.

LUCK CHARMS
Misc. short story.
Detective Fiction Weekly,
November 1, 1930.

GANGSTERS' GOLD
Senor Lobo novelette.
Detective Fiction Weekly,
November 15, 1930.

ONE MAN LAW
Misc. short story.
Clues, November 25, 1930.

THE DAISY-PUSHER
Paul Pry novelette.
Gang World, December
1930.

MUSCLING IN
Misc. short story.
Underworld, December
1930.

DEAD MEN'S TALES
Misc. novelette.
Detective Action Stories,
December 1930.

RED HANDS
Senor Lobo short story.
Detective Fiction Weekly,
December 6, 1930.

PRIESTESS OF THE SUN
Whispering Story short
story.
Argosy, December 6, 1930.

**LESTER FRAMES A
FENCE**
Lester Leith novelette.
Detective Fiction Weekly,
December 13, 1930.

A HORSE ON FANE
Western short story.
Clues, December 25, 1930.

THE VALLEY OF FEUDS
Misc. novelette.
Prize Air Pilot Stories,
approx. 1930.

BLIND MAN'S BLUFF
Misc. novelette.
All Star Detective, approx.
1930.

TELL-TALE SANDS
Fish Mouth McGinnis
short story.
Complete Stories, approx.
1930.

1931

**WIKER GETS THE
WORKS**
Paul Pry novelette.
Gang World, January
1931.

**THE MYSTERIOUS MR.
MANSE**
Mr. Manse novelette.
Detective Action Stories,
January 1931.

**WHAT CHANCE HAS
THE NEW WRITER?**
Article.
Writer's Digest, January
1931.

STRANGER'S SILK
Sidney Zoom novelette.
Detective Fiction Weekly,
January 3, 1931.

**THE MAN WITH
PIN-POINT EYES**
Misc. novelette.
Argosy, January 10, 1931.

THE DEATH PENALTY
Sidney Zoom novelette.
Detective Fiction Weekly,
January 17, 1931.

COLD CLEWS
Lester Leith novelette.
Detective Fiction Weekly,
January 24, 1931.

AIRTIGHT ALIBIS
Misc. short story.
Clues, January 25, 1931.

COFFINS FOR SIX
Misc. novelette.
All Star Detective Stories,
February 1931.

**A DOUBLE DEAL IN
DIAMONDS**
Paul Pry novelette.
Gang World, February
1931.

PLANTED BAIT
Mr. Manse novelette.
Detective Action Stories,
February 1931.

DICE OF DEATH
Misc. novelette.
Amazing Detective,
February 1931.

A MATTER OF IMPULSE
Senor Lobo novelette.
Detective Fiction Weekly,
February 7, 1931.

KILLED AND CURED
Senor Lobo short story.
Detective Fiction Weekly,
February 21, 1931.

THE PURPLE PALM
Mr. Manse novelette.
Detective Action Stories,
March 1931.

RIDDLED WITH LEAD
Paul Pry novelette.
Gang World, March 1931.

**THE LIGHTHOUSE
MURDER**
Misc. novelette.
Amazing Detective Stories,
March 1931.

TABLES FOR LADIES
Misc. short story.
Clues, March 10, 1931.

THE CANDY KID*
Lester Leith novelette.
Detective Fiction Weekly,
March 14, 1931.

BORROWED BULLETS
Sidney Zoom novelette.
Detective Fiction Weekly,
March 21, 1931.

THE MURDER MARK
Mr. Manse novelette.
Detective Action Stories,
April 1931.

SLICK AND CLEAN
Paul Pry novelette.
Gang World, April 1931.

THE COVERED CORPSE
Misc. novelette.
Amazing Detective Stories,
April 1931.

FIRST AND LAST
Misc. short story.
Clues, April 10, 1931.

BIG MONEY
Lester Leith novelette.
Detective Fiction Weekly,
April 18, 1931.

PAY DIRT
Whispering Story
novelette.
Argosy, April 25, 1931.

HOT TIPS
Misc. novelette.
Detective Action Stories,
May 1931.

HIJACKER'S CODE
Paul Pry short story.
Gang World, May 1931.

HER DOGGY FRIEND
Misc. short story.
Detective Story, May 2,
1931.

CARVED IN JADE
Senor Lobo novelette.
Detective Fiction Weekly,
May 9, 1931.

THE DEVIL'S DUE
Major Brane novelette.
Argosy, May 23, 1931.

HOT CASH
Lester Leith novelette.
Detective Fiction Weekly,
May 23, 1931.

THE THIRD KEY
Misc. novelette.
Detective Action Stories,
June 1931.

THE EASY MARK
Paul Pry short story.
Gang World, June 1931.

A CHINAMAN'S CHANCE
Misc. short story.
Detective Fiction Weekly,
June 6, 1931.

SIGN OF THE SUN
Whispering Story short
story.
Argosy, June 27, 1931.

NOT SO DUMB
Lester Leith novelette.
Detective Fiction Weekly,
June 27, 1931.

ONE MAN GANG
Paul Pry novelette.
Gang World, July 1931.

TOMMY TALK
Ed Jenkins novelette.
Black Mask, July 1931.

A FRYING JOB
Misc. short story.
Clues, July 1931.

THE JELLYFISH
CORPSE
Misc. novelette.
Detective Action Stories,
July 1931.

THE EYES OF THE LAW
Misc. short story.
Gangland Stories, July–
August 1931.

THE GIRL WITH THE
DIAMOND LEGS
Lester Leith novelette.
Detective Fiction Weekly,
July 11, 1931.

COFFINS FOR KILLERS
Senor Lobo short story.
Detective Fiction Weekly,
July 25, 1931.

TWO FLOWERS OF
FATE
Misc. novelette.
Detective Action Stories,
August 1931.

HOODOO
Misc. short story.
Clues, August 1931.

HAIRY HANDS
Ed Jenkins novelette.
Black Mask, August 1931.

CAR FARE TO CHI
Paul Pry novelette.
Gang World, August 1931.

AIN'T THAT TOO BAD
Misc. short story.
Detective Fiction Weekly,
August 1, 1931.

THE VANISHING
CORPSE
Sidney Zoom novelette.
Detective Fiction Weekly,
August 15, 1931.

THE WINNER
Western short story.
Western Adventures,
September 1931.

THE SEAL OF SILENCE
Misc. novelette.
Detective Action Stories,
September 1931.

PROMISE TO PAY
Ed Jenkins novelette.
Black Mask, September
1931.

MUSCLE MAN
Paul Pry novelette.
Gang World, September
1931.

SILENT TONGUES
(pen name, Kyle Corning)
Double Decker short story.
Detective Story, September
5, 1931.

HIGHER UP
Sidney Zoom novelette.
Detective Fiction Weekly,
September 19, 1931.

THE GOLD MAGNET
Lester Leith novelette.
Detective Fiction Weekly,
September 26, 1931.

DEAD FINGERS
Misc. novelette.
Detective Action Stories,
October 1931.

THE HOT SQUAT
Ed Jenkins novelette.
Black Mask, October 1931.

LOADED WITH
DYNAMITE
Paul Pry novelette.
Gang World, October
1931.

STAMP OF THE DESERT
Whispering Story short
story.
Argosy, October 17, 1931.

THE FIRST STONE*
Sidney Zoom novelette.
Detective Fiction Weekly,
October 24, 1931.

THE GLOVED MYSTERY
Rex Kane short story.
Detective Action Stories,
November 1931.

THE CAT-EYED WENCH
Paul Pry novelette.
Gang World, November
1931.

THE CRIMSON MASK
Lester Leith novelette.
Detective Fiction Weekly,
November 7, 1931.

SINGING SAND
Whispering Story
novelette.
Argosy, November 7, 1931.

ROLLING STONES
Lester Leith novelette.
Detective Fiction Weekly,
November 21, 1931.

TURN OF THE TIDE*
(pen name, Kyle Corning)
Double Decker short
story.
Detective Story, November
21, 1931.

STRICTLY PERSONAL
Ed Jenkins novelette.
Black Mask, December
1931.

THE KNOCKOUT GUY
Paul Pry novelette.
Gang World, December
1931.

BETWEEN TWO FIRES
Rex Kane novelette.
Detective Action Stories,
December 1931.

NO ROUGH STUFF
Senor Lobo novelette.
Detective Fiction Weekly,
December 5, 1931.

SAUCE FOR THE
GANDER
Senor Lobo novelette.
Detective Fiction Weekly,
December 12, 1931.

THE HUMAN ZERO*
Misc. novelette.
Argosy, December 19, 1931.

RED HERRING
Lester Leith novelette.
Detective Fiction Weekly,
December 26, 1931.

PAYOFF AT SPILLWAY
(pen name, Kyle
Corning (?))
Western short story.
Western Stories, approx.
1931.

FAIR PLAY
Misc. short story (?)
Western Trails (?), approx.
1931.

SNOWY DUCKS FOR
COVER
Misc. short story.
No publication informa-
tion. Approx. 1931.

1932

HELL'S FIREWORKS
Paul Pry novelette.
Gang World, January
1932.

FACE UP
Ed Jenkins novelette.
Black Mask, January 1932.

LOCAL COLOR
Article.
Writer's Digest, January
1932.

THE CORKSCREW KID
Misc. short story.
Black Aces, January 1932.

HONEST MONEY
Ken Corning novelette.
Black Mask, November
1932.

FALSE ALARM
Lester Leith novelette.
Detective Fiction Weekly,
November 5, 1932.

TRUMPS
Senor Lobo short story.
Detective Fiction Weekly,
November 12, 1932.

MARKED MONEY
Dane Skarle novelette.
Dime Detective, December
1932.

THE TOP COMES OFF*
Ken Corning novelette.
Black Mask, December
1932.

THE LAW OF THE
BORDERLAND
Steve Raney novelette.
Clues, December 1932.

HANDS OF DEATH
Dave Barker novelette.
Rapid Fire Detective,
December 1932.

A CLEAN GETAWAY
Senor Lobo novelette.
Detective Fiction Weekly,
December 3, 1932.

NEW WORLDS*
Misc. novelette.
Argosy, December 17,
1932.

JUGGLED GEMS
Lester Leith novelette.
Detective Fiction Weekly,
December 24, 1932.

TICKETS FOR TWO
Senor Lobo novelette.
Detective Fiction Weekly,
December 31, 1932.

THE PINK DUCK
Major Brane short story.
Argosy, December 31,
1932.

MAKE IT SNAPPY
Misc. novelette.
Detective Action Stories,
approx. 1932.

CRIME CONDITIONS
IN THE ORIENT
Article-filler.
Clues, approx. 1932.

THE COLD KILL
Dick Bentley novelette.
Dime Detective, approx.
1932.

1933

CLOSE CALL
Ken Corning novelette.
Black Mask, January 1933.

FRAMED IN GUILT
Dane Skarle novelette.
Dime Detective, January
1933.

INSIDE JOB
Sidney Zoom novelette.
Detective Fiction Weekly,
January 7, 1933.

THE SPOILS OF WAR
Senor Lobo novelette.
Detective Fiction Weekly,
January 14, 1933.

THE LAND OF PAINTED
ROCKS
Whispering Story
novelette.
Argosy, January 28, 1933.

THE DANCE OF THE
DAGGER
Steve Raney novelette.
Clues, February 1933.

SMUDGE
Misc. novelette.
All Detective, February
1933.

THE HOUR OF THE
RAT
Ed Jenkins novelette.
Black Mask, February
1933.

FROZEN MURDER
Small, Weston & Burke
novelette.
Dime Detective, February
1933.

ONE JUMP AHEAD
Lester Leith novelette.
Detective Fiction Weekly,
February 4, 1933.

THE KID MAKES A BID
The Patent Leather Kid
short story.
Detective Fiction Weekly,
February 18, 1933.

RED JADE
Ed Jenkins novelette.
Black Mask, March 1933.

FINGERS OF FONG*
Misc. short story.
All Detective, March 1933.

THE WORD OF A
CROOK
Misc. novelette.
Clues, March 1933.

LAW OF THE ROPE
Whispering Story short
story.
Argosy, March 11, 1933.

LEADEN HONEYMOON
Senor Lobo novelette.
Detective Fiction Weekly,
March 11, 1933.

EARLY BIRDS
Misc short story.
Detective Fiction Weekly,
March 25, 1933.

HOG WILD
Article.
Field & Stream, April
1933.

THE CITY OF FEAR
Misc. novelette.
All Detective, April 1933.

CHINATOWN MURDER
Ed Jenkins novelette.
Black Mask, April 1933.

THE RADIO RUSE
Lester Leith novelette.
Detective Fiction Weekly,
April 1, 1933.

DEATH'S DOORWAY
Go Get 'Em Garver
novelette.
Dime Detective, April 1,
1933.

THE KID MUSCLES IN
The Patent Leather Kid
short story.
Detective Fiction Weekly,
April 15, 1933.

THE DANCE OF THE
SNAKES
Small, Weston & Burke
novelette.
Dime Detective, April 15,
1933.

LAW OF THE GHOST
TOWN
Whispering Story short
story.
Argosy, April 22, 1933.

A LOGICAL ENDING
Misc. short story.
Detective Fiction Weekly,
April 29, 1933.

BOTH ENDS
Misc. short story.
All Detective, May 1933.

THE WEAPONS OF A
CROOK
Ed Jenkins novelette.
Black Mask, May 1933.

RESULTS
Senor Lobo novelette.
Detective Fiction Weekly,
May 6, 1933.

THE KID TAKES A CUT
The Patent Leather Kid
short story.
Detective Fiction Weekly,
May 20, 1933.

**THE WATCHFUL EYES
OF TAIPING**
Major Brane short story.
Argosy, May 27, 1933.

MURDER APPRENTICE
Dudley Bell novelette.
All Detective, June 1933.

MAKING THE BREAKS
Ken Corning novelette.
Black Mask, June 1933.

**DEAD MAN'S
DIAMONDS**
Go Get 'Em Garver
novelette.
Dime Detective, June 1,
1933.

THIN ICE
Lester Leith novelette.
Detective Fiction Weekly,
June 10, 1933.

**THE HAND OF
HORROR**
Misc. novelette.
Dime Detective, June 15–
July 1, 1933.

CARVED IN SAND
Whispering Story
novelette.
Argosy, June 17, 1933.

CATCH AS CATCH CAN
Misc. short story.
All Detective, July 1933.

DEVIL'S FIRE
Ken Corning novelette.
Black Mask, July 1933.

CROOKS' VACATION
Lester Leith novelette.
Detective Fiction Weekly,
July 8, 1933.

AS FAR AS THE POLES
Misc. novelette.
Short Stories, July 25,
1933.

**WHO OWNS THE
MOUNTAINS?**
Article.
Field & Stream, August
1933.

**BLACKMAIL WITH
LEAD**
Ken Corning novelette.
Black Mask, August 1933.

THE BROKEN LINK
Dudley Bell short story.
All Detective, August
1933.

NIGHT BIRDS
El Paisano novelette.
Argosy, August 5, 1933.

**THE KID BEATS THE
GUN**
The Patent Leather Kid
novelette.
Detective Fiction Weekly,
August 5, 1933.

WHISPERING JUSTICE
Ed Jenkins novelette.
Black Mask, September
1933.

SECOND-STORY LAW
Bob Crowder short story.
All Detective, September
1933.

DRESSED TO KILL
Paul Pry short story.
Dime Detective,
September 1, 1933.

THE BIG CIRCLE
Whispering Story
novelette.
Argosy, September 2,
1933.

**SNATCH AS SNATCH
CAN**
Paul Pry novelette.
Dime Detective,
September 15, 1933.

THE SIRENS OF WAR
Senor Lobo novelette.
Detective Fiction Weekly,
September 16, 1933.

**THE CLEARING HOUSE
OF CRIME**
Perry Burke—The
Clearing House of
Crime short story.
Clues, October 1933.

COMMITTEE OF ONE
Misc. short story.
All Detective, October
1933.

THE MURDER PUSH
Ed Jenkins novelette.
Black Mask, October
1933.

**THE CRIMSON
SCORPION**
Small, Weston & Burke
novelette.
Dime Detective, October
15, 1933.

LIFTED BAIT
Sidney Zoom novelette.
Detective Fiction Weekly,
October 21, 1933.

PITCHED BATTLE
Perry Burke—The
Clearing House of
Crime novelette.
Clues, November 1933.

RESTLESS PEARLS
Bob Crowder short story.
All Detective, November
1933.

THE MANIAC MYSTERY
Misc. short story.
Strange Detective,
November 1933.

**THE KID COVERS A
KILL**
The Patent Leather Kid
novelette.
Detective Fiction Weekly,
November 4, 1933.

DOMINOES OF DEATH
Misc. novelette.
Short Stories, November
10, 1933.

BORDER JUSTICE
El Paisano short story.
Argosy, November 11,
1933.

**THE CROSS-STITCH
KILLER**
Paul Pry novelette.
Dime Detective,
November 15, 1933.

COSTS OF COLLECTION
Senor Lobo novelette.
Detective Fiction Weekly,
November 18, 1933.

THE DEATH TRAIL
(pen name, Les Tillray
(?))
Misc. short story.
Startling Detective,
December 1933.

BEHIND THE MASK
Bob Crowder short story.
All Detective, December
1933.

DEAD MEN'S SHOES
Ed Jenkins novelette.
Black Mask, December
1933.

**THE BURDEN OF
PROOF**
Lester Leith novelette.
Detective Fiction Weekly,
December 2, 1933.

THE CASE OF THE
VELVET CLAWS
Perry Mason book.
Morrow, March 1933;
Pocket, September 1940.

THE CASE OF THE
SULKY GIRL
Perry Mason book.
Morrow, September 1933;
Pocket, January 1941.

1934

A GUEST OF THE
HOUSE
Ed Jenkins novelette.
Black Mask, January 1934.

TIME FOR MURDER
Misc. novelette.
Dime Detective, January
15, 1934.

THE CODE OF A
FIGHTER
Senor Lobo novelette.
Detective Fiction Weekly,
January 27, 1934.

THE JACK OF DEATH
Bob Crowder novelette.
All Detective, February
1934

LANDLUBBIN' DOWN
THE MEXICAN COAST
Article.
Serialized in *Pacific Motor
Boat*, February–May
1934.

THE KID CLEARS A
CROOK
The Patent Leather Kid
novelette.
Detective Fiction Weekly,
February 3, 1934.

THE LIZARD'S CAGE
El Paisano novelette.
Argosy, February 10, 1934.

LOST, STRAYED AND
STOLEN
Lester Leith novelette.
Detective Fiction Weekly,
February 24, 1934.

LAWLESS WATERS
Misc. novelette.
Short Stories, February 25,
1934.

COP KILLERS
Ed Jenkins novelette.
Black Mask, March 1934.

SILENT DEATH
Misc. novelette.
All Detective, March 1934.

THE IVORY CASKET
Major Brane novelette.
Argosy, March 17, 1934.

NEW TWENTIES
Ed Jenkins novelette.
Black Mask, April 1934.

CHISELER'S CHOICE
Misc. novelette.
Dime Detective, April 1,
1934.

A MATTER OF
ACCOUNTING
El Paisano novelette.
Argosy, April 21, 1934.

THE KID CLIPS A
COUPON
The Patent Leather Kid
novelette.
Detective Fiction Weekly,
April 21, 1934.

SILVER STRANDS OF
DEATH
Misc. novelette.
Super Detective, May
1934.

THE SMOKING CORPSE
Misc. novelette.
Dime Detective, May 1,
1934.

BROKEN EGGS
Senor Lobo novelette.
Detective Fiction Weekly,
May 5, 1934.

PROOFS OF DEATH
Major Brane novelette.
Argosy, May 12, 1934.

STOLEN THUNDER
Sidney Zoom novelette.
Detective Fiction Weekly,
May 19, 1934.

BURNT FINGERS
Ed Jenkins novelette.
Black Mask, June 1934.

THE FACE LIFTER
Misc. novelette.
All Detective, June 1934.

DEAD TO RIGHTS
Lester Leith novelette.
Detective Fiction Weekly,
June 2, 1934.

WHITE RINGS
Jax Bowman—White
Rings novelette.
Argosy, June 30, 1934.

CROCODILE TEARS
Lester Leith novelette.
Detective Fiction Weekly,
June 30, 1934.

THE WAR LORD OF
DARKNESS
Misc. novelette.
Adventure, July 1934.

THE KID COOKS A
GOOSE
The Patent Leather Kid
novelette.
Detective Fiction Weekly,
July 14, 1934.

SAND BLAST
Whispering Story
novelette.
Argosy, July 21, 1934.

THE HEAVENLY RAT
Ed Jenkins novelette.
Black Mask, September
1934.

HUNDRED GRAND
Misc. novelette.
Serialized in *This Week*,
September 9–October 28,
1934.

NO QUARTER
Jax Bowman—White
Rings novelette.
Argosy, September 22,
1934.

THE MAN WHO
COULDN'T FORGET
The Man Who Couldn't
Forget novelette.
All Detective, October
1934.

OPPORTUNITY
KNOCKS TWICE
Senor Lobo novelette.
Detective Fiction Weekly,
October 27, 1934.

HOT CASH
Ed Jenkins short story.
Black Mask, November
1934.

THE KID STEALS A
STAR
The Patent Leather Kid
novelette.
Detective Fiction Weekly,
November 17, 1934.

THE PURRING DOOM
Small, Weston & Burke
novelette.
Dime Detective, December
1934.

THE BLACK EGG
Misc. novelette.
Short Stories, December
10, 1934.

SUICIDE HOUSE
Small, Weston & Burke
novelette.
Dime Detective, December
15, 1934.

THE CASE OF THE
LUCKY LEGS
Perry Mason book.
Morrow, February 1934;
Pocket, May 1941.

THE CASE OF THE
HOWLING DOG
Perry Mason book.
Serialized in *Liberty
Magazine,* January 13–
March 17, 1934.
Morrow, June 1934;
Pocket, August 1941.

THE CASE OF THE
CURIOUS BRIDE
Perry Mason book.
Serialized in *Liberty
Magazine,* July 7–
September 15, 1934.
Morrow, November 1934;
Pocket, October 1942.

1935

WINGED LEAD
Black Barr novelette.
Black Mask, January 1935.

HARD AS NAILS
Misc. novelette.
Dime Detective, January
15, 1935.

QUEENS WILD
Lester Leith novelette.
Detective Fiction Weekly,
January 26, 1935.

STRONG MEDICINE
El Paisano novelette.
Argosy, January 26, 1935.

AN AUTHOR LOOKS
AT AGENTS
Article.
*American Fiction Guild
Bulletin,* February 15,
1935.

THE DARK BLOND
(pen name, Carleton
Kendrake)
Misc., book-length.
Serialized by NEA
syndicate in various
newspapers, beginning
in March 1935.

THE VAULT OF DEATH
The Man Who Couldn't
Forget novelette.
Detective Fiction Weekly,
March 9, 1935.

MURDER BAIT
Misc. novelette.
Dime Detective, March
15, 1935.

SMALL DEER OF
CEDROS
Article.
Field & Stream, April
1935.

A CHANCE TO CHEAT
Ed Jenkins novelette.
Black Mask, May 1935.

FUGITIVE GOLD
Misc. novelette.
Serialized in *This Week,*
May 26–July 7, 1935.

THE MAN IN THE
SILVER MASK
The Man in the Silver
Mask novelette.
Detective Fiction Weekly,
July 13, 1935.

CRIMSON JADE
Misc. novelette.
Dime Detective,
September 1935.

THE MAN WHO
TALKED
The Man in the Silver
Mask novelette.
Detective Fiction Weekly,
September 7, 1935.

BUNCHED KNUCKLES
Jax Bowman—White
Rings novelette.
Argosy, September 21,
1935.

CRASH AND CARRY
Ed Jenkins novelette.
Black Mask, October 1935.

FACE DOWN
(pen name, Charles J.
Kenny)
Misc. novelette.
Serialized in *Photoplay,*
October 1935–March
1936.

SCREAMING SIRENS
Lester Leith novelette.
Detective Fiction Weekly,
November 2, 1935.

THE SILVER MASK
MURDERS
The Man in the Silver
Mask novelette.
Detective Fiction Weekly,
November 23, 1935.

ABOVE THE LAW
Ed Jenkins novelette.
Black Mask, December
1935.

THE FRAME-UP*
Misc. novelette.
Serialized in *This Week,*
December 15, 1935–
January 19, 1936.

THE CLUE OF THE
FORGOTTEN MURDER
Sidney Griff book.
Originally published as
"The Clew of the For-
gotten Murder" under
pen name, Carleton Ken-
drake.
Morrow, January 1935;
Pocket, June 1947.

THE CASE OF THE
COUNTERFEIT EYE
Perry Mason book.
Morrow, April 1935;
Pocket, May 1942.

THIS IS MURDER
Sam Moraine book.
Originally published
under pen name, Charles
J. Kenny.
Morrow, June 1935;
Pocket, May 1948.

THE CASE OF THE
CARETAKER'S CAT
Perry Mason book.
Serialized in *Liberty
Magazine,* June 15–
August 17, 1935.
Morrow, September 1935;
Pocket, January 1942.

*MOTION PICTURE
RELEASES:*

(Based on Mr. Gardner's
published material and
scripts were edited by
him)

THE CASE OF THE
HOWLING DOG. Warner
Bros., 1935.

THE CASE OF THE
CURIOUS BRIDE. Warner
Bros., 1935.

THE CASE OF THE
LUCKY LEGS. Warner
Bros., 1935.

FUGITIVE GOLD. RKO
under title "Special
Investigator," 1935.

THIS IS MURDER. East-
ern Service Studios, approx.
1935.

1936

SLATED TO DIE
Misc. novelette.
Argosy, January 11, 1936.

BALD-HEADED ROW
Lester Leith novelette.
Detective Fiction Weekly,
March 21, 1936.

THE SCORE CARD
DOESN'T COUNT
Article.
International Sport Digest,
April 1936.

COME-ON GIRL
(pen name, Charles J.
Kenny)
Sam Moraine novelette.
The American Magazine,
May 1936.

BEATING THE BULLS
Ed Jenkins novelette.
Black Mask, May 1936.

COMPLETE DESIGNS
Misc. short story.
Short Stories, July 25,
1936.

DESERT MADNESS
Article.
Field & Stream, September
1936.

THE COMING FICTION
TREND
Article.
Writer's Digest, September
1936.

TEETH OF THE
DRAGON
Misc. novelette.
Serialized in *This Week,*
September 13–October
18, 1936.

TWO STICKS OF DEATH
Small, Weston & Burke
novelette.
Dime Detective, November
1936.

STUMP-HUNTING
STUNTS
Article.
Ye Sylvan Archer,
December 1936.

THE CASE OF THE
SLEEPWALKER'S NIECE
Perry Mason book.
Morrow, March 1936;
Pocket, December 1944.

THE CASE OF THE
STUTTERING BISHOP
Perry Mason book.
Morrow, September 1936;
Pocket, March 1943.

*MOTION PICTURE
RELEASES:*

THE CASE OF THE
VELVET CLAWS. Warner
Bros., 1936.

THE CASE OF THE
CARETAKER'S CAT.
Warner Bros., under title
"The Case of the Black
Cat," 1936.

1937

THIS WAY OUT
Ed Jenkins novelette.
Black Mask, March 1937.

UNDER THE KNIFE
Win Layton—Girl
Reporter novelette.
Serialized in *This Week,*
March 21–April 11, 1937.

INTRODUCTION TO
ARCHERY
Article.
Ye Sylvan Archer, April
1937.

THE LOWER BRACKET
BOYS
Article.
Ye Sylvan Archer, June
1937.

AMONG THIEVES
Pete Wennick novelette.
Black Mask, September
1937.

STUMP HUNTING IN
SEATTLE
Article.
Ye Sylvan Archer,
October 1937.

DOING IT THE HARD
WAY
Article.
Writer's Digest Year Book,
1937.

SKETCH ON DON
BLANDING
Article.
Carmel Pine Cone.
Approx. 1937.

THE D. A. CALLS IT
MURDER
Doug Selby, the D.A.,
book.
Serialized under title
"The Thread of Truth"
in *Country Gentleman,*
September 1936–January
1937.
Morrow, January 1937;
Pocket, July 1944.

THE CASE OF THE
DANGEROUS DOWAGER
Perry Mason book.
Morrow, April 1937;
Pocket, March 1944.

THE CASE OF THE
LAME CANARY
Perry Mason book.
Serialized in *The Saturday
Evening Post,* May 29–
July 17, 1937.
Morrow, September 1937;
Pocket, July 1943.

MURDER UP MY
SLEEVE
Terry Clane book.
Cosmopolitan, September
1937.
Morrow, November 1937;
Pocket, April 1946.

*MOTION PICTURE
RELEASE:*

THE CASE OF THE
STUTTERING BISHOP.
Warner Bros., 1937.

1938

BLIND DATE WITH
DEATH
Win Layton—Girl
Reporter novelette.
Serialized in *This Week,*
January 30–February 20,
1938.

LEG MAN
Pete Wennick novelette.
Black Mask, February
1938.

MUSCLE OUT
Ed Jenkins novelette.
Black Mask, April 1938.

SALESMANSHIP FOR
WRITERS
Article.
Author & Journalist, May
1938.

TWICE IN A ROW*
Misc. novelette.
Cosmopolitan, June 1938.

THE FINISHING
TOUCH
Paul Pry novelette.
Dime Detective, August
1938.

WITHIN QUOTES
Article.
Writer's Digest, August
1938.

THE CASE OF THE
HOLLYWOOD SCANDAL
Misc. novelette.
Serialized in *Photoplay,*
September 1938–January
1939.

IT'S A WILD COUNTRY
Article.
Ye Sylvan Archer,
November 1938.

THE HOUSE OF THREE
CANDLES*
Misc. short story.
This Week, November 6,
1938.

PLANTED PLANETS
Lester Leith novelette.
Detective Story, December
1938.

BARNEY KILLIGEN
Barney Killigen novelette.
Clues, December 1938.

THE CASE OF THE
SUBSTITUTE FACE
Perry Mason book.
Morrow, April 1938;
Pocket, December 1943.

THE CASE OF THE
SHOPLIFTER'S SHOE
Perry Mason book.
Morrow, September 1938;
Pocket, September 1945.

THE D. A. HOLDS A
CANDLE
Doug Selby, the D. A.,
book.
Serialized in *Country
Gentleman,* September
1938–January 1939.
Morrow, November 1938;
Pocket, March 1945.

1939

THE MONKEY MURDER
Lester Leith novelette.
Detective Story, January
1939.

WITHOUT GLOVES
Barney Killigen novelette.
Clues, January 1939.

IT'S THE McCOY
Paul Pry novelette.
Dime Detective, January
1939.

GETTING LOCAL
COLOR
Article-filler.
Clues, January (or
February), 1939.

UNSTUFFING ONE
SHIRT
Barney Killigen short
story.
Clues, February 1939.

THE SEVEN SINISTER
SOMBREROS
Lester Leith novelette.
Detective Story, February
1939.

WHAT'S HOLDING US
BACK?*
Article.
The Writer, February
1939.

THE JOSS OF TAI WONG
Misc. short story.
Adventure, March 1939.

THE FOURTH
MUSKETEER
Lester Leith novelette.
Detective Story, March
1939.

TAKE IT OR LEAVE IT*
Pete Wennick novelette.
Black Mask, March 1939.

WITH RHYME AND
REASON
Lester Leith novelette.
Detective Story, April
1939.

THE QUEEN OF
SHANGHAI NIGHT*
Lester Leith novelette.
Detective Story, May 1939.

DOGS OF DEATH
Barney Killigen novelette.
Clues, May 1939.

TREEING STUMPS
WITH BLOODHOUNDS
Article.
Ye Sylvan Archer, May
1939.

THE EYEBROW MOON
Misc. novelette.
Toronto Star Weekly,
May 13, 1939.

THE RING OF FIERY
EYES
Lester Leith novelette.
Detective Story, August
1939.

THEY WANTED
"HORROR"
Article.
Writer's Digest, August
1939.

THE MAN WHO KILLED
THE WILDCAT
Article.
Ye Sylvan Archer, August
1939.

DARK ALLEYS*
Ed Jenkins novelette.
Black Mask, September
1939.

LESTER LEITH,
MAGICIAN*
Lester Leith novelette.
Detective Fiction Weekly,
September 16, 1939.

A THOUSAND TO ONE*
Lester Leith novelette.
Detective Fiction Weekly,
October 28, 1939.

MYSTERY BY INCHES
Misc. novelette.
Serialized in *Toronto Star
Weekly,* October 28–
December 23, 1939.

A HEARSE FOR
HOLLYWOOD
Jax Keen novelette.
Double Detective,
November 1939.

FAIR EXCHANGE
Lester Leith novelette.
Detective Fiction Weekly,
November 18, 1939.

A HEADACHE FOR
BUTCH
Ed Migrane, the
Headache, novelette.
Double Detective,
December 1939.

AT ARM'S LENGTH*
Misc. short story.
Detective Fiction Weekly,
December 9, 1939.

WHERE ANGELS FEAR
TO TREAD*
Misc. short story.
Detective Fiction Weekly,
December 30, 1939.

THE BIGGER THEY
COME
(pen name, A. A. Fair)
Donald Lam–Bertha Cool
book.
Morrow, January 1939;
Pocket, October 1943.

THE CASE OF THE
PERJURED PARROT
Perry Mason book.
Morrow, February 1939;
Pocket, September 1947.

THE CASE OF THE
ROLLING BONES
Perry Mason book.
Morrow, September 1939;
Pocket, November 1947.

THE D. A. DRAWS A
CIRCLE
Doug Selby, the D.A.,
book.
Morrow, November 1939;
Pocket, March 1946.

1940

TWO-WAY RIDE
Ed Migrane, the
Headache, novelette.
Double Detective,
January 1940.

PASSING THE BUCK
Article.
Ye Sylvan Archer,
January 1940.

SUGAR
Lester Leith novelette.
Detective Fiction Weekly,
January 20, 1940.

SLEEPING DOGS
Jax Keen novelette.
Double Detective,
February 1940.

HOT GUNS
Ed Migrane, the
Headache, novelette.
Double Detective, March
1940.

MONKEYSHINE
Lester Leith novelette.
Detective Fiction Weekly,
March 16, 1940.

INDIAN MAGIC
Misc. short story.
This Week, May 5, 1940.

TONG TROUBLE
Ed Jenkins novelette.
Black Mask, June 1940.

STICKING STUMPS ON
STILTS
Article.
Ye Sylvan Archer, June
1940.

ADD ANOTHER NAME
Article.
Ye Sylvan Archer,
November 1940.

JADE SANCTUARY
Ed Jenkins novelette.
Black Mask, December
1940.

THE ALIBI GIRL
Misc. short story.
Sketch, approx. 1940.

TURN ON THE HEAT
(pen name, A. A. Fair)
Donald Lam—Bertha Cool
book.
Morrow, January 1940;
Dell, May 1944.

THE CASE OF THE
BAITED HOOK
Perry Mason book.
Morrow, March 1940;
Pocket, January 1947.

THE D. A. GOES TO
TRIAL
Doug Selby, the D. A.,
book.
Serialized in *Country
Gentleman,* April–July,
1940.
Morrow, June 1940;
Pocket, November 1946.

GOLD COMES IN BRICKS
(pen name, A. A. Fair)
Donald Lam—Bertha Cool
book.
Morrow, September 1940;
Dell, May 1945.

THE CASE OF THE
SILENT PARTNER
Perry Mason book.
Morrow, November 1940;
Pocket, February 1948.

*MOTION PICTURE
RELEASE:*

THE CASE OF THE
DANGEROUS DOWAGER.
Warner Bros., 1940, under
title "Granny Get Your
Gun." (Was not released
as a Perry Mason picture.)

1941

THE EXACT OPPOSITE*
Lester Leith novelette.
Detective Fiction Weekly,
March 29, 1941.

THE PHANTOM CROOK
Ed Jenkins novelette.
Black Mask, May 1941.

THE LAST BELL ON
THE STREET
Pete Quint short story.
*The Saturday Evening
Post,* May 3, 1941.

THAT'S A WOMAN FOR
YOU!
Pete Quint short story.
*The Saturday Evening
Post,* May 31, 1941.

THE BIG SQUEEZE*
Pete Quint short story.
*The Saturday Evening
Post,* November 15, 1941.

A SUGAR COATING
Lester Leith novelette.
Flynn's Detective Fiction,
November 29, 1941.

RAIN CHECK
Ed Jenkins novelette.
Black Mask, December
1941.

MARRY FOR MONEY
(pen name, Grant
Holiday)
Misc. novelette.
Toronto Star Weekly,
approx. 1941.

THE ALLEYS OF
HONGKONG
Article.
Chinese Relief Committee,
approx. 1941.

Article (untitled)
Hobby Guild, approx.
1941.

THE CASE OF THE
HAUNTED HUSBAND
Perry Mason book.
Morrow, February 1941;
Pocket, June 1949.

SPILL THE JACKPOT
(pen name, A. A. Fair)
Donald Lam—Bertha Cool
book.
Morrow, March 1941;
Dell, May 1946.

THE CASE OF THE
TURNING TIDE
Gramp Wiggins book.
Morrow, July 1941;
Pocket, September 1948.

THE CASE OF THE
EMPTY TIN
Perry Mason book.
Morrow, October 1941;
Pocket, September 1949.

DOUBLE OR QUITS
(pen name, A. A. Fair)
Donald Lam—Bertha Cool
book.
Morrow, December 1941;
Dell, March 1947.

1942

COME ON IN, THE
WATER'S FINE
Article.
Ye Sylvan Archer,
January 1942.

TWO DEAD HANDS
Ed Jenkins novelette.
Black Mask, April 1942.

THE FALSE FIRE
Misc. short story.
This Week, December 6,
1942.

LITERATURE OF
RELAXATION
Article.
Cleveland News, Special
Christmas Book Supple-
ment, approx. 1942.

THE D. A. COOKS A
GOOSE
Doug Selby, the D. A.,
book.
Serialized in *Country
Gentleman,* September
1941–January 1942.
Morrow, January 1942;
Pocket, January 1949.

THE CASE OF THE
DROWNING DUCK
Perry Mason book.
Morrow, May 1942;
Pocket, November 1949.

OWLS DON'T BLINK
(pen name, A. A. Fair)
Donald Lam–Bertha Cool
book.
Morrow, June 1942; Dell,
January 1948.

THE CASE OF THE
CARELESS KITTEN
Perry Mason book.
Serialized in *The Saturday
Evening Post,* May 23–
July 11, 1942.
Morrow, September 1942;
Pocket, October 1950.

BATS FLY AT DUSK
(pen name, A. A. Fair)
Donald Lam–Bertha Cool
book.
Morrow, September 1942;
Dell, November 1948.

1943

SOMETHING LIKE A
PELICAN*
Lester Leith novelette.
Flynn's Detective Fiction,
January 1943.

THE INCREDIBLE
MISTER SMITH
Ed Jenkins novelette.
Black Mask, March 1943.

AVERAGE AMERICAN
Misc. short story.
This Week, April 18, 1943.

CAWS AND EFFECT
Lester Leith novelette.
Flynn's Detective Fiction,
July 1943.

THE GONG OF
VENGEANCE
Ed Jenkins novelette.
Black Mask, September
1943.

EULOGY IN B FLAT
Article.
Ye Sylvan Archer,
September 1943.

Article (untitled)
Author & Journalist,
approx. 1943.

THE CASE OF THE
SMOKING CHIMNEY
Gramp Wiggins book.
Morrow, January 1943;
Pocket, January 1950.

THE CASE OF THE
BURIED CLOCK
Perry Mason book.
Morrow, May 1943;
Pocket, March 1950.

CATS PROWL AT
NIGHT
(pen name, A. A. Fair)
Donald Lam–Bertha Cool
book.
Morrow, August 1943;
Dell, July 1949.

THE CASE OF THE
DROWSY MOSQUITO
Perry Mason book.
Morrow, September 1943;
Pocket, June 1950.

*NEWSPAPER COVERAGE
OF MURDER CASE:*

THE OAKES MURDER
MYSTERY
DeMarigny Trial in
Bahamas.
*New York Journal-
American,* October 14–
November 12, 1943.

*RADIO PRESENTA-
TIONS:*

THE NEW ADVENTURES
OF PERRY MASON
Daily broadcasts of serials
under many different
titles (can be supplied),
edited by Mr. Gardner,
October 18, 1943–Decem-
ber 30, 1955. CBS.

1944

THE GREATEST
DETECTIVES I KNOW
Article.
McClurg Book News,
January–February 1944.

THE MYSTERY OF
WOMAN
Article.
Ladies' Home Journal,
part of symposium which
bore the above title, July
1944.

A METHOD TO
MYSTERY
(pen name, A. A. Fair)
Article.
The Writer, August 1944.

ERLE STANLEY
GARDNER CLAIMS
MYSTERY READERS
BEST DETECTIVES
Article.
The Pocket Bookseller,
September 1944.

THE EYES OF CHINA*
Misc. short story.
This Week, October 29,
1944.

THE CASE OF THE
PERFECT SECRETARY*
Article.
Chatelaine, November
1944.

ARMED FORCES
DESTINED TO HAVE
PERMANENT EFFECT
ON STYLE OF
MYSTERY STORY
Article.
Chicago Daily News,
December 1944.

IT'S OUR WAGON
Article-Blurb.
Treasury Department
War Bond Drive,
approx. 1944.

THE D. A. CALLS A
TURN
Doug Selby, the D. A.,
book.
Serialized in *Country
Gentleman,* November
1943–March 1944.
Morrow, January 1944;
Pocket, January 1949.

THE CASE OF THE
CROOKED CANDLE
Perry Mason book.
Morrow, May 1944;
Pocket, February 1951.

GIVE 'EM THE AX
(pen name, A. A. Fair)
Donald Lam–Bertha Cool
book.
Morrow, September 1944;
Dell, March 1950.

THE CASE OF THE
BLACK-EYED BLONDE
Perry Mason book.
Morrow, November 1944;
Pocket, June 1951.

1945

DEATH RIDES A
BOXCAR*
Misc. short story.
The American Magazine,
January 1945.

TRAVELER'S REPORT
Article.
New Horizons, October–
December 1945.

EXPLAINING HEADLESS
MURDERS
Article.
The American Weekly,
October 14, 1945.

IS THIS THE PERFECT
CRIME?*
Article.
The American Weekly,
October 21, 1945.

GREENER GRASS
Article.
Authors' League Bulletin,
November 1945.

ONE ARROW WILL DO
IT
Article.
Archery, November 1945.

DEAD OPEN AND SHUT
Misc. photo crime.
Look, November 13, 1945.

THE CASE OF THE
GOLDDIGGER'S PURSE
Perry Mason book.
Morrow, May 1945;
Pocket, July 1951.

THE CASE OF THE
HALF-WAKENED WIFE
Perry Mason book.
Morrow, September 1945;
Pocket, September 1951.

1946

THE JOB AHEAD
Article.
Labor Reports, Jewish
Labor Committee,
January 1946.

THE CASE OF THE
MOVIE MURDER*
Article.
True, June 1946.

DON'T QUIT
Article.
Author & Journalist,
July 1946.

WHITE CANARY*
Misc. short story.
This Week, September 15,
1946.

A MAN IS MISSING*
Misc. novelette.
The American Magazine,
November 1946.

THE CASE OF THE
EARLY BEGINNING
Article.
Included in book, *The Art
of the Mystery Story,*
edited by Howard
Haycraft, 1946.

THE D. A. BREAKS A
SEAL
Doug Selby, the D. A.,
book.
Serialized in *The Saturday
Evening Post,* December
1, 1945–January 12, 1946.
Morrow, February 1946;
Pocket, June 1952.

CROWS CAN'T COUNT
(pen name, A. A. Fair)
Donald Lam—Bertha Cool
book.
Morrow, April 1946; Dell,
January 1951.

THE CASE OF THE
BACKWARD MULE
Terry Clane book.
Morrow, July 1946;
Pocket, December 1951.

THE CASE OF THE
BORROWED BRUNETTE
Perry Mason book.
Morrow, November 1946;
Pocket, March 1952.

*RADIO PRESENTA-
TION:*

TURN ON THE HEAT
(Donald Lam—Bertha Cool
book) adapted by Wel-
bourn Kelley for the U.S.
Steel Hour. ABC, June 23,
1946.

1947

TOO MANY CLUES
Sheriff Bill Eldon
novelette.
Serialized in *Country
Gentleman,* February–
May 1947.

THE CASE OF THE
RED-HEADED KILLER
Article.
True Police Cases, May
1947.

THE CASE OF THE
CRYING SWALLOW*
Perry Mason novelette.
The American Magazine,
August 1947.

COME RIGHT IN, MR.
DOYLE
Article.
The Atlantic Monthly,
September 1947.

SEQUOIA NATIONAL
PARK*
Text on back of scenic
view given out by
Standard Oil Company,
1947.

WHO PAYS WHOM
Article.
Author & Journalist,
approx. 1947.

TWO CLUES
Sheriff Bill Eldon book,
consisting of 2 novelettes.
"The Clue of the Run-
away Blonde," serialized
under title "Clues Don't
Count" in *Country
Gentleman,* July–October
1945; and "The Clue of
the Hungry Horse."
Morrow, February 1947;
Pocket, August 1953.

THE CASE OF THE FAN-
DANCER'S HORSE
Perry Mason book.
Morrow, June 1947;
Pocket, August 1952.

FOOLS DIE ON FRIDAY
(pen name, A. A. Fair)
Donald Lam—Bertha Cool
book.
Morrow, September 1947;
Dell, October 1951.

THE CASE OF THE
LAZY LOVER
Perry Mason book.
Morrow, October 1947;
Pocket, December 1952.

1948

STEP *OFF* THE GAS*
Article.
The Atlantic Monthly,
April 1948.

BAJA CALIFORNIA
Article.
Holiday, April 1948.

DeMARIGNY'S FAMOUS
FINGER
Article.
Serialized in *Argosy,*
April–May 1948.

THE CASE OF THE
CRIMSON KISS*
Perry Mason novelette.
The American Magazine,
June 1948.

IS CLARENCE BOGGIE
INNOCENT?
Court of Last Resort
article.
Argosy, September 1948.

SHOULD CLARENCE
BOGGIE BE
PARDONED?
CLR article. (From here
on initials CLR stand
for Court of Last Resort)
Argosy, October 1948.

THE KEYS CASE
CLR letter.
Argosy, "Cooking with
Dynamite" Department,
October 1948.

BATTLE FOR A MAN'S
LIFE
CLR article.
Argosy, November 1948.

ARGOSY UNCOVERS
TRAIL OF REAL KILLER
IN BOGGIE CASE
CLR article.
Argosy, December 1948.

Article (untitled)
Adventurers' Club, approx.
1948.

THE CASE OF THE
HOMELESS CHILD
Brochure.
Children's Home Society
of Missouri, approx. 1948.

HOW I CAME TO
CREATE
PERRY MASON*
Article.
Lintas Proprietary, Ltd.
Wellington, approx.
1948.

THE CASE OF THE
LONELY HEIRESS
Perry Mason book.
Morrow, February 1948;
Pocket, February 1953.

THE LAND OF
SHORTER SHADOWS
Non-fiction book.
Morrow, April 1948.

THE CASE OF THE
VAGABOND VIRGIN
Perry Mason book.
Morrow, July 1948;
Pocket, November 1953.

THE D. A. TAKES A
CHANCE
Doug Selby, the D.A.,
book.
Serialized in *The Saturday
Evening Post*, July 31–
September 18, 1948.
Morrow, October 1948;
Pocket, August 1954.

*NEWSPAPER COVERAGE
OF MURDER CASE:*

THERESA FOSTER
MURDER CASE
Daily articles.
The Denver Post,
November 14–25, 1948.

*RADIO PRESENTA-
TION:*

THE D. A. TAKES A
CHANCE
Adaptation of first install-
ment of *The Saturday
Evening Post* serial for
"Listening Post." ABC,
July 28, 1948.

1949

ARGOSY SEEKS TRUTH
ABOUT MISSING
FINGERPRINT
CLR article.
Argosy, January 1949.

THE CLUE OF THE
SCREAMING WOMAN
Sheriff Bill Eldon
novelette.
Serialized in *Country
Gentleman*, January–
April 1949.

TREACHEROUS
CURRENTS
Article.
National Conference of
Christian and Jews for
Brotherhood Week,
February 20–27, 1949.

THE INCREDIBLE CASE
OF CLARENCE BOGGIE
CLR article.
Argosy, March 1949.

THE WOMAN I ADMIRE
MOST
Article.
Ladies' Home Journal,
April 1949.

THE AFFAIR OF THE
RELUCTANT WITNESS*
Jerry Bane short story.
Argosy, April 1949.

ARE THESE MEN
INNOCENT?
CLR article.
Argosy, August 1949.

WAS GROSS
RAILROADED?
CLR article.
Argosy, September 1949.

LAY OFF THE GROSS
CASE
CLR article.
Argosy, October 1949.

HUNTING IS MORE
FUN THAN KILLING
Article.
Sports Afield, October
1949.

DEMOCRACY BY
DISSENT
Article.
This Week, October 2,
1949.

A PRACTICAL JOKE
IN ACTION
CLR article.
Argosy, "Cooking with
Dynamite" Department,
November 1949.

THE AFFAIR OF THE
PEARL PRINCESS
Jerry Bane novelette.
Argosy, November 1949.

LOUIS GROSS GRANTED
NEW TRIAL
CLR article.
Argosy, "Cooking with
Dynamite" Department,
December 1949.

THE PRESENTATION
OF FACT
Article.
Unpublished, but made
part of course in Police
Administration at Michi-
gan State College, 1949.

BEDROOMS HAVE
WINDOWS
(pen name, A. A. Fair)
Donald Lam—Bertha Cool
book.
Morrow, January 1949;
Dell, July 1952.

THE CASE OF THE
DUBIOUS BRIDEGROOM
Perry Mason book.
Morrow, February 1949;
Pocket, January 1954.

THE CASE OF THE
CAUTIOUS COQUETTE
Perry Mason book.
Morrow, May 1949;
Pocket, June 1954.

THE D. A. BREAKS
AN EGG
Doug Selby, the D.A., book.
Morrow, August 1949;
Pocket, May 1955.

*RADIO PRESENTA-
TIONS:*
(Based on Mr. Gardner's
outlines and ideas, and
scripts were edited by
him.)

A LIFE IN YOUR HANDS
Jonathan Kegg—Amicus
Curiae.
NBC. First show: ran June
7–September 13, 1949.

1950

YOUR COURT VISITS
SCOTLAND YARD
VICTORY FOR COURT
AND GROSS
CLR articles.
Argosy, January 1950.

WHAT ABOUT THE
REAL MURDERER?
CLR article.
Argosy, February 1950.

WILL THEY BE FREED?
CLR article.
Argosy, March 1950.

THE INNOCENT MUST
BE PROTECTED
CLR article.
Argosy, April 1950.

A DEAD MAN WORKS
FOR JUSTICE
CLR article.
Argosy, May 1950.

THE CASE OF THE
SUSPECT SWEET-
HEARTS
(by-line, "Della Street")
Misc. short story
*Radio Mirror and Tele-
vision,* May 1950.

CRIME RECONSTRUC-
TION SMASHES
EVIDENCE
CLR article.
Argosy, June 1950.

COME, COME,
GENTLEMEN
CLR article.
Argosy, July 1950.

DON'T HIDE THE
FACTS
CLR article.
Argosy, August 1950.

WITNESS FOR HARDY
BREAKS CASE WIDE
OPEN
CLR article.
Argosy, September 1950.

THE LAW THAT
LEAKED
Misc. novelette.
Serialized in *Sports Afield,*
September–December
1950.

NEW LIE TEST PROVES
HARDY INNOCENT
CLR article.
Argosy, October 1950.

HARDY CASE NEARS
CLIMAX
CLR article.
Argosy, November 1950.

CIRCUMSTANTIAL
EVIDENCE IN
HOMICIDE CASES
Speech.
Printed in *Michigan State
Bar Journal,* November
1950.

STAY OF EXECUTION
GRANTED CONDEMNED
MAN
CLR article.
Argosy, December 1950.

TRAVELING HOMES
Article.
*Book of Knowledge
Annual,* 1950.

THE WAY OUT
Article.
The Outlook (Walla Walla
Prison), approx. 1950.

THE CASE OF THE
NEGLIGENT NYMPH
Perry Mason book.
Serialized in *Collier's,*
September 17–October
22, 1949.
Morrow, January 1950;
Pocket, November 1954.

THE CASE OF THE
MUSICAL COW
Misc. book.
Serialized under title "The
Case of the Smuggler's
Bell" in *Collier's,* March
25–April 29, 1950.
Morrow, June 1950;
Pocket, December 1955.

THE CASE OF THE ONE-
EYED WITNESS
Perry Mason book.
Morrow, November 1950;
Pocket, February 1955.

*RADIO PRESENTA-
TIONS:*
(Based on Mr. Gardner's
outlines and ideas, and
scripts were edited by
him.)

THE CHRISTOPHER
LONDON SHOW
NBC. January 22–May 29,
1950.

A LIFE IN YOUR HANDS
Jonathan Kegg—Amicus
Curiae.
NBC. Second show: ran
June 20–September 12,
1950.

COMIC STRIPS:
PERRY MASON: "The
Case of the Innocent Thief,"
"The Case of the Nervous
Horse," "The Case of the
Missing Husband," "The
Case of the Constant
Cricket," "The Case of the
Whistling Dog," "The Case
of the Stolen Goddess,"
"The Case of the Desperate
Dupe," "The Case of the
Wanted Woman," "The
Case of the Curious Cop."
Published in U.S. and
Canadian newspapers;
copyrighted October 16,
1950–June 21, 1952.

1951

ADVENTURES IN
JUSTICE
Article.
*American Bar Association
Journal,* January 1951.

TWO MEN WAIT
CLR article.
Argosy, January 1951.

COURT HITS TWO
UNJUST CONVICTIONS
CLR article.
Argosy, February 1951.

THE CORPSE WAS IN
THE COUNTINGHOUSE
Misc. novelette.
Serialized in *Collier's,*
March 3–March 31, 1951.

COURT PROBE
PRODUCES EVIDENCE
THAT SHOULD FREE
A MAN
CLR article.
Argosy, March 1951.

GENTLEMEN OF THE
JURY
CLR article.
Argosy, April 1951.

THE CASE OF THE
BLIND BURGLAR
Article.
Caravan, May 1951.

ERLE STANLEY
GARDNER REPORTS
CLR article.
Argosy, November 1951.

ERLE STANLEY
GARDNER'S FBI VETS
WILL HELP COURT
CLR article.
Argosy, December 1951.

THE CASE OF THE
FIERY FINGERS
Perry Mason book.
Morrow, May 1951;
Pocket, May 1956.

THE CASE OF THE
ANGRY MOURNER
Perry Mason book.
Morrow, October 1951;
Pocket, January 1956.

PLAY:

THE CASE OF THE
SULKY GIRL
  Perry Mason play for
  amateurs.
  Adaptation by The Dra-
  matic Publishing Com-
  pany, Roland Fernand,
  1951.

*RADIO PRESENTA-
TION:*

A LIFE IN YOUR HANDS
  Jonathan Kegg–Amicus
  Curiae.
  ABC: Third show: ran
  June 29–September 21,
  1951.

1952

TO TOM RUNYON
Letter—Article.
Presidio, January 1952.

AN ORCHID FOR
GLADYS
CLR article.
Argosy, March 1952.

THE CREED OF
SALVATION
Article.
  Booklet for Salvation
  Army, March 1952.

SHOULD JUSTICE BE
BLIND?
Article.
Civic Forum, University
of Miami, May 1952.

THE CASE OF WILLIE
SUTTON*
Article.
  Serialized in *Look*, May
  6–May 20, 1952.

FLIGHT INTO
DISASTER*
Misc. novelette.
  Serialized in *This Week*,
  May 11–May 18, 1952.

SALES PSYCHOLOGY
Speech.
  Printed in *Texas Bar
  Journal*, August 1952.

BEWARE THE EYE-
WITNESS
Article.
  The American Weekly,
  August 17, 1952.

TEXAS TAKES THE
LEAD
Article.
  Texas Bar Journal,
  September 1952.

WHO REALLY KILLED
HELEN BEAVERS?
CLR article.
Argosy, October 1952.

JEWELED BUTTERFLY*
Misc. novelette.
Cosmopolitan, October
1952.

THE STRANGE
MURDER OF JOANN
DEWEY
CLR article.
Argosy, November 1952.

MURDER ON THE
APACHE TRAIL
CLR article.
Argosy, December 1952.

ON SWAPPING PLACES
WITH SOMEONE FOR
A DAY
Article.
  Ladies' Home Journal,
  approx. 1952.

TOP OF THE HEAP
(pen name, A. A. Fair)
Donald Lam–Bertha Cool
book.
Morrow, February 1952;
Dell, April 1954.

THE CASE OF THE
MOTH-EATEN MINK
Perry Mason book.
Morrow, April 1952;
Pocket, March 1956.

THE CASE OF THE
GRINNING GORILLA
Perry Mason book.
Morrow, November 1952;
Pocket, June 1956.

THE COURT OF LAST
RESORT
Non-fiction book.
Morrow, November 1952;
Pocket, 1954.

1953

THE EYES OF TEXAS
CLR article.
Argosy, January 1953.

SILENCE IS SECURITY
Article.
  *U.S. Naval Air Station
  Annual*, San Diego,
  January 1953.

THE CASE OF THE
IRATE WITNESS*
Perry Mason novelette.
Collier's, January 17, 1953.

THE CASE OF THE
AUTOGRAPHED
CORPSE
CLR article.
Argosy, February 1953.

JUSTICE IN HIGH GEAR
CLR article.
Argosy, March 1953.

THE IDEAL SLEEPING
BAG
Article.
Argosy, April 1953.

THE SIXTY-FOUR-
DOLLAR QUESTION
CLR article.
Argosy, May 1953.

THE TROUBLE WITH
POLICE
CLR article.
Argosy, June 1953.

THE EMPTY GRAVE OF
JOHNNY HOPKINS
Article.
  Lifetime Living, June
  1953.

TEN STEPS TO JUSTICE
(no author indicated)
CLR article.
Argosy, July 1953.

THE NIGHTMARE
DEATHS OF
HONOLULU*
Article.
Argosy, July 1953.

THE RING OF DEATH
CLR article.
Argosy, August 1953.

THE PRISON RIOT
THAT DIDN'T HAPPEN
CLR article.
Argosy, October 1953.

NEW DEVELOPMENTS
CLR article.
Argosy, December 1953.

BAJA CALIFORNIA—
SUNSET LAND
Article.
*Book of Knowledge
Annual*, 1953.

THE CASE OF THE
HESITANT HOSTESS
Perry Mason book.
Morrow, April 1953;
Pocket, November 1956.

SOME WOMEN WON'T
WAIT
(pen name, A. A. Fair)
Donald Lam—Bertha Cool
book.
Morrow, September 1953;
Dell, November 1954.

THE CASE OF THE
GREEN-EYED SISTER
Perry Mason book.
Morrow, November 1953;
Pocket, July 1957.

1954

THE MYSTERY OF THE
LANDLADY'S DEATH
CLR article.
Argosy, April 1954.

THE STRANGE DEATH
OF SELMA ARVEL
Tape-recorded crime script
and slides.
Also in book *Criminal
Investigation and Inter-
rogation;* also 1962 course
used by law students.
Script and solution copy-
righted April 14, 1954.

MURDER IN LAS VEGAS
CLR article.
Argosy, May 1954.

BAJA CALIFORNIA
Article.
Sportsman's Handbook,
1954–55 issue.

THE CASE OF THE
FUGITIVE NURSE
Perry Mason book.
Serialized in *The Saturday
Evening Post*, September
19–November 7, 1953.
Morrow, February 1954;
Pocket, February 1957.

THE CASE OF THE
RUNAWAY CORPSE
Perry Mason book.
Morrow, June 1954;
Pocket, December 1957.

THE CASE OF THE
RESTLESS REDHEAD
Perry Mason book.
Serialized in *The Saturday
Evening Post*, September
11–October 30, 1954.
Morrow, October 1954;
Pocket, September 1957.

NEIGHBORHOOD
FRONTIERS
Non-fiction book.
Morrow, November 1954.

1955

SAFEGUARDING THE
PUBLIC INTEREST
Speech.
Printed in *Texas Bar
Journal*, February 22,
1955

TOMORROWS IN
PRISON*
Speech.
The Pennsylvania Prison
Society, pamphlet, Febru-
ary 1955.

A RESTATEMENT OF
PURPOSE
CLR article.
Argosy, March 1955.

THE BIG HOUSE*
CLR article.
Argosy, April 1955.

LET'S FIGHT FOR
JUSTICE
CLR article.
Argosy, May 1955.

PROTECTION*
Misc. short story.
Manhunt Detective Story,
May 1955.

A NIGHT ON SKID ROW
CLR article.
Argosy, June 1955.

A GUY CALLED BILL
CLR article.
Argosy, July 1955.

THE STRANGE CASE OF
DON NEAL
CLR article.
Argosy, August 1955.

THE IMPOSSIBLE
HOMICIDE
CLR article.
Argosy, September 1955.

MY CASEBOOK OF
TRUE CRIME—
INTRODUCTION
Article. Introduction to a
group of 28 articles.
The American Weekly,
September 4, 1955.

THE CASE OF THE
INVISIBLE CIRCLE*
Casebook series.
The American Weekly,
September 11, 1955.

THE CASE OF THE
TWO-EDGED KNIFE
Casebook series.
The American Weekly,
September 18, 1955.

THE CASE OF THE
BODY AT THE DESK
Casebook series.
The American Weekly,
September 25, 1955.

THE CASE OF THE
PHANTOM FIREBUG
CLR article.
Argosy, October 1955.

THE CASE OF THE
TELLTALE BOTTLE
Casebook series.
The American Weekly,
October 2, 1955.

STRANGE SEQUEL TO
THE BEDROOM
HOLDUP
Casebook series.
The American Weekly,
October 9, 1955.

THE CASE OF THE
ONYX RING*
Casebook series.
The American Weekly,
October 16, 1955.

THE CASE OF THE
KIND-HEARTED CABBIE
Casebook series.
The American Weekly,
October 23, 1955.

THE CASE OF THE
NERVOUS GRAVE-
DIGGER*
Casebook series.
The American Weekly,
October 30, 1955.

THE AFFAIR OF THE
HYSTERICAL WITNESS
CLR article.
Argosy, November 1955.

THE CASE OF THE
AUTOGRAPHED
BULLET
Casebook series.
The American Weekly,
November 6, 1955.

THE CASE OF THE
KNOCKOUT BULLET*
Casebook series.
The American Weekly,
November 13, 1955.

THE CASE OF THE
WITNESS AT THE
KEYHOLE
Casebook series.
The American Weekly,
November 20, 1955.

THE CASE OF THE
CARELESS
THUMBPRINT
Casebook series.
The American Weekly,
November 27, 1955.

TIME OUT FOR TEXAS
CLR article.
Argosy, December 4, 1955.

THE CASE OF THE
THREE SUITORS*
Casebook series.
The American Weekly,
December 4, 1955.

THE CASE OF THE
204,000 FINGERPRINTS*
Casebook series.
The American Weekly,
December 11, 1955.

CAN WE COPE WITH
CRIME?*
Article.
Fortnight, December 1955–
February 1956.
(Serialized)

THE CASE OF THE
LOST SHAVING KIT
Casebook series.
The American Weekly,
December 18, 1955.

THE CASE OF THE
GUILTY CLIENT*
Article.
Pamphlet for distribution
by Texas Bar Association,
1955.

CRIME AND CRIME
PREVENTION
Article.
*The American People's
Encyclopedia Yearbook:
Events and Personalities
of 1954*, 1955.

THE CASE OF THE
GLAMOROUS GHOST
Perry Mason book.
Morrow, January 1955;
Pocket, January 1958.

THE CASE OF THE SUN
BATHER'S DIARY
Perry Mason book.
Serialized in *The Saturday
Evening Post*, March 5–
April 23, 1955.
Morrow, May 1955; Pocket,
April 1958.

THE CASE OF THE
NERVOUS ACCOMPLICE
Perry Mason book.
Morrow, September 1955;
Pocket, July 1958.

*NEWSPAPER COVERAGE
OF MURDER CASE:*

THE MURDER OF
STEPHANIE BRYAN
Burton Abbott trial.
Daily articles in *San Francisco Examiner*, Novem-
ber 6, 1955–January 20,
1956.

*TELEVISION PRESENTA-
TION:*

THE BIGGER THEY
COME
Adaptation of Donald
Lam—Bertha Cool book
for the Chrysler Climax
show. CBS, January 6,
1955.

1956

TOM RUNYON: THE
WAY BACK
CLR article.
Argosy, January 1956.

THE CASE OF THE
CLUE THAT COST A
QUARTER
Casebook series.
The American Weekly,
January 1, 1956.

THE CASE OF THE
SMUDGED POSTMARK
Casebook series.
The American Weekly,
January 15, 1956.

THE CASE OF THE
EXPLODING AIRLINER
Casebook series.
The American Weekly,
January 29, 1956.

CITIZEN FIREPOWER
AND THE CASE OF
ERNEST WOODMANSEE
CRL article.
Argosy, February 1956.

THE CASE OF THE MAN
WHO WAS IN TWO
PLACES AT ONCE*
Casebook series.
The American Weekly,
February 5, 1956.

THE CASE OF THE
BUSY CORPSE*
Casebook series.
The American Weekly,
February 12, 1956.

THE CASE OF THE
CAREFREE KILLERS
Casebook series.
The American Weekly,
February 19, 1956.

THE CASE OF THE
SILENT WITNESS
Casebook series.
The American Weekly,
February 26, 1956.

WRITE TO KNIGHT
TONIGHT
CLR article.
Argosy, March 1956.

THE CASE OF THE
CORPSE THAT WORE
GLOVES
Casebook series.
The American Weekly,
March 4, 1956.

THE CASE OF THE
INCREDIBLE ALIBI
Casebook series.
The American Weekly,
March 11, 1956.

THE CASE OF THE
BLONDE IN THE
BALCONY
Casebook series.
The American Weekly,
March 18, 1956.

THE CASE OF THE
LUCKLESS BROTHERS
Casebook series.
The American Weekly,
March 25, 1956.

THE PURPOSE OF
PAROLE
CLR article.
Argosy, April 1956.

MY MOST BAFFLING
MURDER CASE*
Casebook series.
The American Weekly,
April 8, 1956.

LAW-ENFORCEMENT
AT THE CROSSROADS
CLR article.
Argosy, May 1956.

THE TOM RUNYON
CASE: WHAT PRICE
PAROLE?
CLR article.
Argosy, June 1956.

THE CASE THAT MADE
THE HANGMAN QUIT
Article (not casebook
series).
The American Weekly,
June 17, 1956.

HOW TO KNOW YOU'RE
TRANSPARENT WHEN
YOU'D LIKE TO BE
OPAQUE*
Article.
Vogue, July 1956.

THE CASE OF THE
PEAR-SHAPED
BLOODSTAINS
CLR article.
Argosy, November 1956.

THE HOLMAN CASE:
A NEW LOOK
CLR article.
Argosy, December 1956.

THE CASE OF THE
TERRIFIED TYPIST
Perry Mason book.
Morrow, January 1956;
Pocket, October 1958.

THE CASE OF THE
DEMURE DEFENDANT
Perry Mason book.
Serialized under title "The
Case of the Missing Poi-
son" in *The Saturday
Evening Post,* December
10, 1955–January 28,
1956.
Morrow, May 1956;
Pocket, January 1959.

THE CASE OF THE
GILDED LILY
Perry Mason book.
Morrow, September 1956;
Pocket, June 1959.

BEWARE THE CURVES
(pen name, A. A. Fair)
Donald Lam–Bertha Cool
book.
Morrow, November 1956;
Pocket, September 1960.

1957

THE HOLMAN CASE:
FINAL RECKONING
CLR article.
Argosy, January 1957.

THE CASE OF THE
MISSING MORALS*
Article.
Together, January 1957.

WHERE DO WE GO
FROM HERE?
Article.
Agenda (prison paper),
March–April 1957.

THE WITTING WILL
CASE
Tape-recorded script-
lecture and slides.
Copyrighted March 7,
1957.

THE COFFIN CASE:
A NEW LOOK
CLR article.
Argosy, April 1957.

FEWER CRIMINALS
MAKE FOR LESS CRIME
Article.
Police, May–June 1957.

MAINTAINING THE
STATUS QUO
Article.
McClurg Book News, May
1957.

THE PRISON OF
TOMORROW*
Article.
Presidio (prison paper),
May 1957.

THE IMPORTANCE
OF TRUTH
CLR article.
Argosy, May 1957.

THE DR. SAM
SHEPPARD CASE AND
MEMO RE RUNYON
(HIS DEATH)
CLR article.
Argosy, June 1957.

AND I MEAN *YOU*
Article.
Pamphlet, Research Insti-
tute of America, August,
1957.

THE CASE OF THE
MORAL TRANSIT
Article.
Episcopal Churchnews,
August 1957.

ARE THE SHEPPARDS
TELLING THE TRUTH?
CLR article.
Argosy, August 1957.

THE HUMAN SIDE OF
THE SHEPPARD CASE
CLR article.
Argosy, September 1957.

THE SHEPPARD CASE
BREAKS WIDE OPEN
CLR article.
Argosy, October 1957.

THE CASE OF THE
MURDERER'S BRIDE*
Misc. novelette.
Look, October 15, 1957.

THE OTHER SHOE IN
THE SHEPPARD CASE
CLR article.
Argosy, November 1957.

THE CORPSE THAT
CHANGED CLOTHES
Casebook series.
The American Weekly,
November 3, 1957.

MEET THE
PROSECUTORS
CLR article.
Argosy, December 1957.

CRIME AND CRIME
PREVENTION
Article.
*The American People's
Encyclopedia Yearbook:
Events and Personalities
of 1956,* 1957.

THE CASE OF THE
LUCKY LOSER
Perry Mason book.
Serialized in *The Saturday
Evening Post,* September
1–October 20, 1956.
Morrow, January 1957;
Pocket, August 1959.

YOU CAN DIE
LAUGHING
(pen name, A. A. Fair)
Donald Lam–Bertha Cool
book.
Morrow, March 1957;
Pocket, April 1961.

THE CASE OF THE
SCREAMING WOMAN
Perry Mason book.
Morrow, May 1957; Pocket,
January 1960.

THE CASE OF THE
DARING DECOY
Perry Mason book.
Serialized by the *Chicago
Tribune-New York News*
syndicate under title
"The Proxy Murder,"
September 8, 1957–October
ber 19, 1957
Morrow, October 1957;
Pocket, April 1960.

SOME SLIPS DON'T
SHOW
(pen name, A. A. Fair)
Donald Lam–Bertha Cool
book.
Morrow, October 1957;
Pocket, November 1961.

*TELEVISION PRESENTA-
TIONS:*

PERRY MASON
Scripts based on all the
Perry Mason books or
original scripts by staff
writers, edited by Mr.
Gardner. CBS (Specific
titles can be supplied).
September 21, 1957–May
22, 1966.

THE COURT OF LAST
RESORT
Scripts edited by Mr.
Gardner. (Specific titles
can be supplied.)
NBC. October 4, 1957–
April 11, 1958.

1958

THE IMPORTANCE OF
THE PRISON PRESS*
Article.
Sagebrush (prison paper),
February 1958.

ACQUITTAL OF GUILTY
HELD PERIL AS GRAVE
AS JAILING OF
INNOCENT
Article.
Los Angeles Times,
"Words for the Times"
Department. February 2,
1958.

THE COURT SALUTES
A WARDEN*
CLR article.
Argosy, March 1958.

PAROLE AND THE
PRISONS: AN OPPORTU-
NITY WASTED*
Article. (Publication of
speech, "The Real
Underdog")
The Atlantic Monthly,
March 1958.

A SHIP AND A POEM:
TWO INCIDENTS THAT
SHAPED A MAN
Article.
San Francisco Examiner,
Special Edgewood Maga-
zine Section, March 16,
1958.

FEWELL CASE, etc. (news-
paper headline)
Article.
Birmingham News, April
27, 1958.

THE IMPORTANCE OF
CRIMINAL LAW
Article.
Long Beach Bar Bulletin,
May 1958.

UNITED FRONT
NEEDED: POLICE WORK
IS NEGLECTED BY THE
PUBLIC GARDNER SAYS
Article.
Texas Police Journal, May
1958.

THE IMPOSSIBLE
MURDER
CLR article.
Argosy, June 1958.

THE CASE OF THE
UNSCRATCHED FENDER
Article.
American Motorist, June
1958.

CONFESSIONS OF A
CROSS-EXAMINER
Article.
*Journal of Forensic
Sciences,* July 1958.

MISCARRIAGES OF
JUSTICE
Article.
Police, July–August 1958.

THE CASE OF THE DIS-
INTERESTED LAWYER
Article-Advertisement.
*American Bar Association
Journal,* August 1958.

THE PROBLEM OF
PUBLIC RELATIONS
Article.
Temple Law Quarterly,
Summer 1958.

THE FORK IN THE
ROAD*
CLR article.
Argosy, September 1958.

IF SOCIETY WANTS
REHABILITATION*
Article.
The Spectator (prison pa-
per), September 19, 1958.

THE MURDER CASE
WHICH KEEPS CONTRA-
DICTING ITSELF
CLR article.
Argosy, October 1958.

ERLE STANLEY GARD-
NER REPORTS ON
PUBLIC RELATIONS
Article.
*Michigan State Bar
Journal,* October 1958.

THE COURT OF LAST
RESORT
Article.
Cornell Law Quarterly,
Fall 1958.

THE CASE OF THE
MISSING ERASURE
Article-envelope stuffer.
Eaton Paper Corp. No
publication information.
Approx. 1958.

THE CASE OF THE
LONG-LEGGED MODELS
Perry Mason book.
Serialized under title "The
Case of the Dead Man's
Daughter" in *The Satur-
day Evening Post,* August
10–September 28, 1957.
Morrow, January 1958;
Pocket, August 1960.

THE CASE OF THE
FOOT-LOOSE DOLL
Perry Mason book.
Serialized in *The Saturday
Evening Post,* February
1–March 22, 1958.
Morrow, May 1958;
Pocket, August 1960.

THE COUNT OF NINE
(pen name, A. A. Fair)
Donald Lam–Bertha Cool
book.
Morrow, June 1958;
Pocket, March 1962.

THE CASE OF THE
CALENDAR GIRL
Perry Mason book.
Morrow, October 1958;
Pocket, January 1961.

1959

THE MANY MEANINGS AN "ESCAPE" NOVEL HOLDS FOR ITS MANY READERS
Article.
New York Herald-Tribune Books, January 18, 1959.

THE NATION'S GREAT EDUCATIONAL FACTOR*
Article.
TV Guide, January 31–February 6, 1959.

SPEAKING AS A CITIZEN*
Article.
Federal Probation, March 1959.

NEED FOR NEW CONCEPTS IN THE ADMINISTRATION OF CRIMINAL JUSTICE
Speech.
Printed in *The Journal of Criminal Law, Criminology & Police Science*, May–June 1959.

LETTER MEMORIAL TO TOM RUNYON
Article-Letter.
The Keystone (prison paper), Autumn 1959.

JUST JUSTICE
Article.
Privately printed for Mr. Gardner to be distributed for proposed new Court of Last Resort corporation, 1959.

WE CAN'T BUY GOOD LAW ENFORCEMENT IN THE ECONOMIC BARGAIN BASEMENT
Article.
Fresno Police Annual, 1959.

THE CASE OF THE BOY WHO WROTE "THE CASE OF THE MISSING CLUE WITH PERRY MASON"*
Article.
Booklet, Morrow, 1959.

WHERE DO CRIMINALS COME FROM?*
Article.
The Eye-Opener (prison paper), approx. 1959.

THE CASE OF THE DEADLY TOY
Perry Mason book.
Serialized under title "The Case of the Greedy Grandpa" in *The Saturday Evening Post*, October 25–December 13, 1958.
Morrow, January 1959; Pocket, May 1961.

PASS THE GRAVY
(pen name, A. A. Fair)
Donald Lam–Bertha Cool book.
Morrow, February 1959; Pocket, October 1962.

THE CASE OF THE MYTHICAL MONKEYS
Perry Mason book.
Serialized in *The Saturday Evening Post*, May 2–June 20, 1959.
Morrow, June 1959; Pocket, August 1961.

THE CASE OF THE SINGING SKIRT
Perry Mason book.
Morrow, September 1959; Pocket, January 1962.

1960

THE CITIZENS ARE THE STOCKHOLDERS
Article.
California Peace Officer, January–February 1960.

THE PERENNIAL CRIMES OF CAPTAIN LEE
Article.
Yankee, July 1960.

THE CASE OF THE AVERAGE CITIZEN
Article.
The Episcopalian, September 1960.

A NEW TREND IN CRIMINAL LAW
Article.
MP Journal, December 1960.

THE LITTLE STAR
Article.
This Week, "Words to Live By" Department, approx. 1960.

PUT YOUR BACK-GROUNDS TO WORK
Article.
Popular Photography, approx. 1960.

THE CASE OF THE WAYLAID WOLF
Perry Mason book.
Serialized in *The Saturday Evening Post*, September 5–October 24, 1959.
Morrow, January 1960; Pocket, April 1962.

THE CASE OF THE DUPLICATE DAUGHTER
Perry Mason book.
Serialized in *The Saturday Evening Post*, June 4–July 23, 1960.
Morrow, June 1960; Pocket, August 1962.

KEPT WOMEN CAN'T QUIT
(pen name, A. A. Fair)
Donald Lam–Bertha Cool book.
Morrow, September 1960; Pocket, April 1963.

THE CASE OF THE SHAPELY SHADOW
Perry Mason book.
Morrow, October 1960; Pocket, January 1963.

HUNTING THE DESERT WHALE*
Non-fiction book.
Excerpts in *Sports Afield*, November 1960–January, 1961.
Morrow, December 1960.

1961

THE TRUTH ABOUT SURVIVAL*
Article.
Serialized in *Sports Afield*, February–April 1961.

THE PLEASURES OF PHOTOGRAPHY
Article.
Popular Photography, June 1961.

FISHING BAJA
Article. First in series "Adventuring With Erle Stanley Gardner."
Sports Afield, July 1961.

VIRGIN TERRITORY
Article. "Adventuring With Erle Stanley Gardner."
Sports Afield, August 1961.

THE BLONDE IN LOWER SIX
Ed Jenkins, book-length.
Argosy, September 1961.

WITH LOVING HANDS
Article.
Quest, Winter 1961.

CAREERS AND HOBBIES
Article.
Book of Knowledge, 1961.

A CITIZEN LOOKS AT
LAW ENFORCEMENT*
Article.
Crime, Vol. 2 (Texas Law
Enforcement Association),
1961.

COMMENTS ON
JOURNALISM
Taped message to class in
city schools of Riverside,
California. 1961.

THE CASE OF THE
SPURIOUS SPINSTER
Perry Mason book.
Serialized in *The Saturday
Evening Post*, January
28–March 11, 1961.
Morrow, March 1961;
Pocket, May 1963.

BACHELORS GET
LONELY
(pen name, A. A. Fair)
Donald Lam–Bertha Cool
book.
Morrow, March 1961;
Pocket, August 1963.

THE CASE OF THE
BIGAMOUS SPOUSE
Perry Mason book.
Serialized in *The Saturday
Evening Post*, July 15–
August 26, 1961.
Morrow, August 1961;
Pocket, October 1963.

SHILLS CAN'T CASH
CHIPS
(pen name, A. A. Fair)
Donald Lam-Bertha Cool
book.
Morrow, November 1961;
Pocket, December 1963.

HOVERING OVER BAJA
Non-fiction book.
Sports Afield (excerpts),
September 1961.
Morrow, December 1961.

1962

CAPTAIN FRANCES G.
LEE
Article.
Boston Globe, February 4,
1962.

THE CASE OF THE
MISSING MANNERS*
Article.
Ford Times, March 1962.

THE CASE OF THE
BLUEBELLE'S LAST
VOYAGE
Article.
Family Weekly, March 25,
1962.

WHO OWNS THE
OUTDOORS?*
Article.
Desert Magazine, May
1962.

LOOKING ISN'T SEEING
Article.
Boys' Life, July 1962.

THE CASE OF THE BAJA
CAVES: A LEGENDARY
TREASURE LEFT BY A
LONG-LOST TRIBE
Article.
Life, July 20, 1962.

SOME RIGHTS SHOULD
BE LEFT*
Article.
Sports Afield, September
1962.

THE CASE OF THE
RELUCTANT MODEL
Perry Mason book.
Published under title "The
Case of the False Feteet"
in *Toronto Star Weekly*,
October 7, 1961.
Morrow, January 1962;
Pocket, January 1964.

TRY ANYTHING ONCE
(pen name, A. A. Fair)
Donald Lam–Bertha Cool
book.
Morrow, April 1962;
Pocket, March 1964.

THE CASE OF THE
BLONDE BONANZA
Perry Mason book.
Serialized in *Toronto Star
Weekly*, April 7–14, 1962.
Morrow, June 1962;
Pocket, May 1964.

THE CASE OF THE
ICE-COLD HANDS
Perry Mason book.
Morrow, October 1962;
Pocket, September 1964.

THE HIDDEN HEART
OF BAJA
Non-fiction book.
Morrow, November 1962.

1963

"CODE OF ETHICS" FOR
COURT REPORTERS?
Speech.
Printed in monthly bulle-
tin of International Press
Institute, April 1963.

CAMPFIRE
COMPANIONSHIP*
Article.
Sports Afield, May 1963.

LET'S HELP THE PENAL
PRESS
Article.
The Encourager (prison
paper), 10th Anniversary
Issue, 1963.

PUBLIC RELATIONS
Article.
The Four Wheeler, De-
cember 1963.

THE CASE OF THE
MISCHIEVOUS DOLL
Perry Mason book.
*The Saturday Evening
Post*, December 8, 1962.
Morrow, February 1963;
Pocket, January 1965.

FISH OR CUT BAIT
(pen name, A. A. Fair)
Donald Lam–Bertha Cool
book.
Morrow, April 1963;
Pocket, December 1964.

THE CASE OF THE
STEPDAUGHTER'S
SECRET
Perry Mason book.
Morrow, June 1963;
Pocket, April 1965.

THE CASE OF THE
AMOROUS AUNT
Perry Mason book.
Morrow, September 1963;
Pocket, August 1965.

THE DESERT IS YOURS
Non-fiction book.
Excerpts published in
Desert Magazine, Novem-
ber–December 1963, and
in *Sports Afield*, Decem-
ber 1963.
Morrow, December 1963
(under title "Our Desert
Coyote").

1964

PUNISHMENT WON'T
CURE CRIME*
Article.
Together, March 1964.

POISONED PARADISE
Article.
Sports Afield, May 1964.

THE MAD STRANGLER
OF BOSTON*
Article.
The Atlantic Monthly,
May 1964.

THE CASE OF THE
DARING DIVORCEE
Perry Mason book.
Morrow, February 1964;
Pocket, October 1965.

UP FOR GRABS
(pen name, A. A. Fair)
Donald Lam—Bertha Cool
book.
Morrow, March 1964;
Pocket, February 1965.

THE CASE OF THE
PHANTOM FORTUNE
Perry Mason book.
Morrow, May 1964; Pocket,
January 1966.

THE CASE OF THE
HORRIFIED HEIRS
Perry Mason book.
Morrow, September 1964;
Pocket, April 1966.

THE WORLD OF
WATER
Non-fiction book.
Morrow, December 1964.

*DRAMATIC PRESENTA-
TION:*

PUNISHMENT WON'T
CURE CRIME
  Excerpt for Expression
  Departments. Adapted by
  Wetmore Declamation
  Bureau, edited by Mr.
  Gardner, November 7,
  1964.

1965

GETTING AWAY WITH
MURDER*
Article.
The Atlantic Monthly,
January 1965.

DESERT JUSTICE
Misc. novelette.
Serialized in *Desert Maga-
zine*, April–May 1965.

SPEED DASH (THE
HUMAN FLY)
Article.
The Atlantic Monthly,
June 1965.

WHO IS PERRY MASON?
Article.
Chicago Daily News—
Panorama, October 2,
1965.

MY LOVE AFFAIR WITH
SAND AND WHEELS
Article.
Popular Science,
November 1965.

TRAPPED!
Article.
Sports Afield, November
1965.

THE CASE OF THE
TROUBLED TRUSTEE
Perry Mason book.
Morrow, February 1965;
Pocket, August 1966.

CUT THIN TO WIN
(pen name, A. A. Fair)
Donald Lam-Bertha Cool
book.
Morrow, April 1965;
Pocket, June 1966.

THE CASE OF THE
BEAUTIFUL BEGGAR
Perry Mason book.
Morrow, June 1965;
Pocket, January 1967.

HUNTING LOST MINES
BY HELICOPTER
Non-fiction book.
Morrow, November 1965.

1966

TRAP OUR WILDLIFE,
NO!
Letter-Article.
Sports Afield, March 1966.

THE WEST IS WAITING
TO BE DISCOVERED
Article.
*Ford Times Western
Journeys*, March 1966.

HOW I SEARCH FOR
LOST GOLD MINES—
AND WHY
Article.
Popular Science, March
1966.

MY STORIES OF THE
WILD WEST*
Article.
The Atlantic Monthly,
July 1966.

CRIME AND LAW
ENFORCEMENT
Article.
Included in paperback
book *California—the
Dynamic State* at request
of Governor Brown, 1966.

THE ADVANCEMENT
OF LAW ENFORCE-
MENT
Article.
Crime & Detection
(England), approx. 1966.

WIDOWS WEAR WEEDS
(pen name, A. A. Fair)
Donald Lam—Bertha Cool
book.
Morrow, May 1966; Dell,
May 1967.

THE CASE OF THE
WORRIED WAITRESS
Perry Mason book.
Morrow, August 1966;
Pocket, January 1968.

1967

TRIAL BY JURY*
Article.
This Week, January 22,
1967.

LAWS THAT LEAK
Article.
Sports Afield, March 1967.

I LOVE CAMPING—
MY WAY
Article.
Popular Science, May
1967.

HEALTH FOODS TO
PLEASE THE PALATE
Article.
Let's Live, August 1967.

PEOPLE ARE ENTITLED
TO THE TRUTH
Speech.
Printed in American
Polygraph Association
Newsletter, November–
December 1967.

INTERNATIONAL
UNDERSTANDING
Article.
Amigos, December 1967.

CAN NEW NON-LETHAL
WEAPONS CONTROL
RIOTS?
Article.
Popular Science, December
1967.

THE MEASURE OF A
MAN
Article.
The High Country,
Winter 1967.

Final chapter in book *The
President's Mystery Plot*
by Franklin Delano
Roosevelt and others.
Prentice-Hall, 1967.

THE DEFENSE OF
CRIMINAL CASES
Article.
Crime & Detection
(England), approx. 1967.

TRAPS NEED FRESH
BAIT
(pen name, A. A. Fair)
Donald Lam—Bertha Cool
book.
Morrow, March 1967;
Pocket, June 1968.

OFF THE BEATEN
TRACK IN BAJA
Non-fiction book.
Morrow, April 1967.

THE CASE OF THE
QUEENLY CONTESTANT
Perry Mason book.
Morrow, May 1967;
Pocket, January 1969.

GYPSY DAYS ON THE
DELTA
Non-fiction book.
Morrow, October 1967.

PLAY

A CASE FOR PERRY
MASON. Suspense play by
William McCleery, based
on Mr. Gardner's charac-
ters and situations, and
edited by Mr. Gardner.
1967.

1968

DIP YOUR PEN IN FIRE
Article.
Author & Journalist,
March–April 1968.

IF I WERE A
SECRETARY
Letter—Article.
The Secretary, April 1968.

CRIME IN THE STREETS
Article.
This Week, August 18,
1968.

THE WONDERFUL
WORLD OF FOUR-
WHEEL DRIVE
Article.
Popular Science, August
1968.

STRIPES UNDER THE
STARS
Article.
Sports Afield, September
1968.

THE CASE OF THE
CARELESS CUPID
Perry Mason book.
Morrow, March 1968;
Pocket, January 1970.

MEXICO'S MAGIC
SQUARE
Non-fiction book.
Morrow, November 1968.

1969

CAST LOOSE ALL CARES
Article.
Motor Boating, January
1969.

THE EYES DON'T
ALWAYS HAVE IT*
Article.
This Week, April 20,
1969.

THE CASE OF THE
HOSPITABLE HOUSE-
BOAT
Article.
Popular Science, July 1969.

CLAMMING AT EL
GOLFO
Article.
Desert Magazine, July
1969.

DOWN INTO BAJA—A
Photographic Journey
Through Lower California
Article.
Travel & Camera, August
1969.

ACAMBARO MYSTERY
Article.
Desert Magazine, October
1969.

A MAKER OF MEN
Article.
The High Country,
Winter 1969.

DRIFTING DOWN THE
DELTA
Non-fiction book.
Morrow, January 1969.

THE CASE OF THE
FABULOUS FAKE
Perry Mason book.
Morrow, November 1969;
Pocket, 1971.

HOST WITH THE BIG
HAT
Non-fiction book.
Morrow, December 1969.

THE CASE OF THE
MURDERER'S BRIDE
and Other Stories
Edited by Ellery Queen.
Davis Publications, Inc.
1969.

1970

HELPING THE
INNOCENT
Article.
U.C.L.A. Law Review,
February 1970.

THE CASE OF THE
AGILE ATVs
Article.
Popular Science, February
1970.

COPS ON CAMPUS AND
CRIME IN THE STREETS
Non-fiction book.
Serialized by *Chicago
Tribune—New York News*
Syndicate, Inc., January
25–February 5, 1970.
Morrow, January 30, 1970;
Pocket, 1970.

1971

ALL GRASS ISN'T
GREEN
(pen name, A. A. Fair)
Donald Lam—Bertha Cool
book.
Morrow, March 1970;
Pocket, 1971.

*TELEVISION PRESENTA-
TION:*

DOUG SELBY, D. A.—
"THE D. A. DRAWS A
CIRCLE."
Two-hour film (served as
the pilot for a possible TV
movie series) on NBC
WORLD PREMIERE.
Script based on characters
and situations created by
Mr. Gardner, and edited by
him. Produced by Paisano
Productions, Inc., in asso-

ciation with Twentieth Century-Fox. (Production started in 1969, finished Feb. 9, 1970.)
Date of presentation—NBC. Channel 4 8:30 P.M.P.T. December 17, 1971.

THE CASE OF THE CRIMSON KISS (Reprint anthology)
  A Perry Mason Novelette and Other Stories: (Crooked Lightning; The Valley of Little Fears; Fingers of Fong; At Arm's Length)
  Morrow, March 3, 1971; Pocket, 1972.

THE CASE OF THE CRYING SWALLOW (Reprint Anthology)
  A Perry Mason Novelette and Other Stories: (The Candy Kid; The Vanishing Corpse; The Affair of the Reluctant Witness)
  Morrow, June 8, 1971; Pocket, 1972.

1972

THE CASE OF THE IRATE WITNESS (Reprint Anthology)
  A Perry Mason Mystery and Other Stories: (The Jeweled Butterfly; Something Like a Pelican; A Man is Missing)
  Morrow, March 3, 1972. Pocket, 1973.

THE CASE OF THE FENCED-IN WOMAN
  Perry Mason book.
  Morrow, September 1972. Pocket, 1973.

1973

THE CASE OF THE POSTPONED MURDER
  Perry Mason book.
  Morrow, 1973.
  Pocket, 1974.

INDEX